FORENSIC GENEALOGY

Colleen Fitzpatrick, PhD

Rice Book Press
Fountain Valley, CA

Copyright 2005 © Colleen Fitzpatrick

Published by Rice Book Press

All rights reserved. No part of this book may be reproduced in any form or by any means, electronic or mechanical, including photocopying, recording, or by any information storage and retrieval system, without permission in writing from the Publisher.

Figures 12, 17, 18 of the Digital Detective and Figure 5 in Case Study in Database Detective Work ©2005 MapQuest.com, Inc. The MapQuest.com logo is a registered trademark of MapQuest.com, Inc. Map content ©2005 by MapQuest.com, Inc., GDT, Inc., and AND Products, B.V. The MapQuest trademarks and all map content are used with permission.

Figures 57 and 58 in the Digital Detective, © 1910, 1911, 1899-1909, 1895-1896, The Sanborn Map Company, The Sanborn Library, LLC. All Rights Reserved.

Cover designed by Kimball Clark.

Library of Congress Control Number: 2005902190

ISBN 0-9767160-0-3

Printed in the United States of America.

Third Printing

Dedicated to My Mother
Marilyn Rose Rice

The Daughter of Bernard F. Rice and Margaret Bernard
The Granddaughter of Matthew A. Rice and Viola Brechtel
The Great Granddaughter of Bernard C. Rice and Catherine Swords
The Great Great Granddaughter of John Rice and Ann Byrnes
Natives of the Roman Catholic Parish of Lower Killevy
County Armagh, Ireland

ACKNOWLEDGEMENTS

There are so many people who have made this project fun. I want to thank the large number of people who have contacted me with a family mystery to solve or a photograph to share. My fellow genealogists Dee Brunner and Penny Delery are acknowledged for their encouragement and support and for dedicating so much time and energy to making our Orleans Parish Rootsweb Site the best on the internet. Thanks also to the members of the New Orleans Volunteer Association (NOVA), for the finger power they have dedicated to make so many interesting and usual records available for free on our site. NOVA is #1!

The chapter The DNA Detective was the most difficult to write, and required much discussion with members of the DNA community. I greatly appreciate the interest that Family Tree DNA has shown in the promotion of this book, especially the help I have received from Bennett Greenspan during our discussions on many aspects of DNA testing and for the use of the mtDNA migration map and the phylogenetic tree of Y-chromosome SNP haplogroups. Thanks also to DNA study group leaders who have been generous in discussing their results with me: Terry Barton, Jerry Butler, Mary Haacke, and Michael McManus, and L. David Roper and to the Fitzpatrick DNA study participants for their interest in our surname project.

Finally, I'd like to acknowledge the friends who have been so generous with their time and patience during the preparation of this book: Jackie Johnson, for her help in formatting, Craig Fodness for his assistance in understanding the requirements for printing the book, John Patrick Yeiser for infecting me with his creative energy, and Greg Netherwood and Mike Larkin for office help. Thanks to my friends Louise Butler, Ali Khounsary, Sinika Garey, and Melodie Bell for their constant encouragement, and to my clansman Ronan Fitzpatrick for his insight into Clan history.

TABLE OF CONTENTS

INTRODUCTION	1
THE DIGITAL DETECTIVE	5
Getting Started	6
Location, Location, Location	13
When?	20
Stumpers	58
CASE STUDY IN DIGITAL DETECTIVE WORK	
WHERE, WHO, WHEN AND WHY	61
THE DATABASE DETECTIVE	75
Introduction	75
Getting Started	79
Periodical Databases–Using City Directories	82
Event Databases	103
Unusual Reference Materials	110
Using Multiple Sources to Construct A Family Story	113
Cultural Profiling	117
CASE STUDY IN DATABASE DETECTIVE WORK	
THE HISTORY OF THE ULMER FAMILY	125
THE DNA DETECTIVE	145
About DNA	146
Types of DNA Markers and Mutations	150
Why Surname Studies Use Certain Markers	152
Genealogical DNA Analysis	152
Single Name DNA Studies	156
Connecting with History through Single Name Studies	159
Nonpaternity Events	161
Genetic Genealogy Testing Companies and Testing Options	164
Online Databases	169
The Details Of DNA Markers and Their Genealogical Uses	171
The Most Recent Common Ancestor (MRCA)	179
Cladograms and Pairwise Mismatches	194
There Will Always Be Mysteries Left	217

INTRODUCTION

So much fascinating information is locked in that old family photograph, document, or story just waiting to be brought out! All that's needed is a few new tools and some creative curiosity. This book is intended to give you those tools, all you need to provide is the curiosity.

Every fan of the popular television shows *Forensic Files*, *CSI*, and *Medical Detectives* knows that the FBI uses all the resources it has at its disposal to solve a crime. The FBI does not limit its investigations to conventional sources of evidence such as fingerprints and eyewitness accounts, but makes use of its large reference libraries of plants, carpets, shoes, string, wrapping paper and anything else that can be critical to a successful investigation.

Likewise, a good forensic genealogist makes use of the wealth of information he has available on the internet along with any hard copy, digital and microfilmed reference materials that might be at his disposal. He realizes the value of all sources of information, not just conventional materials such as birth, marriage and death records. My investigations have led me to examine five hundred year old weather records, information on the breeding cycle of mosquitoes, old almanacs, how babies were delivered in the middle ages, old hospital admission records, the 1909 National Cash Register catalog, the history of the railroad in Canada, the backs of photographic prints from the 1950s, the history of the Spanish Armada, and many other unconventional reference materials—resulting in intriguing family insights.

Forensic scientists and genealogists share the same goal—to find out who was who, and who did what and when. Whether you are investigating a crime or researching your family tree, photographs, databases and DNA analysis are the three most important resources that you can use for answering these questions. For this reason, I devote the major sections of this book to how to use these three kinds of sources to best advantage. In explaining how to analyze photographs, to mine databases, and to use DNA analysis to reveal family history, I emphasis the creative parts of an investigation over the mechanics. Have you ever thought of looking at the edges of old photographs to find out if they are from the same roll, or the backs to place them in chronological order? Have you considered looking at a city directory to figure out if your ancestor and his wife lost any children? How about using DNA analysis to tie your family to the history and politics of a religious conflict?

Using the forensic investigation techniques presented in this book you will:
- make unconventional discoveries from surprising sources
- gain an understanding of how your ancestors lived
- develop fascinating insights into your family history

Forensic Genealogy will give you a sense of coming from a long line of real people who are not just names on a page.

Here are some samples of the suggestions and insights you will get from reading *Forensic Genealogy*:

1. Many articles on identifying old photographs don't go beyond suggesting that you should ask older relatives if they recognize anyone in a picture. This is a great start, but it's a mistake to believe that this is all you can do. Because many early photographs in our collections date from the late 1800s to the early 1900s, those who could have identified the people in the pictures are gone. Even older relatives who do have memories to share are often confused about events that happened decades in the past. While talking to elderly relatives is still the first place to start when researching old photographs, there are other powerful tools to use for this purpose. Is there a house number in the picture? Why not use the city directories to find out which family lived at that address and when? The Digital Detective chapter gives many more suggestions for investigating old photographs.

2. You cannot accurately date a photograph by the clothing or hairstyles except in rare cases. How often do you buy new clothes? Because of availability and cost, past generations were less likely to buy new clothes than people today who can shop at the nearest mall. Hand-me-downs to younger children in a family were much more common then. 19th century photographers often had wardrobes available for customers so that someone in an old photograph might not even be wearing his own clothes!

3. You To date a photograph, what can the position of the brand name on the back tell? Are there clues to geographical location in the picture? How can you tell what camera was used to take a picture and when it was in use? How can knowing this tell you who is in the photo? What resources can you use to match items in the picture with a particular time period? These are just some of the questions you might ask when investigating a photo.

4. When looking for specific data such as an address or a birth date, you may be tempted to copy down *only that* piece of information. But in doing so, you may lose important insights by focusing too tightly on individual facts. If your great grandfather was Johann Schmidt, it pays to research all the Schmidts from all the city directories you have available, not just old Johan himself for the year you know he lived on such-and-so street. Several years earlier Johan might have lived with other Schmidts, cousins, aunts, or uncles on this-and-that street. Knowing who lived with whom and when can reveal interesting family dynamics. Expanding your efforts to include variations in spelling like Smith and Smidt will also greatly increases your chances of finding something. The Database Detective chapter gives more tips in this area.

5. General information can point to specific facts. For example, knowing the legal age of marriage can predict a birth date, or lead you to investigate the documents needed to license the marriage of an underage couple. Knowing that it was the practice in some cultures to have children early and often can reveal gaps in the birth dates in a family, leading to the discovery that children are missing from the known birth line-up, either because they were left behind when a family emigrated, because of a child's death or a miscarriage, or because daughters might not appear in civil or legal records like sons do. In The Database Detective chapter, I show that knowing how city directories were compiled can reveal the birth and marriage years of the sons in a family, but not necessarily the daughters.

6. Do not ignore the historical context of your family in your eagerness to fill in names on your family tree. The time your spend studying seemingly unimportant background information may prove most rewarding. Knowing how your ancestors lived can offer more insight to family history than discovering that Great Great Uncle John worked for the gas company in 1875. Wouldn't it be interesting to know that he survived a yellow fever epidemic that year?

7. Look for a name change on immigration only if your family came to the U.S. before 1906. After the immigration station at Ellis Island opened in that year, immigration officials were required to record immigrants' names as they appeared on ship manifests created at embarkation points. The language barrier between arrivals and station officials was non-existent. All Ellis Island immigration officials were fluent in at least three languages, and interpreters were on call 24 hours a day to cover rare dialects, so that even spelling variations were uncommon. From 1906 any name changes or variations in spelling probably occurred after an immigrant's entry into the U.S. See the DNA Detective.

8. In DNA analysis, mismatches can be far more interesting and revealing than matches. In reviewing the implications of two startling mismatches in my own Fitzpatrick DNA study, I came across a possible link between members of my surname group and the sinking of the Spanish Armada. DNA can be a useful tool for more than estimating a date for a Most Recent Common Ancestor (MRCA) or for determining which 50,000 year old clan mother you descend from. DNA can tie you to world history, it can be used to give you the geographical location your ancestors came from in recent centuries, and it can reveal unsuspected liaisons between seemingly unrelated families through nonpaternity events. There is as much information as you probably will want to know about this in The DNA Detective chapter.

9. In estimating the date for the Most Recent Common Ancestor (MRCA) of two people in a DNA study, the math reduces to the binomial expansion, or equivalently, the Poisson

distribution. Don't let anyone tell you otherwise. The DNA Detective chapter gives easy-to-use charts for looking up the MRCA of two people based on how many markers they are tested on and how many mismatches there are between them. The chapter also gives spreadsheet skeletons you can use to perform your own MRCA calculations, as well as the underlying formulas for those who would like to dig deeper.

10. A Y-chromosome cladogram is more than a graphical representation of a surname's genetic structure. The complexity and arrangement of groups within a cladogram are tied to family history and can indicate the diversity of a surname's origins and can be used to identify the main branches of a family. Having a cluster of genetically similar individuals that is well separated from other members of a study indicates that this cluster has a unique history and geography. As the number of name studies grows and online databases of DNA profiles become larger, it will be interesting to combine the DNA results of many surname studies into a single cladogram to identify common genetic histories. You will enjoy finding out more about how to create and interpret cladograms in The DNA Detective chapter.

This book is meant to start every new forensic genealogist on a path of discovery. I hope that each mystery that is solved by using the techniques in this book leaves ten more in its place. A good forensic genealogist realizes that ten new mysteries can only be regarded as ten new opportunities for exciting new genealogical detective work.

THE DIGITAL DETECTIVE

Since the advent of the internet, a digital detective has access to the gencalogical equivalent of the FBI forensics laboratory, including libraries of shoes, hats, jewelry, military uniforms and insignia, plants, photographic backdrops, tools, and almost anything else that could possibly be used in the analysis of a photograph. These libraries include the materials photos are printed on (copper, glass, tin, and types of print papers), the dimensions of photographs produced by a variety of cameras, common practices used by commercial photographers during different time periods, and the specifications of product lines of major camera companies.

Forensic methods of photograph analysis are important tools for recovering at least some of the information missing about a picture. When interpreted correctly, old photographs can yield an abundance of genealogical information, either directly revealing facts about family members, or serving as a point of departure for further investigation. This chapter will give you tips on how to look at a photo, so that you can learn to observe important elements which will allow you to identify its what, when, where, and, most importantly, its who.

Since the very first photograph was produced in 1829 by Nicephore Niépce with an eight hour exposure of the rooftops in Paris, photography has advanced to the present technology of disposable cameras, digital cameras, scanners, and graphic arts software packages. What was once the domain of scientists and the wealthy is now an integral part of our everyday lives.

Throughout the 1800s, photographic techniques became simpler and less expensive. Yet it was not until 1871, when Dr. Richard Maddox invented dry processing, that photography took the first step toward becoming convenient to individuals who had little specialized equipment or scientific knowledge. The subsequent development of celluloid-based film and then the box camera by George Eastman in the 1880s lowered the price of cameras and film, so that along with the increase in convenience, taking photographs now became much more affordable.

The first individuals who could take photos in the convenience of their own homes would now be between 100 to 120 years old. Even though there are many photographs still around today which predate the turn of the 20th century, including those taken during the Civil War, most of the oldest photos we have in our family albums today were taken by these early home-based photographers. Unfortunately, the majority of these people are gone, leaving a void of information about the pictures they took. It is still a good idea to speak to the older members of your family to uncover as much information as possible about your old family pictures. But much valuable information that may no longer be available from your relatives may be obtainable using forensic techniques.

Figure 1.

GETTING STARTED

Here is your first quiz. See Figure 1. Where was this picture taken?

If you answered Paris, you pass the test! You have the makings of a photo-detective. This picture of the Eiffel Tower is an obvious example of how important details to location often lurk in the background, having little to do with the primary subjects of the photograph.

WHAT CAN YOU *REALLY* LEARN FROM A PHOTOGRAPH?

The most important lesson a digital detective can ever learn is to notice what a photograph is *really* saying. There are occasions when a quick look will lead to the wrong conclusions. A good example of this is the photograph in Figure 2 that I was asked to analyze by a friend in Dublin.

At first glance, this picture seems to be the photograph of a wedding around the turn of the 20th century, with the bride and the groom in the center of the picture, surrounded by members of the wedding party. But take a closer look. Is it *really* a wedding photograph?

On closer inspection, the two men in the front row look a lot like women. The man to the left in the back row wearing the top hat has a very smooth face with small hands, and is probably also a woman. In fact, all the 'men' in the photo are women. This cannot possibly be a wedding party. It is the cast of a

Figure 2. The wedding.

play. According to a friend who is knowledgable about the theatre, it is a play called *Charlie's Aunt*, by Brandon Thomas. The mat of the photo carried the logo of Roe McMahon, who according to city directories, was a photographer active in Dublin from about 1909 to 1960. Since the owner of the photograph did not recognize anyone in the photo, nor did his oldest relatives, the picture was probably taken in the earlier part of the 1900s, not for a wedding album, but as a publicity shot to advertize the production.

Knowing what this photograph is really saying is important. Instead of tracing a *bride* in the family, you should be tracing an *actress*.

REMEMBER TO LOOK AT THE BACK!

This might seem silly, but the very first thing you should do in unraveling the history of a photograph is to look at the back. Unbelievable as it may seem, some of our ancestors had the presence of mind to write names on the backs of their photos, and we simply forget to turn them over. Recently, my father presented me with a picture of a little girl apparently taken in the early 1900s that he had found while cleaning out his attic. He did not have the foggiest idea who it was. From past experience, I recognized it immediately as a photo of my grandmother aged about 3 years old, taken when she had the mumps. I had been searching for this picture for the past 25 years. Since my grandmother's house had been cleaned out and sold when she died, I had lost hope of ever seeing it again. But it wasn't necessary to know any of this to figure out who was in the picture and when it was taken – when I turned the photo over, her name was written on the back!

Even if you are not lucky enough to find a specific name on the back of a photo, you might find something else that will help in identifying it. The picture in Figure 3 belonged to a friend who, typically, had found it in her collection of photos but did not know who it was. The photograph carries the logo of Blissenbach Artists, Mankato, MN on the bottom of the front of the mat. She could see that there was some writing on the back, but it was so faint she could not make it out.

Using Microsoft Photo Editor©, I was able to enhance the writing by adjusting the contrast and gamma correction and to pull out the words, "Aged 19 years from Mary to Uncle George". The picture is a typical example of a cabinet card from the late 1880s through the turn of the century. (More on cartes de visite and cabinet cards is found later in this chapter.) The job now was to piece together these clues and find an ancestor named Mary with an Uncle George, who was 19 years old during the 1880s to 1890s, and who lived in Mankato, MN. Although this did not give the exact identity of this young woman, there was now a lot more

Figure 3. Aged 19 years, from Mary to Uncle George.

information to go on. Searching on Google on the keywords 'Mankato' and 'genealogy', I located Shelley Harrison, Archives Assistant of the Blue Earth County Historical Society in Mankato, who told me that Blissenbach Artists appeared in the Mankato city directory between 1888 and 1910. Unfortunately, there was a fire in 1911 that destroyed the business after which Mr. Blissenbach went into insurance, so that his photographic archives no longer exist. To continue the investigation, other ways must be found to identify the woman.

Figure 4. The backs of photos often carry lot numbers that help to identify them.

Besides providing a handwritten note, another possibility is that a photo carries a mark or a number on the back that can help to identify it. Three common marks are: the lot number of the print paper, the logo of the print paper type or its manufacturer, and personal marks made by the photographer who processed the film.

As print paper was manufactured, it was often stamped on the back by the manufacturer with its lot number to designate when and where the film was produced. By grouping photographs that are marked with the same lot number as shown in Figure 4, pictures printed on paper from the same box can be identified. This usually means the pictures were developed from the same roll of film, or from several rolls brought in to be processed at the same time. Information about one photograph can often lead to information on other photographs from the same lot.

The second kind of mark that is useful in dating an old photograph is the logo of the type of print paper used or the company that

Figure 5. The logo on the back of a photo is an important clue.

manufactured the paper. See Figure 5. For example, sometime between the 1920s and the 1940s, Kodak started marking the back of its photographic paper with the VELOX logo[1]. In the early to mid 1950s, the logo was changed to 'Kodak VELOX Paper'.

Agfa made a similar change in its logo about the same time. Prior to the 1950s, Agfa used a two part logo, made up of the name Agfa followed by the brand name (Agfa Brovira, for example). For new products introduced after 1945, and for existing products produced after the mid-1950s, the company dropped the brand name and used the single word Agfa. Table 1 provides a guide in using Kodak and Agfa print paper logos to determine an approximate date when a photograph was taken. For example, if you have a photograph with a two part Agfa logo, you can be sure it was produced before the mid-1950s[1].

The back of an old photograph can also carry a personal mark made by the photographer who processed the picture. This kind of mark can be anything from a handwritten number to a pencil mark. Sometimes a photographer fanned out a group of pictures face down and ran a pencil over the edges. If the pencil mark appears at about the same place on the back of several pictures, chances are they were processed from the same roll of film. See Figure 6.

Table 1. Kodak and Agfa logos[1]

KODAK		AGFA	
Logo	Date	Logo	Date
VELOX	Before early 1950s	Agfa + Produce Name	Before 1950s
Kodak Velox Paper	After early 1950s	AGFA	After 1945 or mid-1950s, depending on product

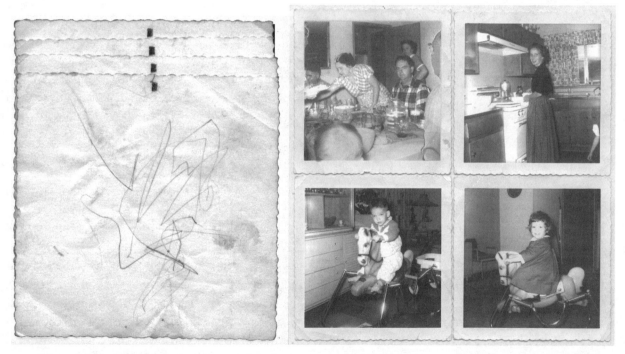

Figure 6. There are often pencil marks on the backs of prints that were made during processing.

OTHER INTERESTING FEATURES

There are other features that you can use to associate photographs with each other. During manufacture, a master roll of paper advances through a cutting machine in increments equal to the width of the final print paper rectangles, with the same blades used each time a cut is made. This means that *every* piece of photopaper from the same run not only has the logo in about the same position on the back, but also that the detailed shape of the corresponding edges of prints cut from the same master roll are identical.

This is especially useful for sequencing prints with serrated or scalloped edges. If the edges are crinkled, photos from the same batch will fit end to end like a jigsaw puzzle, as long as the right edge of one is placed next to the left edge of the other. It does not matter if photo #1 lies next to photo #5 or photo #100 – the edges should fit together and the logo should be in about the same position on each photo cut from the same master roll (Figure 7). In some cases where the cut was made in the middle of a logo, the piece of print paper on each side of the cut carries matching parts (Figure 8).

In general, if the edges and logos of a group of pictures 'fit' together as described, they were probably printed using the same box of print paper so that they are from the same roll, or the same group of rolls.

In the case where the edges or logos fit together, but the photographs have different lot numbers, they were printed using two different boxes of print paper that were manufactured in the same place with the same cutting machine, but that belonged to different lots.

Figure 7. Crinkled edges that match.

Figure 8. Sometimes the logo is divided across two photographs.

One last comment. If the master roll of print paper advanced through the cutting machine at a slower or faster rate than normal, the spacing of the cuts would be different from the spacing of the logos that had already been printed on the back of the roll. In this case, even though the pictures will still fit together as described above, the logo will not appear in the same place on the back of each photo, but will precess or 'creep' in position from one photo to the next. By organizing the photos according to the amount of 'creep', it is possible to place them in chronological order from the earliest to the latest, as in Figure 9.

In summary, a good digital detective will always remember to look at the back of a photograph for clues to its origins. The edges of the print paper can also provide valuable information about the photo.

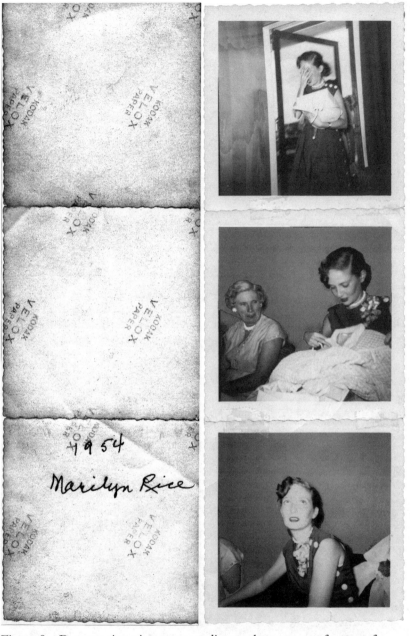

Figure 9. By arranging pictures according to the amount of creep of their logos, the pictures can be put in chronological order.

Things to look for are:
- Names, addresses, inscriptions
- Lot numbers for the paper used to print the negative
- Logos for the type of print paper and its manufacturer
- Pencil marks made by the person processing the film
- Photographs with serrated, scalloped, or crinkled edges that fit together like a puzzle
- Photos with matching halves of logos that have been cut in two during manufacture of the print paper
- Logos that precess or creep along the back of a group of photos with matching edges.

LOCATION, LOCATION, LOCATION

The location where a photo was taken can sometimes be determined by observing details in the picture that otherwise would be considered incidental to the untrained eye. More than likely, you will not have the Eiffel Tower in the background of your picture, so it will be up to you to notice more subtle references to location. For example, photos taken outdoors with scenery in the background, photos which include part of an indoor setting, or photos which include advertisements or signs are prime candidates for this line of investigation. The key to success is to filter out generic references to location such as plants, clothes, furniture, buildings, and focus on the items that make the photograph unique.

Figure 10. A small detail can provide a lot of **information**.

FILTER OUT GENERIC, FOCUS ON SPECIFIC

The photo shown in Figure 10 is a good example of how a small detail can reveal a large amount of information on where a photograph was taken. At first glance, this photo of a little boy playing in front of his house does not give you much to go on. His tricycle, his clothes, and the row of houses he is standing in front of are all generic. He could be standing anywhere. The trick to figuring out where this picture was taken is to filter out the common elements to find more informative details.

Close examination of the boy's picture reveals a number over the door farthest to the right. When the picture is enlarged, the number appears to be '951'. If the city where the photo was taken is known and there is a list of surnames that might go along with the child, a search of the city directories could yield a range of years when a family member lived at 951 something street. It is then a matter of figuring out the names and birthdates of the male children in the family who were two to three years old during that time period. Keep in mind that the little boy might be standing in front of a neighbor's house. But even so, his house number would be close to 951.

The photo of a young girl shown in Figure 11 was taken in New Orleans and has three clues to its location. Before reading any further, can you identify them? The first two are fairly obvious. The third one is a little more difficult to spot.

The first and easiest clue is the name of the street on the telephone pole in the immediate background. Because of the beer sign hanging from the pole, we can be pretty sure that the photo was taken outside of a bar, a restaurant, or a grocery on Duels St.

The second clue, which is less apparent, is the railroad crossing in the background. By looking at a map of the area around Duels St.[2] (Figure 12), the location can be identified as the intersection of Duels and Frenchmen Sts. with the railroad tracks. Notice that on the map the railroad is not exactly on the corner. This makes sense when compared to the photo, since the railroad appears in the background across the street from the restaurant. Notice also that the railroad crossing sign is facing along the street where the car is parked, probably along the curb. The sign hanging from the telephone pole (probably advertising Jax beer, a popular local variety) and the Duels St. sign are pointing at a 45 degree angle to the corner, where they can be seen by cars approaching the intersection along either street.

The third clue is more subtle. The position of the shadows on the telephone pole and on the little girl's face show that the sun is coming in slightly to the left of the people in the picture, and from halfway up in the sky. Since New Orleans at 29.58° N latitude is north of the Tropic of Cancer at 23.5° N latitude, the sun always shines from the south. The girl is facing south along Frenchmen St. into the sun, which is consistent with the railroad tracks appearing to the north of the intersection behind her in the photo. While the shadows alone could not tell you where the photograph was taken, they can confirm clues

Figure 11. Can you spot the three clues to the location of this photograph?

Figure 12. Map corresponding to Figure 11.

from other sources. Note that the picture was taken in the late afternoon, when then sun was in the western sky.

THE TYPE OF LOCATION CAN BE IMPORTANT

Sometimes knowing the kind of place where a picture was taken can lead to more specific information. In the example in Figure 13, there are a number of details which indicate that this group was associated with a Catholic (not Protestant) church. The most obvious one is the nun standing in the back row. Knowing that the picture was taken in front of a Catholic church, you can search for more specific hints to the location.

Figure 13.

The Latin inscription on the façade of the building reads, "Annumeratus Est Cum Undecim". Any online Latin dictionary can be used to translate this as, "He was numbered with the eleven". Searching an online bible will tell you that this phrase is found in the New Testament in Acts 1:26 and refers to the apostle Matthew. Note that the name Matthias is inscribed on a panel in the middle of this phrase. The building must be a Catholic church, probably named St. Matthias or St. Matthew. It is likely that the group of children in the picture is under the supervision of the nun and the two priests. Judging by the white dresses the girls are wearing, the photo could be of a graduating class or of a group of children making their first Holy Communion. A more in-depth online investigation of the habit worn by the nun in the picture could also lead to her order, perhaps associated with a specific church or parochial school.

The possible name of the church, the order of the nun, the approximate age of the children in the photo, and the likelihood that they are dressed for graduation or for their first Holy Communion can be matched with listings for churches in the city directories and compared to family history to determine the location and the date the photo was taken. Knowledge of the birth dates of the children in the family would narrow down which family member appears in the picture.

MAKING A LIST OF LOCATION-RELATED ITEMS

The photo in Figure 14 has circulated over the internet as a joke about women drivers. While it does not relate to genealogy, I include it here because it is an excellent example of how combining several details in a photograph can be the key to determining its location, and how knowledge of the location can lead to the answer of the more important question, "Who is in the picture?" Believe it or not, with a bit of digital detective work, it is possible to figure out the address of the gas station in the right background of the photo. This photograph is also an example of how luck and coincidence can play a role in forensic science. Were it not for privacy considerations, I could tell you the name of the woman driving the car.

Figure 14. Where was this photograph taken?

When working with a picture that is rich in details, it is a good idea to start by making a list of interesting features that might be location-related. This will help you filter out the generic and focus on more important items. As you progress, you can always add to your list if you uncover more interesting details. After looking at the photo for a few minutes, I found the following items:
- License plate on the car
- Street Signs (State, U.S., and Interstate)
- Sign on the car in front of the one dragging the hose
- Sign on the back of the truck in the right lane of traffic
- Texaco gas station on the right side of the street
- Ads and other signs along the right side of the road

I also found some generic items that I put in a stockpile in case they turned out to be relevant later. They include the speed limit sign on the left side of the street, the position of stoplights (probably at intersections), and the types and models of cars in the picture.

It is unfortunate that the photograph is not of higher resolution. That would make it much easier to read the words above the numbers on the license plate, and to figure out the country or the state where the photo was taken. This would be a dead giveaway. Fortunately, there are many other items in the picture that are just as useful.

The two highway signs to the left of center in Figure 15 show that the photo was taken in the U.S. The sign in the center with the arrow below it carries an outline of the State of Louisiana. Of the two U.S. highway signs, one is easily read as 'Hwy 90'. A quick look at a map confirms that this is a possibility. Hwy. 90 runs the width of southern Louisiana from the Texas border in the west to New Orleans in the east (Figure 16). The shape of what is written above the number '90' reveals that it is Hwy. 90 West. While the details of the other U.S. highway sign are not as distinct, at least we can see that the other highway is designated by three digits. The word on top of this second U.S. Hwy. sign is too long for north, south, east, or west. It possibly reads 'junction'.

Figure 15. Close-up of the traffic signs in the photograph in Figure 14.

Another important clue is the piece of the interstate sign along the upper right, which shows the letters 'Ex', probably representing the first two letters of 'Expressway'. Usually, these signs have further directions on how to access the Expressway, or where it is going, so that the 'S' showing on the second line probably indicates 'Second', as in 'Second Left', 'South', or might even be the name of the next town down the road. There is a smaller sign attached to the bottom of the larger one, with the letter 'L' visible. This would commonly indicate 'Left Lane'.

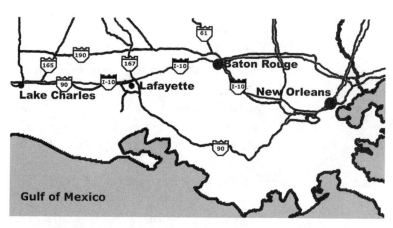

Figure 16. Hwy. 90 runs through southern Louisana.

Using the state, U.S., and interstate highway signs has given us a general location for the picture, but can we get more specific? We are looking for a location in Louisiana where:

- Hwy 90 runs close to an Interstate highway, possibly accessed through the left lane. Either the Interstate entrance is the second left, or else the next city along the freeway begins with an 'S', where
- It joins with a three digit U.S. highway, and where
- It intersects or is a short distance away from a Louisiana state highway.

The map of Hwy 90 shown in Figure 16 indicates that the highway is about 350 miles long, and runs close to Interstate 10 for a very short distance in the east near New Orleans. Going west, it veers away from I-10 towards the very south of the state. It then turns north approaching Lafayette, and runs more or less parallel to the interstate through the rest of the state. We can eliminate much of the early part of the route between New Orleans and Lafayette from consideration, because Hwy. 90 is located so far away from Interstate 10.

The remaining 200-mile long stretch of Hwy. 90 runs parallel to I-10 from Lafayette to the Texas border. The job now is to find locations along this stretch where Hwy 90 joins with a three-digit U.S. highway. Tracing the highway the rest of the way to Texas, there are only two places where this happens. One is just outside of Lafayette, where it meets U.S. Hwy 167, and the other is near Iowa, LA, just east of Lake Charles, where it joins with U.S. Hwy 165. Cross checking this with the photo, the first two of the three digits of this highway could be '16'.

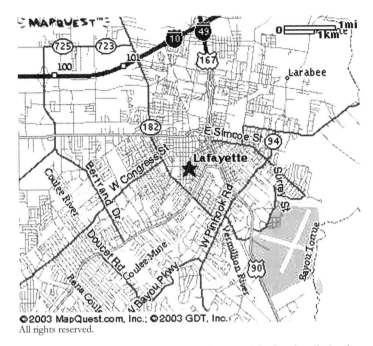

Figure 17. This location is consistent with the details in the photograph in Figure 14[3].

Using the other clues in the picture makes it possible to choose between these two locations. Remember the Expressway sign? If the 'S' on the second line on the sign indicates 'Second Left', we are looking for a place where Hwy 90 meets U.S. Hwy 16X, and then junctions with I-10 to the left a short distance later. This fits the map of the westbound section of the highway outside Lafayette[3] (Figure 17).

Is it possible to go even further than this by using some of the remaining items on the list? What about the Texaco gas station? If there is a service station on the right hand side of the road near the intersection of Hwys. 90 and 167, we could claim success. If the station is no longer a Texaco, knowing when the station changed hands would help narrow down the date when the photograph was taken.

Using the Mapquest.com[4] Yellow Pages feature to map the service stations in the immediate area (Figure 18), it is not surprising that there are quite a few located near such a busy intersection. Yet only one is on the immediate right hand side of the road – station #4. According to Mapquest, there is a Jiffy Mart at 1339 SE Evangeline Thruway, Lafayette, LA that fits our requirements. In case there is still a doubt that this is the correct location, a closer look at the picture reveals that traffic on the road is only going in one direction. The signs on opposite sides of the street are facing the same way, since there are no lanes of oncoming traffic. In fact, the Jiffy Mart is located several blocks after the Evangeline Thruway turns into a divided highway, two major intersections south of the junction with I-10. Note that the details of the traffic flow were not on our list of interesting features nor were they in our stockpile of items of potential interest.

As an interesting postscript to this detective work, a friend of mine often drives through southern Louisiana in connection with his work decorating parks for Christmas. When shown this photograph, he immediately recognized it as near a park in Lafayette that he had decorated in the last couple of years. By coincidence, this friend also works as a reserve state policeman who has access to the state's database of license numbers. If it were not for privacy considerations, he told me he would run the license plate of the car to identify the owner so he could tell me the name of the owner, who would know the name of the woman driving the car.

By making a list of the items in this picture that might yield clues to its location, and by creating a stockpile of items of potential interest, with a bit of luck we have been able to identify the exact intersection where this picture was taken, and aside from privacy considerations, it would be possible to obtain the identity of the woman driving the car. What's more, if the woman were ever contacted, she would know the exact date she made her famous mistake, the time of day, where she was headed, as well as what was in her trunk at the time.

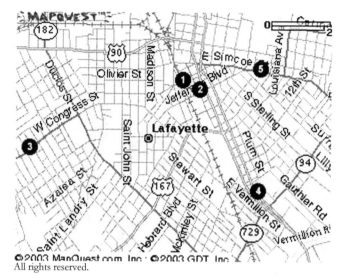

Figure 18[4].

WHEN?

The answer to the question 'When' is valuable in digital detective work. If you can determine approximately when a photograph was taken, you might be able to identify who is in it, or at least rule out who is not. Often a photograph contains things that are associated with a certain time period, for example, an advertisement for a product that was on the market only for a limited time, indication of an event that happened on a certain date, or a store that is no longer in business. Even the photograph itself – the paper it was printed on, its color, its relative length and width (known as the aspect ratio), or how it is framed can often provide valuable information.

DATING PHOTOGRAPHS BY CLOTHING STYLES

It is a common misconception that the style of dress can lead to the date a picture was taken. While clothing styles can serve as a starting point, they can rarely provide 'the' detail that identifies the date of a photograph. Men's clothing styles are relatively more stable than women's, making it is difficult to associate a given type of suit with a specific date. Men's hats generally also fall into the same category. Although a particular style of hat might have become popular on a specific occasion, men's hat styles tend to remain in style indefinitely. Bowlers, straw boaters, fedoras, and Stetsons created over a century ago are still worn today.

Women's clothing styles change more frequently with major changes usually, but not always, appearing as an accumulation of many smaller ones. Countless variations in collars, bodices, sleeves, and other features often blur transitions from one style to the next, making it almost impossible to link the style of dress in a photograph to a narrow period of time.

There are other reasons why costume can only serve as a general guideline for dating a photograph. People usually do not buy the latest fashion the moment it comes out. This is expensive for all but the very wealthy. Until modern times fashion spread slowly, so that the latest style might have taken a long time to reach a small town far away from a major city. Assuming the clothes a person is wearing in a photograph were his 'good' clothes, they were probably several years old, expensive to replace, and might not have been the leading fashion at the time of purchase. They might also have been hand-me-downs from older siblings. Sometimes the clothes someone is wearing in a photograph might not even have belonged to him, since it was common for photographers to have a wardrobe for a customer to select from when getting his picture taken. Although there are several very good web sites that describe clothing trends over the ages[5], most resources on clothing styles rely on illustrations from well known magazines of the times, or on styles worn in photographs of famous people. There are very few resources on common, everyday clothing.

PHOTOGRAPH STYLE IS IMPORTANT

Figure 19.

Even if a photograph does not contain any unusual items that could lead to a specific date, the style of the photograph itself might give some useful hints on its origins. A rule of thumb in dating a photograph from around the turn of the 20th century is that if it was taken at home instead of in a studio, it was probably taken after the first Kodak Brownie camera came on the market in 1900. Because the Brownie sold for only $1 (equivalent to about $20 today), after 1900 photography became an inexpensive and convenient part of everyday life[6]. The box camera had already been developed by George Eastman in 1886, and photographic film (as opposed to sensitized plates) was first produced by John Corbutt in 1888. This was followed by several more innovations: the invention of roll film by George Eastman in 1889, the introduction of the first daylight loading film by Eastman Kodak in 1894[7], and the marketing of the Kodak Pocket Folding Camera in 1898, considered to be the ancestor of all modern roll film cameras[8]. The Brownie was the first inexpensive, mass-produced camera available to the public. The Brownie made it possible for an individual to own and use his own camera conveniently at home, without advanced technical knowledge. From this time forward, photographs could be taken at home in informal settings. An excellent history of Kodak cameras and film can be found at: http://members.aol.com/Chuck02178/brownie.htm[9]. These early home-based Brownie photographs represent quite a few of the unidentified pictures we find in our family albums today.

The photograph in Figure 19 was sent to me by someone who knew that the woman in the picture was either her great great grandmother or her great grandmother. Her great great grandmother was born in 1860, her great grandmother in 1886, and her grandmother in 1910. Because the photograph was taken outside someone's house, it was probably taken by an early home photographer in 1900 or later. Also, by accident or intention, the subjects are not nicely centered. An older child has been half cut out of the picture. This could be due to bad framing, to printing out only part of the negative, to the fact that the photographer was not interested in the older child, or simply because of clumsiness. All of these possibilities indicate that the photographer was an amateur.

If the woman was the great great grandmother, judging from the ages of the children in the picture, the photograph was taken between 1886 and 1890. If the woman was the great grandmother, the photograph dates from around 1910 to 1914. Since home photography was uncommon in the mid to late 1880's, the photo was most likely taken during the later time period. The woman in the photograph was probably the great grandmother. From other information, the picture's owner knew her grandmother had only one sibling who was several years younger, so that the picture was taken about 1914 and the little girl in the picture was the grandmother.

The photo in Figure 20 is an interesting example of how even the most generic picture of someone can give itself away. This picture was found in the family collection of another friend. There is a note written in the upper left hand corner, which reads, "My grandfather, M. Noonan". She knew of several possible M. Noonans in her family, but did not know which one was referred to. She also did not know whether M. Noonan was the man in the picture or the person who wrote the note.

Figure 20.

The list of possible M. Noonans supplied by the picture's owner is:
1. Maurice/Morris Noonan, b. abt 1831, d. 1885,
2. Michael, a brother to the Maurice who was born about 1831. There is not too much known about Michael other than it is reasonably certain he died about 1900, at the age of about 60,
3. Maurice Noonan, b. 1918, still living,
4. Michael, b. 1949, still living.

As before, it is a good idea to start by making a list of the contents of a photograph. In this case, there are only a few simple items to consider: the hat, the chair, the dog, and the tree.

Although clothing is not usually a strong indicator of time period, the clue that is the most likely to lead to a specific date is the hat the man is wearing (Figure 21). The top of the hat is high with a dip running from front to back. The narrow brim is rolled up on the sides, but not in the front. The web site http://www.villagehatshop.com/hats_categories.html[10] gives a picture gallery of all kinds of hat styles – men's hats, women's hats, sport hats, and many more. By comparing the hat to the styles on this web site, the hat can be identified as a Homburg. This style came into style in 1890 when King Edward VII of England visited Germany for a vacation and returned home wearing such a hat. This dates the picture to no earlier than 1890.

©2005 The Village Hat Shop

Figure 21.

This photograph was not taken in a photographic studio – it was probably taken outside the man's home or outside the home of the photographer. The high probability that a Brownie camera was used to take the picture pushes the earliest date forward to about 1900. Although this eliminates M. Noonans #1 and #2 from the list, it is still not enough information to narrow down which of the M. Noonans is associated with the note.

A better estimate of the photograph's date is obtained from the physical characteristics of the photograph itself. The ratio of the length to the width of a picture, called the aspect ratio, depends on the dimensions of the negative used to print it. The aspect ratio of the print will be the same as that of the negative, assuming the print is not cropped, and is characteristic of the type of camera. In this case, the photo has an aspect ratio of 1.25 to 1. A typical film size with these proportions has the dimensions 4" x 5", or 5" x 4" if the camera is held on its side.

Film sizes 103, 104, 109, 110, and 123 all fit this description. There were several early Kodak cameras that used this size film, starting in 1896 with the Bullet Camera[9]. The most recent of these was the No. 4 Folding Pocket Camera, which was on the market from 1907 to 1915. Assuming one of these cameras was used to take this picture, and that whoever bought it used it for several years, the range of years for the photograph is 1896 through about 1918. Assuming that the picture was taken after the introduction of the Brownie camera slightly improves the range to 1900 through 1918.

The two remaining M. Noonans were born after 1918, so that none of the M. Noonans on this list matches the facts – at least not if the 'M. Noonan' denotes the person in the picture. However, the owner's Uncle Maurice (the M. Noonan born in 1918) swears that the man is the photograph is his father John Jeremiah Noonan (b. abt. 1868, d. May 20, 1935). If so, John Jeremiah would have been between 32 and 47 years old during 1900–1918. In 1907 when the Kodak Pocket Camera was introduced, he would have been 39. This all fits well with the appearance of the man in the picture, who seems to be in his mid 30s to late 40's.

Since we have exhausted all the possible M. Noonan's who could appear in the photograph, M. Noonan must be the person who wrote (and signed) the note. The evidence provided by the dimensions of the photograph indicates that Uncle Maurice is right, and that the man in the picture is probably his father. The task now is to find if John Jeremiah had a grandchild named M. Noonan who could have written the note.

BRIEF HISTORY OF PHOTOGRAPHY IN THE 19TH AND EARLY 20TH CENTURIES

What if a photograph was taken in a studio before 1900? How can it be identified? A brief discussion on the history of photography can answer these questions. During the 19th century, the style of photographs changed as techniques advanced, so that different types of photographs are associated with certain time periods. Once the general kind of photograph has been identified, specific details can sometimes narrow the possible date to within a few years.

The four main kinds of photographs that were common during the 19th and early 20th centuries are: Daguerreotypes, ambrotypes, tintypes, and albumen prints. Each of these types can be identified by unique characteristics relating to both the visual appearance of the image and to the type of deterioration it may exhibit. The development of each of these kinds of photographs was directed towards making photography less expensive and more convenient. Although the first Daguerreotypes were affordable only by the more well-off, later tintypes and albumen prints were relatively cheap and widely available.

A timeline of the major types of photographs of the 19th and early 20th centuries is given in Table 2[11]. Although a specific time period is given for each, none of the styles ceased production entirely. Daguerreotypes for example, are still occasionally produced today. The discussion here focuses on the four most popular types, with a brief mention of salt prints. Information on less common types of photographs such as cyanotypes can be found in the references provided for this chapter.

Table 2. Timeline of major photographic styles[11].

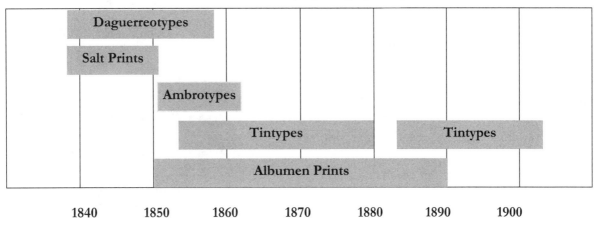

Daguerreotypes were invented by Louis Daguerre in 1839. They were the earliest type of photograph commercially available to the public. Daguerreotype images usually exhibit fine detail associated with a small aperture camera lens and high resolution, long exposure film (Figure 22). They were most popular during the late 1840s to early 1850s, and rarely produced after 1860. Photographs dating from the Civil War are often mislabeled as Daguerreotypes, but by that time, they had been replaced by the less expensive ambrotypes and tintypes.

Daguerreotypes were made by coating a layer of silver onto a highly polished copper plate, and then exposing the surface to sensitizing chemicals such as iodine or bromine vapor. This created a light sensitive silver halide layer on the surface of the silver coating. Exposing the plates to light reduced the silver halide in the exposed areas to metallic silver, which formed silver mercury amalgam when developed with mercury vapor. The silver halide remaining in unexposed areas was washed away in a final rinse with a fixative to prevent further development. The result was a positive, monochromatic mirror image of the original scene, with more highly exposed areas appearing bright due to the diffuse light scattering properties of the silver mercury amalgam, and unexposed areas appearing dark from off-axis reflection of the underlayer of bulk silver. To protect the image from damage, a brass mat was often placed directly on top of the photo edges to serve as a spacer for a protective glass cover.

The image of a Daguerreotype can only be seen through a limited range of viewing angles. Outside this range, the image appears as a negative because the off-axis reflection from the silver substrate is in the direction of the observer, causing the unexposed areas to appear much brighter than the exposed, more diffusely reflecting areas. If the seal protecting the copper plate, brass mat, and cover glass is damaged so that the image is exposed to the elements, a Daguerreotype will typically deteriorate from the edges inward (Figure 23).

Daguerreotypes can be identified by:
- Narrow viewing angle
- Image appearing as a negative outside of viewing angle
- Image reversed left to right
- Copper back
- High detail
- High contrast
- Glass cover protecting image
- Deterioration usually starting from the edges

Figure 22. A typical Daguerreotype.

Daguerreotypes had certain disadvantages. As every image was one-of-a-kind, a subject had to sit for each individual portrait. This was inconvenient in that the exposure time could be as long as 20 minutes and supports were often required to keep him in place. Plates could not be stored once they were sensitized, so that the development process had to take place within a few minutes of exposure.

Figure 23. Daguerreotypes deteriorate from the edges inward.

Ambrotypes were introduced by Frederick Scott Archer in 1851 and reached their peak popularity between 1855 and 1860. (See Figure 24). They died out after the introduction of the carte de visite (CdV) in the early 1860s. Ambrotypes became popular because they were cheaper and were more convenient to produce than Daguerreotypes, requiring shorter exposure times. The glass substrate of the ambrotype was also less easily damaged than the thin copper plate of the Daguerreotype.

The process required to make an ambrotype was similar to that used for producing a Daguerreotype, but resulted in a negative image of the original scene. The areas that were not exposed were washed away during processing just as for the Daguerreotype, but the absence of the underlying bulk silver layer caused the unexposed areas of the ambrotype to be clear and to seem brighter than the exposed areas where metallic silver remained in the collodion layer. The result was a negative image, but when backed by black velvet, the clear (unexposed) areas appeared black and caused the picture to appear as a positive. The plate could also be positioned face down on the backing, meaning the final product would not be reversed left to right. Unlike a Daguerreotype, an ambrotype can be seen through a wide viewing angle.

Figure 24. A typical ambrotype.

Ambrotypes can be identified by:
- Positive image visible through a wide viewing angle
- Not reversed left to right
- Glass substrate
- Black background in the form of black paint, metal, or fabric
- Removal of the black backing will cause the image to appear as a negative
- Relatively low contrast

Although ambrotypes exhibited many advantages over Daguerreotypes, the glass substrate was fragile. Ambrotypes were also relatively expensive to produce. Like Daguerreotypes, each portrait was one-of-a-kind.

Tintypes were invented by Adolphe Alexander Martin in 1853 as a less expensive and more rugged alternative to the ambrotype (Figure 25). The tintype was produced on an iron (not tin) sheet instead of a glass plate. The black backing required by an ambrotype to produce a positive image was replaced by a layer of lamp black applied to the surface prior to the application of the silver halide-carrying collodion film. Both sides were coated by varnish to protect the image from scratches and the metal from corrosion.

Tintypes became popular during the Civil War because it was possible for soldiers to send them to their families through the mail. They were less likely to break than the glass plates of ambrotypes or the copper plates of Daguerreotypes. In addition, up to twelve images could be produced on a plate in a single exposure with a multiple lens camera. It is said that the tintype got its name from the tin shears used to cut individual images from the multiply exposed sheet. Brown or chocolate tintypes were popularized by the Phenix Co. during the years 1870 through 1885. Another development was the 'rustic' look introduced around 1870 which made use of painted backgrounds of rural themes[12]. Tintypes were popular until the late 1880s, when they were superceded by gelatin dry emulsion plates, although in more rural areas they were produced until much later. Tintypes experienced a resurgence in popularity in the late 1890s, as a type of cheap and quick photograph sold at carnivals and boardwalks. The last tintypes were produced in about 1930.

A tintype can be identified by:
- Attraction to a magnet
- Wide viewing angle
- Image reversed left to right
- Whitish gray appearance of relatively low contrast

Figure 25. A typical tintype.

Two important developments at this time led to a great reduction in the cost and time required to produce photographs with improved quality. One was the ability to produce multiple photographic prints on paper and the second was the development of the glass negative.

From the very early days of photography, there was an effort to print photographs on paper from a negative with the goal of producing multiple, inexpensive copies of the same image. The first successful photograph of this kind was the **salt print**. The sensitized paper required by a salt print was created by dipping paper in a salt solution and then floating it on a solution of silver nitrate. The paper was printed from a negative through exposure to sunlight and then washed with water and fixed with sodium thiosulfate. Since the chemicals were absorbed into the paper, the surface features of the paper appeared as part of the final image, reducing the resolution. Although the salt print could produce multiple copies of the same image, its resolution could not compete with that of the Daguerreotype. Salt prints tended to fade easily and very few have survived to present times.

It was known that an increase in the resolution of a printed photograph could be accomplished by using a glass negative, but it was difficult to find a binder which would adhere to a glass surface. Many substances were tried, even snail slime. In 1848 Abel Niépce, the nephew of Nicephore Niépce, discovered that this problem could be solved by using albumen (egg white) salted with potassium iodide. After the suspension was applied to the surface, it was sensitized by exposure to a silver nitrate solution, and after exposure, developed with gallic acid.

The eventual result of being able to print photographs on paper from a glass negative was the **albumen print** (Figure 26). In 1850, two years after the discovery of albumen as a binding agent for glass negatives, Blanquart-Ervrard perfected albumen printing paper which offered the same convenience as salted paper but with much higher resolution and shorter exposure times. Albumen prints produced on paper still retained some trace of the surface features, but not to the degree of salt prints, since the coating filled the space between the fibers on the paper surface. Although the glossiness of its surface was not initially accepted, the albumen print became the most popular form of photograph through the end of the century. The albumen print was much more detailed than the salt print, but still required a very long exposure time, up to 30 minutes. For this reason, albumen prints were frequently used for landscapes and architectural scenes.

Figure 26. A typical albumin print

Albumen prints can be identified by:
- Glossy surface
- Some trace of the surface features of the paper in the image
- Fine cracks in the surface can be seen under low magnification
- Strong tendency to curl
- Most are attached to card stock
- Yellowing of bright areas (Figure 27)
- Loss of details in bright areas
- Fading inward from the edges[12]
- Inability to produce true back and white tones

Figure 27. Light areas in albumen prints can turn yellow with age.

Two very popular forms of the albumen print that deserve special mention are the **carte de visite** (**CdV**) and the **cabinet card**. Initially, CdVs were more popular and dictated the style of the cabinet card. In later years, when their popularity was reversed, the cabinet card set the standard for the CdV. Changes in card styles occurred gradually in parallel with developments in photography and according to popular demand. The longevity and spread of particular styles also depended on economics – expensive cameras could not be replaced every time a new trend appeared. For all of these reasons, attempts to date CdVs and cabinet cards should take into account overlap in the use of particular styles.

The CdV (Figure 28) was introduced in 1854 by Andre Adolphe Disderi[13] when he developed a method of producing eight images on a single 8" x 10" glass negative, allowing eight prints to be produced at one time. It is said that the CdV first became popular when the Emperor Napoleon stopped his army at Disderi's studio to have his photograph taken in full uniform during his march to Italy in 1859. The popularity of the CdV spread quickly throughout Europe and the United States, where collecting CdVs became quite a fad. Queen Victoria was an avid collector, owning several hundred.

Cartes de Visite are albumen prints that are typically 2 1/8" x 3 1/2", mounted on 2 1/2" x 4" card stock. Prints can deviate somewhat from this standard size because each print had to be cut by hand from the original multiple-image master print. The size of

Figure 28. A typical Carte de Visite.

the card stock is more regular since it was usually bought by the photographer from a commercial supplier. Upon the introduction of the photo album in about 1860, the standard size of the CdV was slightly reduced to be compatible with album pockets. Because the photographer attached a print to the card stock himself, the image is sometimes crooked with respect to the stock. CdVs were popular throughout the Civil War because like tintypes, they could be sent through the mail without being broken. CdVs reached their peak in popularity in 1866, after which they were gradually replaced by the cabinet card until production died out in the early 1880s.

There are guidelines for dating CdVs[14] based on card thickness, shape of card corners, image size, and borders. Since commercial card stock was sometimes stored and used at a later date to mount a print, the date derived for a CdV from its card stock can be different from the date the image was produced. It is also not uncommon to find an earlier Daguerreotype or ambrotype that was copied later as an albumen print. In the extreme case, the dates for the stock and the image can differ by as much as fifty years. An excellent guide to dating CdVs can be found at http://www.phototree.com/phototree/main/history/hist_cdv.htm[14]. Several of the guidelines that appear on this website are shown in Tables 3, 4, and 5.

Card thickness: The thickness of the CdV card stock was increased in 1870 and then again in 1880.

Table 3. CdV thicknesses of according to year.

Thickness	Year
0.01 – 0.02"	1858 – 1869
0.02 – 0.03"	1869 – 1887
0.03 – 0.04"	1880–1900

Card corners were mostly square until about 1870. After this, corners became rounded to make them less prone to wear and tear. Older cards might appear to have rounded corners, but close examination will reveal that corners that were originally square have become rounded through handling. Square corners that have been damaged in this way are generally more ragged than corners that were originally round.

Image size gradually became larger due to the improvement of photographic equipment. This improvement did not relate to the technical ability to take larger photographs. It related to the technical ability to take larger photographs with higher quality and adequate resolution, since the larger the image, the more noticeable an imperfection. In general, the smaller the photograph, the earlier it was produced, with dime-sized photographs dating from before 1865.

Table 4. CdV image sizes according to year.

Image Size	Year
Less than 3/4"	1860 – 1864
About 1"	1862 – 1867
Between 1 1/2" – 1 3/4"	1865 – 1872
2 1/8" – 3 1/2"	1874–1910

<u>Borders</u> can be used to date a CdV according to how many lines were used and how wide they were. A rule of thumb for dating a CdV according to its borders is that the fewer the lines used to border the photograph, and the thinner these lines are, the earlier the CdV was produced.

Table 5. CdV borders according to year.

Number of Lines	Year
None	1860 – 1863
One or Two Thin Lines One Wide and One Thin Line	1863 – 1869
Wide Lines	1874–1880

Props, backgrounds and card styles developed in parallel, starting from the very basic and ending with the ornate and imaginative. Early props and backgrounds consisted only of a chair or a table that the subject could lean on. Initially, card stock was white with straight edges. But around 1870, backdrops became much more inventive, and from about 1874 forward, colored card stock appeared sometimes with gilt and beveled edges. After 1863, CdV were sometimes displayed behind a rectangular or oval mat.

The *Photo Tree* web site in Reference 14 gives a convenient *Quick Identification Chart* summarizing CdV characteristics in relation to the time frames in which they were most popular. This chart is reproduced in Table 6.

Table 6. Guide to dating Cartes de Visite[14]

Feature	59-62	63-66	66-69	70-73	74-77	78-81
Card						
Square Corners	●	●	●			
Round Corners			○	●	●	●
Thin Stock	●	●	○			
Thick Stock			○	●	●	●
Tax Stamps (Sep 1, 1864 – Aug 1, 1866)		●	●			
Border–2 Thin Lines	●	○	○			
Border – 1 Thin, 1 Thick Line		●	●	○		
Border – 1 Very Thick Line					○	●
Colored Cards				○	●	●
Gilt and Beveled Edges					●	●
Image Size						
Very Small	●	○				
Medium		●	●			
Large				●	●	●

● = Commonly Used ○ = Sometimes Used

The **cabinet card** was introduced as a larger format albumen print by Windsor & Bridge in London in 1863 (Figure 29). It became known as a cabinet card because photographic albums were not large enough to accommodate it, so that it were usually displayed in cabinets. A standard cabinet card consists of a 4" x 5 1/2" image mounted on 4 1/4" x 6 1/2" card stock. Because of the larger size of the cabinet cards, retouching became a necessary part of the photographic process. Usually a test print was made first to identify changes and corrections to the negative from which final prints were made[15]. Cabinet cards were popular 1870–1890, but by the end of the century were declining in popularity due to the introduction of the snapshot (an unmounted paper photograph[16]). Cabinet cards continued to be produced until the early 1920s.

The styles of cabinet cards have not been researched as thoroughly as those of the CdVs, but as in the case of the CdV, the date can be estimated from the type of card stock used. The cabinet card can be recognized at first glance by its larger image and, for cabinet cards produced after about 1880, the photographer's logo and address at the bottom of the mat. Typically, the more elaborate the style of the card, the later in the century it was produced. In the 1880s and 1890s a number of colored card stocks were used, and by 1885 gold beveled edges were in style. In the 1890s scalloped and notched edges appeared, with elaborate patterns on the back. Until about 1895, cabinet cards were albumen prints, from 1895 through 1905, gelatin silver printing-out prints, and from 1905 forward, gelatin silver developing prints[17]. Cabinet cards from the 1890s often resemble later black and white photographs, printed on matte collodion, gelatin or gelatin bromide paper[18].

One of the most often quoted references on dating cabinet cards is Willis, *Photography as a Tool in Genealogy*[19]. While the information shown in Table 7 reproduced from Willis is not quite consistent with that above for CdVs, it is one of the few sources available.

Figure 29. A typical cabinet card.

Special Stamps

From August 1, 1864 through August 1, 1866, a special tax was placed on proprietary items to raise Civil War revenues for the Union Army. Manufacturers of goods such as matches, medicines, perfumes, and playing cards took advantage of the 5 to 10% discount allowed for producing their own stamps, and regarded them as an opportunity for advertising. These stamps are found in *Scott U.S. Specialized Catalog* and are known as 'Private Die Proprietary Stamps', or 'Matches and Medicines'[20].

Photographers opposed the tax, and refused to print their own stamps. They felt it was not worth the discount for the relatively small volume of photographs they produced, nor did they need the advertising, as the studio logo was more than likely printed on the back of the picture. For this reason, there are no equivalent private die stamps for photography studios. Photos from this era carry official government-issued tax stamps on their reverse sides.

Table 7. A guide to dating cabinet cards[19].

Card Colors	
1866–1880	White card stock of a light weight
1880–1890	Different colors for face and back of mounts
1882–1888	Face of buff, matte-finished, with a back of creamy-yellow, glossy
Borders	
1866–1880	Red or gold rules, single and double lines
1884–1885	Wide gold borders
1885–1892	Gold beveled edges
1889–1896	Rounded corner rule of single line
1890–1892	Metallic green or gold impressed border
1896	Impressed outer border, without color
Corners	
1866–1880	Square, lightweight mount
1880–1890	Square, heavy board with scalloped sides

The tax on photographs was also called the 'sun picture' tax, after one method used for printing the most popular (and therefore the most tax-worthy) albumen prints. The tax covered all types of photographs, including copies of engravings and artwork, photos used as book illustrations, and photographic portraits. It was paid in the case of an individual portrait by affixing a stamp to the back. (See Figure 30 and Figure 31.) A stamp was canceled immediately upon being used. Sometimes the cancellation was made by a simple pencil mark or the date, but sometimes a photographer printed his name or stamped his initials. In this case, the cancellation mark can provide clues to the origin of the photograph. Many photograph tax stamps have survived because photographs were the only items exempt from the stipulation that stamps be destroyed when opening a package[21].

The amount of tax depended on the value of the item: 2 cents for up to 25 cents, 3 cents for 25 to 50 cents, 5 cents from 51 cents to $1 and 5 additional cents for each additional $1 or fraction thereof. Some stamps are quite rare. The blue Playing Card stamp was used only during the summer of 1866[22], shortly before the tax was repealed. Stamps were most commonly placed on ambrotypes, tintypes, and CdVs. It is rare to find a cabinet card bearing a tax stamp. Because Daguerreotypes were not commonly produced during this period, they were not included in the tax.

Figure 30. Photographs from the Civil War era carry special tax stamps.

Figure 31. Tax stamp on a portrait photograph mounted in a cartouche mat typically used in the mid 1860s.

Union Cases

Even if the type of photograph is uncertain, the way a photograph is packaged can provide information on its date. Each of the two photos in Figure 32 was framed in a 2 ½" x 3" molded brown or black case with brass hinges. The case enclosing the photo on the left bears the inscription 'S. Peck & Co.', while the one enclosing the photo on the right reads, "Littlefield, Parsons, and Co." The portraits are two of a set of six photographs discovered by an individual while researching his Opdenweyer family.

Figure 32. Two photographic portraits enclosed in Union Cases.

The portraits themselves do not present too many details for further examination, but the frames and their cases certainly do. The first items to research of course are the companies 'S. Peck & Co.' and 'Littlefield, Parsons & Co.', to see when they were in business. The web site www.digimuse.usc.edu gives the following information[23]:

'A Case for Early Photography'

Except for paper-based images, most early photographs were customarily enclosed in miniature cases. Frequently containing portraits, cases protected Daguerreotypes, ambrotypes, and even tintypes from light, moisture, pollution, and abrasion; they also allowed the photographs to be easily and safely carried about.

Early cases were constructed of wood with leather or cloth coverings, metal fasteners, hinges, and fabric interior linings. The actual photograph, protected by glass and a brass mat, was snugly inserted into the back portion

Figure 33. The interior and exterior of a Union Case.

of the case. Opening the case like a book gave the viewer a chance to relate intimately to the image, and to its called-up memory. (See Figure 33.)

"Except for some well documented instances [of] success in this highly competitive and volatile industry, few manufacturers of the cases are known by name… Scovill Manufacturing Co.; Littlefield, Parsons & Company; [and] Edward T. Anthony Co."

The following detailed description of the history of the molded cases can be found on the web site http://www.plastiquarian.com/critchlo.htm[24].

Figure 34. Alfred Critchlow.

"Alfred P. Critchlow (Figure 34) was born in 1813 in Nottingham, England and manufactured horn buttons in Birmingham. He emigrated to the US and continued his trade in Haydenville, Mass., before moving to Florence, Mass. where he began experimenting in the early 1850s with shellac and gutta percha moulding compounds. He claimed to have invented a shellac-based moulding material (he called it Florence Compound) which he, and others, used to manufacture Union Cases. These highly decorated cases, used to protect Daguerreotype photographic images, were among the first mass-produced plastic mouldings. In an 1856 patent relating to the manufacture of Union Cases, Critchlow merely referred to the compound as being composed of various materials, well known to those whose business it is to manufacture such cases. Critchlow entered into partnership with Samuel Hill and Isaac Parsons in 1853 but in 1857, when the popularity of Union Cases was approaching its peak, he sold his interest in the business and its name was changed to Littlefield, Parsons & Company. However, by the mid 1860s, ambrotypes had taken over from Daguerreotypes and the need for the Union Case was gone. In 1866, Littlefield, Parsons & Co. changed their name to the Florence Manufacturing Co. and produced a number of beautiful shellac hand mirror and brush sets."

From this discussion, it can be deduced that the photo of the woman and her child on the left in Figure 32 was taken between 1853 and 1857 when the company was known as 'Samuel Peck & Co.', and the photo of the older man posed next to the chair on the right in Figure 32 was taken between 1857 and 1866, when the company was known as 'Littlefield, Parsons & Co.'.

IS THERE AN EVENT DEPICTED IN THE PHOTOGRAPH THAT CAN DATE IT?

Sometimes a photograph will contain explicit information on date through the depiction of an event. There aren't many of us that are lucky enough to have a picture of our great grandfather taken at the coronation of Queen Victoria or at the inauguration of President Lincoln. We more likely have pictures of birthday parties or Christmas dinners. Yet any kind of picture can contain hidden details that can directly relate to the date and even the time of day it was taken.

Figure 35.

The two photographs in Figure 35 provide a good example of a detail related to an event that can be a dead giveaway in dating a picture. These two photos were in the collection of a friend. She could not identify the women although she knew they were probably two of her many aunts. She also knew that the pictures were taken in New Orleans. By comparing the background scenery in the two photos, it is obvious that the pictures were taken about the same time and in the same place, possibly with the women exchanging the camera to take photos of each other with their children.

The key to unlocking the occasion of the photos as well as the identities of the two mothers is the snow on the ground. New Orleans has a subtropical climate, and the number of snow days in a century can be counted on two hands. Believe it or not, there is a web site listing all the

Table 8. New Orleans snow days.

Date	Snowfall	Date	Snowfall
Jan. 12, 1853	4"	Feb. 13, 1960	0.6"
Jan. 5, 1879	1"	Dec. 31, 1963	4.5"
Jan. 23/24, 1881	3"	Feb. 9, 1973	0.8"
Feb. 14/15, 1899	3"	Jan. 21, 1985	0.4"
Jan. 22, 1935	0.1"	Dec. 22, 1989	0.5"
Feb. 12, 1958	1.3"		

snow days in New Orleans for the last 150 years. See http://www.suite101.com/welcome.cfm/-french_quarter[25]. The snow dates listed are shown in Table 8.

From this list of rare snow dates, we can obviously rule out those prior to the turn of the century. My friend could also narrow down the date to the late 1950s, or early 1960s, when her aunts still had small children. Fortunately, there are only three dates that fall into the acceptable range, those in 1958, 1960 and 1963. The woman on the left is holding a child who is about two years old, and the woman on the right is holding a slightly younger child, and she also appears pregnant. (One way to tell the child on the left is probably younger is that he is not as heavy as the one on the right, judging by the posture of the two mothers.) Comparing these facts to the birthdates of her cousins, the picture's owner was able to say that the photos were taken February 12, 1958. The two women were her Aunt June (on the right) and her Aunt Bev (on the left). Aunt Bev was holding her daughter Alicia who was 21 months old, and Aunt June was holding her son Peter who was 16 months old. Aunt June was six months pregnant with her daughter Cynthia, who was born the following May.

The pictures were taken either at sunrise or at sunset. But in a subtropical climate, chances are that it had snowed during the night and the women were out early in the morning to see it before it melted. According to http://www.timeanddate.com/worldclock/astronomy.html[26], the sun rises at 6:43 a.m. every year on this date in New Orleans. Aunt June's picture was snapped about this time because the sun was just peeping over the house in the background. Aunt Bev got her picture taken slightly before this, when the sun had not yet made its appearance over the rooftops. Both women were facing northwest into the camera.

RESEARCHING DATE-RELATED ITEMS

Unique packaging or models of consumer products such as cars, cigarettes, foods, beer and wine are often on the market only for a limited time period. If such an item appears in a photograph, chances are that the photograph was taken about the same time that the item was available. The reference materials used for dating consumer products are as varied as the products themselves. Catalogs, almanacs, city directories, newspaper ads, and even other photographs can be used. Web sites associated with collectibles are a great resource for this purpose. If several items appear in a single photograph, they can be used as a group to narrow the date.

Two great examples of pictures that show what good digital detective work can accomplish with little or nothing to go on are the photographs shown in Figures 36 and 40. Success in dating them depended on many of the consumer items in the pictures. Typically, the owner of these photographs had almost no information about their origins. She had found them among her deceased mother's belongings and guessed that they were taken in New Orleans.

Most of the items in the picture in Figure 36 are generic and could be found anywhere, at any time. The woman in the poster behind the cash register seems to be dressed in the style of the late 1800s or early 1900s. This poster could be a reproduction of an earlier one and located in a more modern barroom, but the handlebar mustache of the bartender on the left is also consistent with the turn of the 20th century. Neither of these details is specific enough to date the photograph, however.

Figure 36.

The cash register has great potential for further investigation (Figure 37). It is an item that was probably manufactured for only a certain period of time, superceded by later models with more advanced capabilities. The cash register also has potential as a collectible, that is, there might be individuals or organizations that collect antique registers who could identify its make and the dates it was available. The design of the case, the number and position of the keys, even the style of the sale indicator showing through the window might be useful in getting an estimate of when this style of register was in common use.

Figure 38. Model 349 NCR cash register.

Figure 37. Cash register in the photograph in Figure 36.

This cash register has two rows of keys, thirteen on the top and fourteen on the bottom. According to the National Cash Register Catalog for 1909[27], which can be found on the web site http://brasscashregisters.com/page4a.html[28], the key pattern corresponds to that of Models 346, 347, and 349. The catalog states that the Model 349 was made especially for bars and cafes, with a security feature to prevent an employee from stealing from the till. For this reason, the register in the picture was probably a Model 349, which sold for $125 in 1909 (Figure 38). According to the web site, the case is the dolphin design that was in use from 1902 through 1915. Since the Model 349 register probably appeared in the NCR catalog for several years around 1909, and it was likely used in the bar for a period of time, 1909 is only an approximate year for the picture. But this is a good starting point for further research.

CREATING A TIME LINE

If you are dating a photograph containing a large number of potentially date-related items in it, it is a good idea to create a time line showing when each of the items was on the market. The timeline can be drawn as a table in Microsoft Word® or Excel®, or simply freehand on paper, and can have a row for each item being investigated. A row can be colored in to indicate the earliest and latest date an item could have been produced. The overlap in time periods for all the items is when the photograph was probably taken.

The barroom photograph shown in Figure 40 has quite a few things in it that might helpful in dating it. It also had an important clue to location. The picture's owner discovered an address penciled on the back – 761 Baronne St., a location downtown in the New Orleans business district. (Remember to look at the back!)

Because Prohibition was in effect from October 1919 through April 1933, the bar had to be in operation before 1919 or after 1933. The bartender in this picture is the same as the man on the left in the first barroom and he looks about the same age. The approximate date of this second picture must be around 1909, with 1919 as the latest year that the barroom could have been in existence. Our initial time line stretches between these two dates. See Figure 39.

Appearance of register in NCR catalog ▼														Prohibition ▼
					Total									
1904	1905	1906	1907	1908	1909	1910	1911	1912	1913	1914	1915	1916	1917	1918

Figure 39. Initial timeline for dating the items in the barroom in Figure 40.

Don't forget to make a list of items that merit investigation:
- Pictures on the wall behind the bar
- Beer signs behind the bar
- Whiskey bottles
- Ad on the door leading to the street
- The car in the street
- The sign on the next building seen through the open door

Other items of interest that we can put in a stockpile for further reference are the sign (calendar?) in the window, and the picture on the wall between the door and the bar. We might also make a note of the sunlight that is glaring through the windows as a possible key to location.

Most of these items have very interesting histories that could lead to a date for the picture. They are shown in Figure 41 highlighted over the original photo. A timeline showing when these items were on the market is shown later in Figure 51.

Figure 40. Bar located at 761 Baronne St., New Orleans, LA

Figure 41. Items in the barroom that could help date the picture.

Figure 42 shows the picture hanging to the left on the wall behind the bar. When it is enlarged, the writing above the woman's portrait can be read as 'Harvard Rye'. According to http://www.awa.dk/whisky/windex.htm[29], Harvard Rye was a type of whiskey distilled by the Klein Bros. in Cincinnati, O. The 'pre-pro.com' Web site, "a Web Site Devoted to the Appreciation of Pre-prohibition Shot Glasses," indicates that the Harvard Rye brand was in use between 1899-1918. See http://www.pre-pro.com/Dataweb/pages/Klein_Bros_Cincinnati.html[30]. The distillery was listed in the Williams' Cincinnati, Ohio General & Business Directory as early as 1881. In 1911 it is shown as, "KLEIN BROS., Distillers and Wholesale Liquor Dealers; proprietors [sic] Live Oak Distillery Co., 212".

Figure 42. Picture on left.

Figure 43.

The Falstaff shield (Figure 43) with the name 'Lemp' under the Falstaff name and 'St. Louis' appearing below that, dates from between 1903 and 1918. The Lemp family were the original owners of the brewery and licensed the name in 1903. The brewery was closed in 1918 after the family experienced a string of personal and professional misfortunes[31]. The Falstaff shield with the Lemp name and the St. Louis designation were introduced at the 1904 St. Louis World's Fair.

The cash register shown in Figure 44 is the same type as the one in the first barroom picture. (It might be the same register.) It is an NCR Model 349 with a Dolphin style pattern from the 1909 National Cash Register Catalog. The register has an additional Dolphin style marquee across the top reading, "Amount Purchased"[32].

Figure 44.

The Cook & Rice City Brewery was established in 1853 in Evansville, IN (Figure 45). In 1885, the name was changed to the F. W. Cook Brewing Company until the brewery was closed in 1919 because of Prohibition. In 1933, it reopened as the F. W. Cook Co. Some of the Cook labels included Cook's Bock Beer, Cook's 500 Ale, and Cook's Goldblume, the beer advertised by the pennant hanging to the left of the cash register. See

Figure 45.

Figure 46.

http://www.beercollections.com/BCIN190.htm[33].

The key to this strange picture on the wall (Figure 46) is the picture on the wall in the picture. The scene takes place in a parlour, with one couple seated to the left and the other dancing to the right. The parlour is decorated with a mantelpiece behind the dancing couple, a potted plant in the far left corner, and a tiger skin rug on the floor. The foreground displays a whiskey bottle, so that this must be another liquor ad. On the rear wall of the parlour there is a picture carrying a logo. If we could read it, we'd probably know the name of the whiskey being advertised.

The logo becomes legible when this section of the picture is scanned at high resolution and enlarged. It reads 'Harvard' above a country scene with a field and some sort of building. The writing on the bottom is not quite readable even at high resolution, but it appears to say, "____ Bros, _____ O." But we already found that Harvard Rye was produced by the Klein Bros. in Cincinnati, O. The black robes and square hats that the two men are wearing must be graduation robes and mortar boards. The tassels on the hats are to the observer's right, indicating the two men are celebrating their graduation from Harvard. The man who is standing is raising a glass in a toast to their accomplishment. Since this is evidently another ad for Harvard Rye, it represents the same time period 1899–1918 as the woman's portrait to the left.

Figure 47.   Figure 48.

The caption at the bottom of the picture on the right of the wall behind the bar (Figure 47) is a giveaway. It says, "Anheuser Busch" and includes the company's logo of an eagle superimposed on a large capital 'A'. The picture is that of the well-known Red Dress Budweiser® Girl from 1907. This image appears on one of a set of four collectible beer mugs offered for sale on the web site:

http://www.beer-steins.com/budsteins/P002593_jp60.jpg [34], (Figure 48) each depicting a famous Budweiser® girl.

Unfortunately, there are only a couple of whiskey bottle labels on the shelves (Figure 49) that can be read even at high resolution, Oxford Club Dry Gin (A), and Hill's Horehound Irish Moss (B). There are also a couple of bottles of Falstaff Beer on the bottom shelf in the image to the far left (C). Many of the same whiskey and beer bottles appear several times on the shelves behind the bar. Unfortunately, most of the labels are not legible or are turned away from the camera. Curiously, the only reference to Hill's Horehound Irish Moss that I could find on the internet was for a cold medication by the same name.

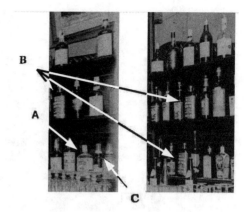

Figure 49.

The identification of the Budweiser® Girl from Anheuser Busch in St. Louis and the Harvard Rye logo from a distillery in Cincinnati gives an interesting insight into how New Orleans obtained its liquor stocks. Evidently, the most popular whiskeys and beers were manufactured in cities further north, and shipped down the Mississippi River for sale to barrooms in the city.

Figure 50 shows the ad for Bull Durham tobacco hanging on the door to the bar. I could not find any reference to this particular ad on any of the collectible sites I visited, but I did find an interesting history on Bull Durham tobacco at www.rabbitbrush.com/hickson/BullDurham.html[35]. John Ruffin Green was a tobacco farmer in North Carolina during the Civil War. While troops from both sides were camped in the area they sampled his tobacco. They enjoyed it so much that after the war requests came to Green from all over the country for more. Green realized his opportunity, and expanded his business. He coined the term 'Bull Durham' after the bull on the label of Coleman's Mustard that he mistakenly believed was manufactured in Durham, England. Originally known as, 'Genuine Durham Smoking Tobacco', it was later known simply as 'Bull Durham'[36]. It was the most popular brand of tobacco in the world throughout the latter part of the 1800s.

Figure 50.

So far, from dates associated with the pictures, the beer ads and the cash register, we have narrowed the date to around 1910. This is consistent with the approximate date of 1909 we found for the first barroom photograph.

Prohibition ▼

	Figure 45. Cook's Goldblum Beer
	Figures 42 & 46. Harvard Rye Pictures
	Figure 43. Falstaff Shield
			Figure 47. Budweiser Girl											
					Figures 37 & 44. Cash Register									
					>>>Total for Items inside Bar<<<									
1904	1905	1906	1907	1908	1909	1910	1911	1912	1913	1914	1915	1916	1917	1918

Figure 51. Timeline for items in the bar.

Figure 52.

The timeline relating to the items in Figures 42 through 50 is given in Figure 51. The latest date that the bar could have opened is given by the appearance of the cash register in the 1909 NCR catalog. The latest date it could have been in existence was October 1919 when Prohibition began. None of the other items helps to narrow down the time period.

I have saved the best for last. The final two details on the list are the most important in dating this photo. They are not items seen in the bar. Both of them can be seen through the open door outside on the street. The first is the car parked on the curb (Figure 52), and the second is the sign on the shop next door. Through minor changes in the contrast and gamma correction, the glare through the door can be reduced so that both of these items are visible in more detail.

When the car is cropped from the image, enlarged, and enhanced on its own, it appears to be a Ford Model T. It has several features that can be compared to online

Figure 53.

Ford Motor Company catalogs to identify the model[37] (Figure 53). The body of the car is compact so that it is much shorter than a touring car. The top seem to be curved down towards the front somewhat, which rules out the Ford Coupe. The back window is rectangular. While the window does not appear to be centered, the opening is probably eclipsed by part of the frame of the car, so that it looks off center and smaller than it really is.

Still another feature is the shape of the back. There seems to be a hood pulled up over the seats and the differential can be seen between the rear wheels where the back flattens out. There is a small bright spot on the passenger side about half way to the top of the hood. This could be the rear view mirror that could be ordered with the car as an accessory. In addition, wedged in the corner just above the wheels and to the right of the passenger side, there is the hint of a round headlight. The best matches for the car in this time period are the 1911 and 1912 Ford Model T Runabout, popularly known as the Roadster (Figure 54). The body of earlier Runabout models is too long; later models had a different style back. Since the Roadster rolled off the production line from Oct. 1, 1910 through Sept. 30, 1912, if our identification of the car is correct, the photo had to have been taken after October 1, 1910[38].

Figure 54.

Even though Ford motor cars were sold all over the country, the number of cars of this model that were produced was not very high[39]. (See Table 9.)

According to the city directory, New Orleans did not have a Ford dealership at this time. There were probably fewer Model T Fords in New Orleans than in other large cities that did have dealerships such as Houston, St. Louis, and Chicago. On the basis of the low production numbers and the lack of a New Orleans dealership, it might be possible to discover the actual owner of the car. But according to Wayne Everard, Archivist at the Louisiana Division of the New Orleans Public Library, city automobile registration or licensing records began only in about 1924, and records that do still exist tend to be summary records rather than those for individual vehicles or drivers[39]. The state of Louisiana did not require vehicle registration until the 1930s, so there is probably no information available on the identity of the owner of the vehicle in the picture.

Table 9.

Year	No. Produced
1911	7,845
1912	13,376

							Total for Items Inside Bar								
							Model T*								
							>>Total<<								
1904	1905	1906	1907	1908	1909	1910	1911	1912	1913	1914	1915	1916	1917	1918	

Figure 55. Timeline including the Model T Ford Roadster. *Assumes the car was in use for at least three years after it was purchased.

When the dates of manufacture for the Model T Roadster are included in the time line, the range of dates when the picture could have been taken becomes narrower. See Figure 55.

The sign on the shop next door is the last item on the list and perhaps the most tantalizing clue of all. When the sign is cropped from the photo and its contrast enhanced, part of the name of the neighboring shop can be read. The sign appears to say G_N_ M_R __ (Figure 56). Is it possible to use these scraps of letters to figure out the name of the business at this location when the picture was taken? If the company was around only for a short time, it might be possible to narrow the date of the photograph even further.

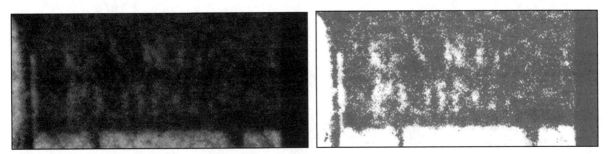

Figure 56. The sign on the next building.

<u>Was the Barroom in the Picture Really Located at 761 Baronne St.?</u> Before proceeding with an investigation of the establishment next door, it's probably a good idea to confirm that the barroom was located at 761 Baronne St. and that the address on the back is not the mailing address of someone who wanted to receive a copy of the picture.

The United States is above the Tropic of Cancer so that the sun always shines from the south, so with glare coming through the windows and the door, the bar had to be facing southerly into the sun. The car was parked on the west side of the street pointing towards the south, too. The door was located in the corner of the barroom and there was apparently no building next door to block the sun from the

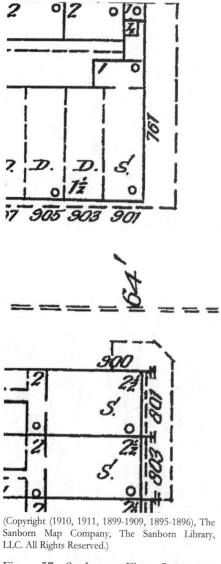

(Copyright (1910, 1911, 1899-1909, 1895-1896), The Sanborn Map Company, The Sanborn Library, LLC. All Rights Reserved.)

Figure 57. Sanborn Fire Insurance Map from 1895 – 1896.

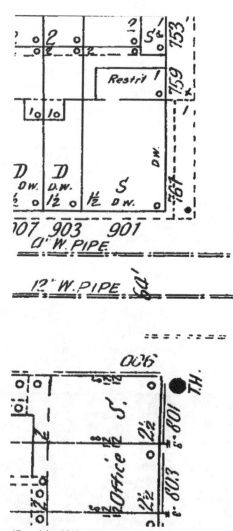

(Copyright (1910, 1911, 1899-1909, 1895-1896), The Sanborn Map Company, The Sanborn Library, LLC. All Rights Reserved.)

Figure 58. Sanborn Fire Insurance Map from 1908 – 1909.

windows, so that the bar was probably located on the northwest corner of the street. The car and the sign seen through the door seem a bit far away to be right next door. If the bar was on a corner, the next shop was probably across a side street intersecting the main road. All this information is useful for confirming the barroom's address using old city maps.

The Sanborn Fire Insurance Maps were created by the Sanborn Company beginning in the late 19th century[40]. They provided data for insurance underwriters, such as building materials (wood frame vs. brick, shingle vs. slate roof, etc.) and other information useful for determining insurance rates. They were made for cities all over the U.S. Excerpts from the Sanborn maps for New Orleans for 1895–1896 and for 1908–1909 show that 761 Baronne was indeed on the northwest corner of the intersection of Baronne and Julia Sts. (Figure 57 and Figure 58)[41]. The maps also show that the numbers on Baronne St. run from north to south, with the odd numbers on the west side of the street. The number on the northwest corner has to be the highest odd number on that block. This is consistent with the address 761 Baronne written on the back of the photo.

While the maps do not explicitly say that the establishment at this address was a bar, they indicate that there was a restaurant next door that could be accessed through a door between the two businesses. This would be close to the place where the photographer was standing when he took the picture.

The Sign across the Street–Clues from City Directories. The New Orleans city directories give additional information on the businesses that were located near the corner of Baronne and Julia Sts. around this time. The directories show that the saloon located at 761 Baronne St. changed hands several times between 1908 and 1919, and was owned in 1912 by Paul DiMaggio, the maternal great grandfather of the owner of the photograph (She was not aware of this.) He is shown at that address through the 1919 city directory, meaning he owned the bar until Prohibition began.

Since the city directory for a particular year was compiled over a period of several months during the previous year, the listings provided by the directories indicate that the picture was taken between mid 1911 (after the neighborhood had been surveyed for the 1912 directory) and 1919 when Mr. DiMaggio had to close the bar because of Prohibition. Now that we have confirmed the address of the bar as 761 Baronne and that it is indeed the one shown in the picture, we can continue to investigate the sign on the building located across Julia St.

An updated timeline is shown in Figure 59. The earliest date the picture could have been taken is still late 1910, due to Paul DiMaggio's appearance in the 1912 directory. The latest date is still

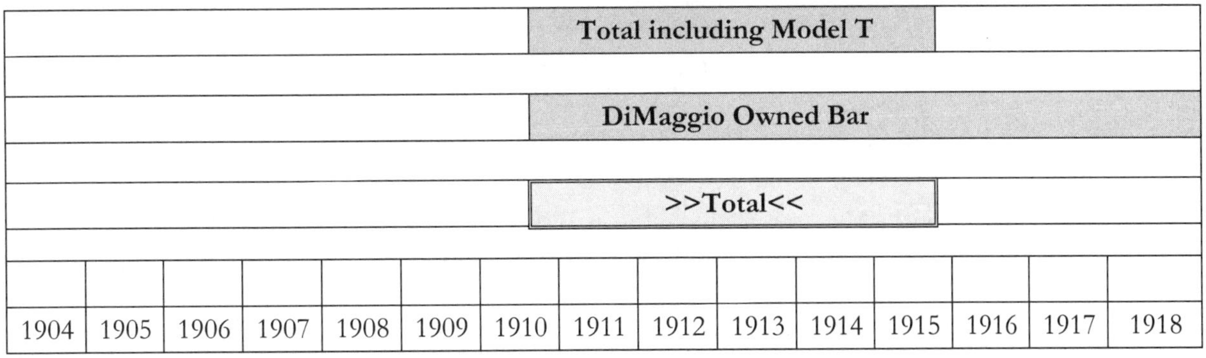

						Total including Model T								
						DiMaggio Owned Bar								
						>>Total<<								
1904	1905	1906	1907	1908	1909	1910	1911	1912	1913	1914	1915	1916	1917	1918

Figure 59. The timeline now includes the dates Paul DiMaggio owned the bar.

determined by the Model T as around late 1915, assuming the car was used for no more than three years after it was purchased.

The 1911 New Orleans city directory is available online through Ancestry Plus[42]. The businesses listed in the neighborhood of 761 Baronne in 1911 are given in Table 10.

Table 10. Listings on Baronne St. in the 1911 New Orleans city directory.

\multicolumn{3}{c}{1911}		
Street No.	**Name**	**Business Type**
761	Williams, Shannon L.	Saloon
801	So. Packing Mfg. Co.	Insulation
803	McCann, Mrs. Lena	Boarding House
805	Strouse Distillery Co.	Distillery
811	Go-Ro Mfg. Co.	Water Heaters

Checking the directories of other years for these listings might narrow down the time period. The Southern Packing Mfg. Co. was listed at 801 Baronne from 1911 until 1915, after which time it relocated to 820 Baronne on the opposite side of the street and a few doors to the south. By 1916, the Southern Co. was no longer listed in the directory, nor were Mrs. McCann and her boarding house. Since the name 'Southern Packing Mfg. Co.' is too long to match what little can be read of the sign, it's likely that the picture dates either from before the Southern Co. appeared at that address or after it moved down the street – before mid 1910 or after mid 1914, the years the 1911 and 1915 directories were prepared. An interesting inconsistency is emerging between the dates derived from the city directories and the start date of October 1, 1910 for the manufacture of the 1911 Ford Roadster. (But see below.)

Correlating the letter fragments that appear on the sign with the types of businesses that are shown in the directories might give clues to what the sign says. Tables 10 and 11 show the variety of listings in the neighborhood. The top word on the sign could be the surname of the business owner, such as *Smith*, as in *Smith's Carpets*. It could also be a word describing the kind of business, such as *retail* auto parts or *wholesale* furniture. The bottom could be the name of a service, such as *painter*, the name of a product, such as *tires*, or the name of an activity such as *manufacturing*. Comparing the bottom line of the sign with the possibilities given by the directories, it seems 'PLUMBING' fits what can be seen of the number and shape of the letters. The letter we originally thought was an M could instead be PL and the R could have been mistaken for the middle strokes of UM. In comparison, the upper word on the sign seems to have six letters resembling G _ M _ _ _, with a round letter in between the G and the M.

Comparing the directory listings for all the plumbing supply stores and all the plumbers with the top row of the sign successfully produced a match. The Go-Ro Mfg. Co. was owned by Nicolas G. Goreau.

Table 11. Listings near the address 761 Baronne taken from the 1916 New Orleans city directory. The Southern Packing Manufacturing Co. was no longer listed in the neighborhood.

1916		
Street No.	Name	Business Type
761	DiMaggio, Paul	Saloon
805	Stechmann, Carl	Plumber & Gasfitter
809	Vorhaben, T. J. & Bro.	Jeweler
811	Jalemak, J.	Leather and Findings
813	Roser, Andrew	Auto Tire Service, Vulcanizing
826	Go-Ro Mfg. Co.	Water Heaters

There was also a Thomas W. Goreau, a plumber, listed at 751 Carondelet for most of this time period. The name Goreau has six letters, and starts with a G. Its second letter is round. It is possible that the letter identified earlier as an M is really an R. The sign says 'Goreau Plumbing'.

The directories show that the Go-Ro Mfg. Co. was located at 801 Baronne St. through 1909 and that it produced water filters. According to his biography that appears on the New Orleans Rootsweb site[43], Thomas W. Goreau was the older brother of Nicholas G. Goreau, and was the inventor of the then 'well-known' Goreau water filter. In 1910 when the Goreaus relocated to 811 Baronne, the 801 address is not listed. The building was probably left vacant, after which the Southern Packing Mfg. Co. arrived sometime in 1910, in time to be listed in the 1911 directory.

The Go-Ro Co. also manufactured hot water heaters. The Southern Packing Mfg. Co. manufactured packing for hot water heaters, so there is a logical connection between the two companies. The landlord could have leased the property out to a second business similar to the first, especially if the two companies required the same kind of facilities. Alternatively, the owners of the two companies might have been friends or professional colleagues and negotiated a sublease when the Goreaus moved out. The directories indicate that there were several plumbing companies in this block around 1910, and that they seemed to occupy many of the same addresses as they appeared and disappeared over the years.

A comparison between the owners of the saloon at 761 Baronne and the tenants at the corner of Baronne and Julia Sts. and is given in Table 12, with an updated timeline in Figure 60.

Table 12. Listings from 1908 through 1912 at the corner of Baronne and Julia St.

Year	Go-Ro Mfg. Co.	Southern Packing Manufacturing Co.	List of Saloon Owners at 761 Baronne St.
1908	801 Baronne	Not Listed	Haydel, Sydney F.
1909	801 Baronne	Not Listed	Haydel, Sydney F.
1910	811 Baronne	Not Listed	Garner, Edward
1911	811 Baronne	801 Baronne	Williams, Shannon L.
1912	811 Baronne	801 Baronne	DiMaggio, Paul

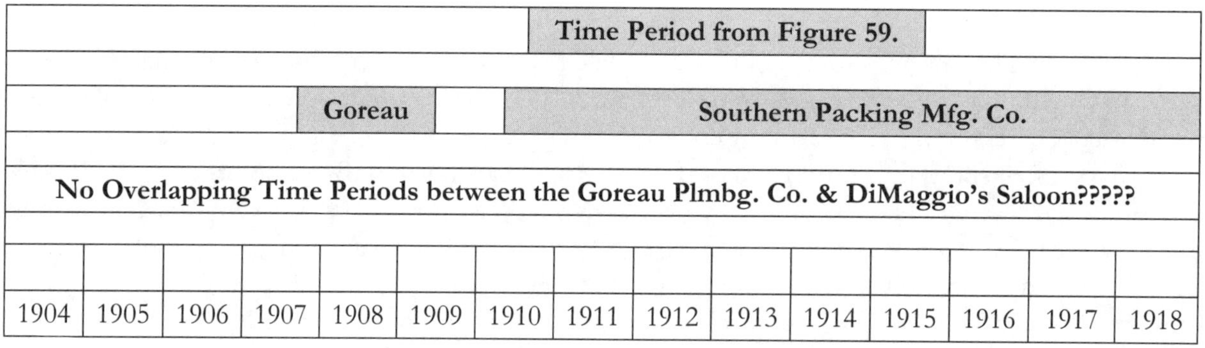

		Time Period from Figure 59.	
	Goreau		Southern Packing Mfg. Co.
No Overlapping Time Periods between the Goreau Plmbg. Co. & DiMaggio's Saloon?????			
1904	1905	1906	1907	1908	1909	1910	1911	1912	1913	1914	1915	1916	1917	1918

Figure 60. The Goreau Plumbing Co. had already relocated from 801 Baronne by the time Paul DiMaggio took ownership of the bar. They were not located on the corner at the same time.

The Solution to the Mystery. The puzzle is how the photo can show Paul DiMaggio in the bar at 761 Baronne at the same time a sign saying 'Goreau Plumbing' hung in front of the corner shop across the street. Go-Ro moved out of 801 Baronne before late 1909, but DiMaggio did not buy the bar until after late 1910.

The only possible explanation is that the Southern Packing Mfg. Co. leased the property at 801 Baronne early in 1910, but the company did not move in right away. The old Goreau Plumbing sign remained in place while the property was left vacant. Only after DiMaggio took over the saloon later in 1910 did the Southern Co. physically move into their new location across the street and take down the sign. The Go-Ro Manufacturing Co. might not have overlapped with Paul DiMaggio, but the Goreau Plumbing sign certainly did.

We know from the Model T car parked in the street that Paul Dimaggio moved in after October 1, 1910. Since this was too late for him to be listed in the 1911 directory, we can use October 1 as the nominal date by which the neighborhood around the intersection of Baronne and Julia Sts. was surveyed for the next year's directory. While the Southern Co. could have left the property vacant the entire time they were listed at that location (mid 1910 through mid 1914), this is not too likely. It's seems safe to assume that they relocated to the corner later in 1910, at which time they removed the Goreau Plumbing sign.

The end of the story is that the photo was taken between October 1, 1910 and October 1, 1911. My guess is that the photograph was taken on the opening day for DiMaggio at his new saloon. The three men in the picture are not customers. They are friends or relatives who came by for the grand opening. There are no glasses on the bar indicating they were not there to buy a drink. The rubbish on the floor near the bar might have been left over from the party the night before celebrating the change of ownership. Shannon L. Williams locked up one evening, and Paul DiMaggio took over the following morning. If these assumptions are correct, a future search of the conveyance records in the New Orleans Notarial Archives might produce the exact date the photo was taken.

Going by the dates provided by the car, the sign on the building next door, and information from the city directories, there were eight events that had to occur in a specific order for the picture to look as it does:

- The Goreau Plumbing Co. relocated from 801 Baronne St. sometime between late 1908 and mid 1909, leaving the building vacant for the next year or so,
- The city directory company surveyed the neighborhood in mid 1909 for the 1910 city directory listings,
- The Southern Packing Manufacturing Co. leased the location between late 1909 and mid 1910,
- The city directory company surveyed the neighborhood in mid 1910 for the 1911 city directory listings,
- Paul Dimaggio opened his saloon at 761 Baronne St. between Oct. 1, 1910 and October 1, 1911,
- The photographer took the picture of Paul in his saloon on opening day with the Goreau sign still hanging on the vacant building across Julia St.,
- The Southern Packing Manufacturing Co. relocated to 801 Baronne St.,
- The city directory company surveyed the neighborhood in mid 1911 for the 1912 city directory listings.

A final timeline including all these events is shown in Figure 61. Note that the exact date that the sign was removed is not important, as long as it was hanging at 801 Baronne on the day that Paul DiMaggio and his three patrons got their picture taken.

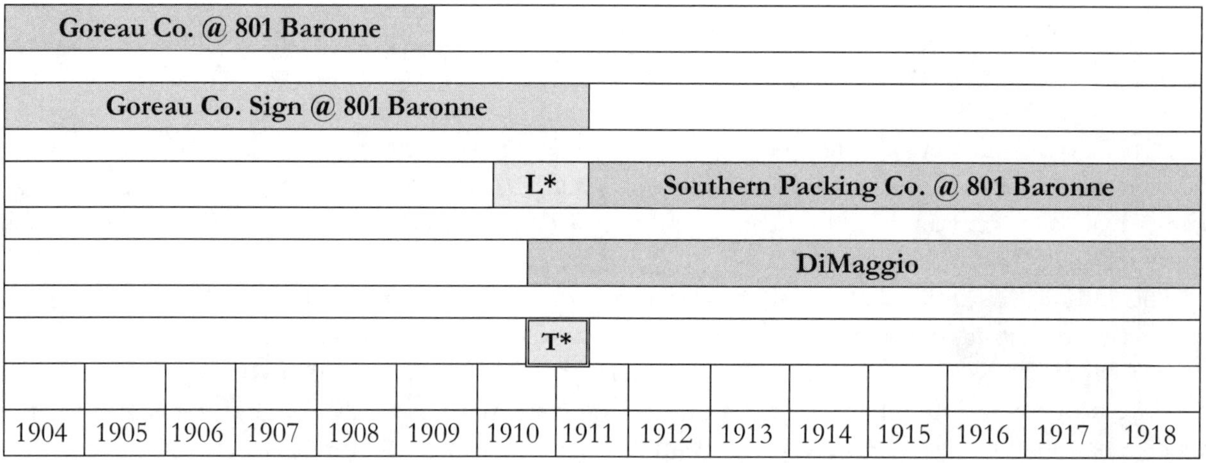

	1904	1905	1906	1907	1908	1909	1910	1911	1912	1913	1914	1915	1916	1917	1918
Goreau Co. @ 801 Baronne	■	■	■	■											
Goreau Co. Sign @ 801 Baronne	■	■	■	■	■	■									
Southern Packing Co. @ 801 Baronne							L*	■	■	■	■	■	■	■	■
DiMaggio								■	■	■	■	■	■	■	■
T*							T*								

Figure 61. The Goreau sign stayed on the building until after Paul DiMaggio took over ownership of the bar. *L = The Southern Packing Mfg. Co. leased 801 Baronne sometime before mid 1910. *T = Total period of overlap between the Goreau sign hanging on the building at 801 Baronne and Paul DiMaggio's ownership of the bar.

SOMETIMES THE MAGIC WORKS AND SOMETIMES IT DOESN'T – STUMPERS

There are some pictures which are frustrating to work with because they contain almost, but not quite enough information for analysis. This picture (Figure 62) is one which was sent to me by a woman who told me that she had found it in old family papers. She was puzzled about who Francis C. Brady could have been because the Brady name was not in her family.

Although this photo is a prime candidate for location analysis, it does not provide enough information to do anything except wonder where it was taken. There is no unique detail that gives away its location or date. The style of the tombstone is generic, as is the type of plants which appear in the picture. Even if a FBI-style genealogical library of tombstones and plants were available, these clues are probably not much help. The shadows on the two black cones on the back corners of the grave enclosure could possibly be used to determine either the time of day or day of the year the photo was taken, or else the location, but not both. Since neither in known in this case, we are out of luck.

Figure 62.

---

[1] "A Method for Dating Photographs relative to 1950", Paul Messier, Conservator of Photographs, Boston Art Conservation, http://paulmessier.com/PM/PDF/AIPAD4W3.pdf
[2] http://www.mapquest.com. Search on 2199 Duels St., New Orleans, LA 70119.
[3] http://www.mapquest.com. Search on Lafayette, LA, and increase the zoom factor.
[4] http://www.mapquest.com. Search on Lafayette, LA, and click on Yellow Pages.
[5] See for example, http://www.geocities.com/vintageconnection/, http://costumes.org/pages/timelinepages/timeline.htm, and http://www.geocities.com/vintageconnection/VintageConnection--LinksTimelinesEtc.html
[6] http://www.kodak.com/US/en/corp/aboutKodak/kodakHistory/milestones78to32.shtml
[7] http://www.rleggat.com/photohistory/
[8] http://www.kodak.com/US/en/corp/kodakHistory/1878_1929.shtml
[9] http://members.aol.com/Chuck02178/brownie.htm
[10] http://www.villagehatshop.com/hats_categories.html

[11] "Identification of Major 19th C. Photographic Print Processes", Paul Messier, Boston Art & Conservation & Art Conservation Department, Buffalo State College, http://albumen.stanford.edu/id/messier2000.htm
[12] http://www.city-gallery.com/learning/types/tintype/index.php
[13] http://www.photographymuseum.com/histsw.htm
[14] http://www.phototree.com/phototree/main/history/hist_cdv.htm
[15] O. Henry Mace, *Collector's Guide to Early Photographs*, Krause Publications, 1999, p. 134.
[16] http://www.city-gallery.com/learning/types/cabinet_card/index.php
[17] http://www..cycleback.com/earlyphotos/three.html
[18] http://www.city-gallery.com/learning/types/cabinet_card/index.php
[19] http://www.city-gallery.com/learning/guide/cabinet-date.php
[20] http://www.pipeline.com/~ciociola/baryla/m&m.htm
[21] http://www.pipeline.com/~ciociola/baryla/civilwar.htm
[22] http://www.pipeline.com/~ciociola/baryla/4c-pc.htm
[23] http://www.digimuse.usc.edu
[24] http://www.plastiquarian.com/critchlo.htm
[25] http://www.suite101.com/welcome.cfm/french_quarter
[26] http://www.timeanddate.com/worldclock/astronomy.html
[27] http://www.brassregisters.com/ncr/cat/1909cat300class.htm
[28] http://brasscashregisters.com/page4a.html
[29] http://www.awa.dk/whisky/windex.htm
[30] http://www.pre-pro.com/Dataweb/pages/Klein_Bros_Cincinnati.html
[31] http://www.beerhistory.com/library/holdings/lemp1.shtml
[32] http://members.aol.com/ErgoFred/ncr/info/5ts.htm
[33] http://www.beercollections.com/BCIN190.htm
[34] http://www.beer-steins.com/budsteins/P002593_jp60.jpg
[35] http://www.rabbitbrush.com/hickson/BullDurham.html
[36] http://www.rabbitbrush.com/hickson/BullDurham.html
[37] http://www.mtfca.com/encyclo/
[38] http://www.mtfca.com/encyclo/1909.htm
[39] Wayne Everard, Archivist, Louisiana Division, New Orleans Public Library, 219 Loyola Ave., New Orleans, LA 70112, private communication.
[40] http://fisher.lib.virginia.edu/sanborn/about.html
[41] http://sanborn.umi.com/HelpFiles/about.html
[42] http://www.gale.ancestry.com/ggmain.htm
[43] http://ftp.rootsweb.com/pub/usgenweb/la/orleans/biographies/g-000031.txt

A CASE STUDY IN DIGITAL DETECTIVE WORK
WHERE, WHO, WHEN, AND WHY

Sometimes a picture comes along that is so full of details that it is possible to answer just about any question about it. These photographs are the most exciting and offer the greatest potential for digital detective work.

The railroad photograph in Figure 1 was given to me by my distant cousin Paddy during a recent trip to Ireland. It is hard to convey the sorry condition of the original. It was torn, and dirty and the top of it had been burned. I could drape it over my hands like a dishrag. My cousin knew that one of the men in the picture was his namesake, Uncle Patrick Swords, who had moved to Canada to work for the railroad at the turn of the century.

When handling a photo in such poor condition, it is a good idea to preserve it electronically. This not only gives you a copy that you can restore to close to its original state, it also allows you to put away the original to protect it from further damage. Scanning the picture and adjusting the brightness, contrast, and the gamma correction using Microsoft Photo Editor® produced the corrected image in Figure 2.

Here is the approach we'll use to analyze this picture:
1) Decipher the writing across the top of the picture
2) Examine the writing on the railroad car behind the men on the left
3) Make a list of significant or unusual items for closer study
   - The papers held by the man standing to the left of the front row
   - The papers in the pockets of the two men standing in the middle of the back row
   - The certificate held by the man in the center of the front row
   - The white hat worn by the man seated in the front row to the left.

Figure 1.

Figure 2.

As we examine the picture, it's likely we will find more items of interest. We can add to our list as we go along.

Where? Who? When? Why? Let's address one question at a time.

WHERE?

The most interesting clue to the photograph's origin is the writing to the right and across the top. Some of it is legible in the corrected version of the photo as "…..Street, Winnipeg, Man." (Figure 3). If this is a clue to the location where the photograph was taken, it is probably also a clue to where Patrick Swords lived at the time.

Figure 3. Part of the writing corrected a second time.

This section can be cropped, enlarged and examined on its own to get a closer look at the writing. The contrast of just this portion of the picture can be enhanced. While correction of the brightness and contrast of the whole photo restored much of its original appearance, further processing of this particular section of writing brought out additional interesting details. Part of the street name could now be read as __he_urn.

More of the writing can be seen by taking an even smaller excerpt of the photo, and again increasing the contrast (Figure 4). Even though nothing can be done about the part of the word that was destroyed when the picture was burned, an 'S' can now be made out as the initial letter of the street name. A logical choice for the missing letter is 'b' so that the name is Sherburn. According to a modern street map of Winnipeg, Sherburn Street is a main street in the downtown area of the city.

The Henderson's city directories for Winnipeg in the early 1900s list a Michael Swords at 951 Sherburn St. from 1910 through 1914. A further clue is given by the 1915 directory, which lists "Kate, wid. Michael, 951 Sherburn St."

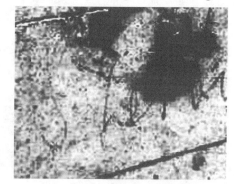

Figure 4.

Figure 5.

There is still one other hint to location - the writing on the boxcar in the left background (Figure 5). An investigation of the history of Winnipeg shows that by the 1880s, Winnipeg had become a major hub for the Canadian Pacific Railroad. The word on the boxcar is "Pacific". A map of modern Winnipeg shows that Sherburn St. deadends close to the main depot of the Canadian Pacific Railroad.

Michael Patrick Swords owned a house at 951 Sherburn St., Winnipeg, Manitoba from 1910 through 1914, when he was married to Kate and worked for the Canadian Pacific Railroad.

He died between 1914 and 1915.

WHO?

We already know a lot about who is in the picture – Patrick Swords and the group of men he worked with at the Canadian Pacific Railroad. But can we find out more?

Figure 6.

The writing across the top of the photo presents more of a challenge, as it is very faded, and runs into the damaged part of the picture. But by isolating and processing this section of the photograph on its own, the script in this area can be enhanced as before (Figure 6).

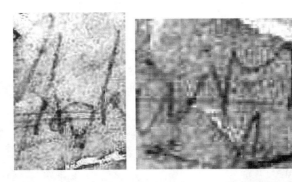

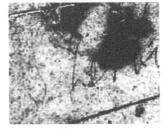

Figure 7.

We can use the letters in the address as templates against which to compare this section of writing. At first glance, several letters can be deciphered, "P__k _w_". By comparing the shapes of the missing letters to those in the words in the address that have already been deciphered, several more letters can be identified (Figure 7). The letter after the 'P' in the first word is tall. It is followed by a small letter that resembles the 'r' in 'street', written somewhat like the letter 'v'. The first word now reads 'Ptrk'. The first letter in the second word resembles the 'S' in 'Sherburn', and the 'w' is followed by a small round letter. "Ptrk. Swo…". Aha!

There are about thirty other men in the photo. Is it possible to identify any of them? Does any man have a unique feature that might lead us to who he was? Even with a list of their names it might be impossible to assign them to the right people, but maybe some of the men can be identified according to their position with the railroad.

Let's check our list of clues. What about the papers in the pockets of the two men standing in the back row (Figure 8). Are there any other identifying marks that would give away who these men were and what documents they were carrying?

How about the pocket watch worn across the vest of the man on the right? One man working for the railroad has need for a watch. This man with the watch was the conductor with the assistant conductor on his right. The papers tucked into their pockets were railroad timetables.

Figure 8.

Even though clothing cannot usually be used to give an accurate date for a photograph, it can be useful in identifying occupations. For example, there are two men on the left in the second row wearing white shirts (Figure 9). The one standing on the far left of the row had his sleeves rolled up. But who would wear a white shirt while working in a railyard? A telegraph operator, of course! From his rolled up sleeves, his hatless condition, and the fact he was standing on the end of the row, the man on the left must have been the telegraph operator on duty at the time the rail crew assembled to get their picture taken, and was called to join the group only at the last moment before the shutter was opened. He ran from the office still holding onto his paperwork, and didn't have a chance to grab his cap. The man sitting next to him was wearing a white shirt, too. But his sleeves were rolled down, and he looks like he had time to take a seat among the rest of the group. He was probably another telegraph operator who was not on duty at that moment. It can be argued that both of these men appear well scrubbed compared to the other workers in the photo, indicating that they did not work in the yard itself, but rather in the railroad office.

Figure 9.

There are two other unusual individuals that should be mentioned. The first is the man in the front row wearing a white hat and a tie (Figure 10). He, too, appears to be better scrubbed than

Figure 10.   Figure 11.

most of the others in the picture. He was also much better dressed, yet he was still sitting in the dirt. My guess is that he was a manager or perhaps a local official of the railroad. Although he had to work in the yard to some extent, he also had office responsibilities during which he was expected to deal with outside customers, and had to dress appropriately for these two different responsibilities.

The other person of note is the man sitting on a platform in the middle of the second row, slightly higher than the men standing on the ground to his left and his right (Figure 11). From his posture and position above his colleagues, I would guess that this person was the boss or the leader of a work crew.

WHEN?

A true digital detective realizes that the next question is "*When?*". The one piece of evidence in the photograph that can help to determine exactly when this photograph was taken is the size of the shadows. If there is one item in the photo whose relative width and depth are known that has well defined shadows, the day of the year can be determined from the length of the shadow, and the time of day determined from its width. It is not necessary to know exact dimensions. Everything can be done in relative sizes, read directly from the photograph in centimeters or inches. Knowing the date that the photograph was taken can be helpful in searching the Winnipeg newspapers in case the photo was ever published.

Figure 12.

An item that proved ideal for shadow work was the square fence post in the background on the far right of the photo (Figure 12). Incidentally, the fence itself (and hence the post) was probably five feet high, comprising five one-foot boards. This is consistent with the height of the men standing along the back row in front of the fence. Referring to Figure 13, the width of the post is $W_p = 64$ mm and the thickness is $T_p = 24$ mm when measured on the screen at the highest magnification of my photoediting program. The corner of the shadow of the post appears $H_s = 43$ mm from the top of the fence, and measures $L_s = 62.5$ mm from the front of the post to the fence.

To be useful in calculating the time of day and day of the year, these measurements have to be corrected for three things:

- the position of the post with respect to the center, or vanishing point of the photograph (to correct the post's dimensions and those of its shadow for the effects of perspective),
- the angle of the fence with respect to true north (to correct the size of the shadow for the post not facing directly into the sun), and
- the latitude of the railyard in Winnipeg.

To make the picture a little easier to work with, it first needs to be rotated so that the horizontal edges (the top of the boxcar, the top of the fence, and the platform where the back row of men are standing) are parallel to the edge of the picture.

Finding the vanishing point to get the first correction takes the most thought. Fortunately the picture has features that can be used for this. Since the interior of the railroad car can be seen through its open door, the laws of perspective dictate that the vanishing point lies on the line that passes through the upper left corner of the door facing towards the camera (A, Figure 14), and the upper left corner of the door facing away from the camera (B, Figure 14).

The platform the men are standing on gives the best hint to the horizontal centerline. The camera had to be no more than a few inches higher than the top surface of the platform since the camera was looking almost directly at the shoes of the men standing on it. The vanishing point is located at the intersection of the line through the corners and the horizontal centerline. In Figure 15 an additional vertical centerline has been drawn through the vanishing point for reference. Now the vertical and horizontal positions of any item in the photo can be determined relative to the center in order to correct its size for the effects of perspective.

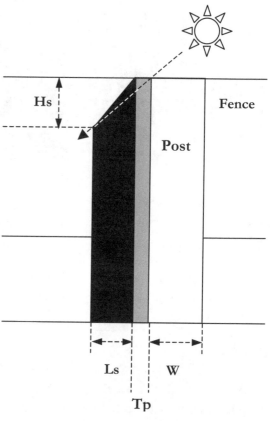

Figure 13. The direction of the sun with respect to the post and the shadow it casts.

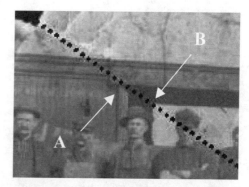

Figure 14. The vanishing point of the picture must lie along the line that passes through A and B.

Figure 15. The vanishing point in the picture is at the intersection of these three lines.

A good atlas gives the information necessary for the next two corrections. The center of the main railyard in Winnipeg is located at 49.95° N latitude. It is reasonable to assume that the picture was taken on one of the tracks in the yard, which, according to a modern map of the town, are located an average of 21.5° north of west. These two facts will be important for correcting the length and the width of the shadow for the time of day and the day of the year.

While each of these three corrections depends on a good guess or two, they are probably accurate enough to get an estimate of when the picture was taken. The parameters I used for my calculations are given in Table 1. The procedure for computing the time of day and day of the year based on shadows is too long to be included here. If you are interested only in obtaining the final result without an in-depth explanation, the CD offers a premade spreadsheet already set up to do the calculations, along with instructions on how to perform your own shadow analysis.

My results showed that the photograph was taken at 12:50 in the afternoon 6.36 days (or 6 days, 8 hours and 36 minutes) either after the spring equinox or before the autumnal equinox. The date of the picture was around March 27 or September 15, with the exact date and time depending on when the equinox occurred that year in Winnipeg. (Because of the irregularity of the earth's rotation and orbits of the sun, earth, and moon, the date of the equinox can vary.)

It is not possible to narrow down the year without further investigation, as the sun transits almost the same path in the sky every 365 days. But if the time of day calculated from the fraction of days before or after the time of the equinox matches with the time of day calculated from the shadows (12:50 p.m.), we will have a probable date for the picture.

To do this, we have to know the exact time of the spring and fall equinoxes for 1910 through 1915. The web site http://www.hermetic.ch/cal_sw/ve/ve.htm[1] allows the calculation of both equinoxes for any year between –100 CE and 4000 CE. The results are given in terms of Greenwich Mean Time (GMT) and must be converted to sidereal time, (the time of day as measured by the sun's position and not according to which time zone a location belongs to). The web site http://www.xylem.f2s.com/kepler/sidereal.htm[2] offers a program called Interactive Computer Ephemeris (ICE) for this purpose. The results are shown in Table 2 for the spring equinox and Table 3 for the fall equinox.

Table 1. Information needed to calculate time of day and day of the year.

Parameter	Value
Width of post* = Wp	64 mm
Thickness of post* = Tp	24 mm
Height of shadow * = Hs	43 mm
Length of shadow * = Ls	62.5 mm
Degrees post is off centerline	31.6°
Latitude of Winnipeg train depot	49.95°N
Direction of tracks in railyard	21.5° south of west

*As measured directly from the picture.

Table 2. Time of day and date of the spring equinox, 1910 – 1915.

Year	GMT*	Winnipeg Sidereal Time	Date
1910	11:55	6:16	21-Mar
1911	17:44	12:05	21-Mar
1912	23:33	17:54	20-Mar
1913	5:22	23:43	21-Mar
1914	11:11	5:32	21-Mar
1915	17:00	11:21	21-Mar

*Greenwich Mean Time

Table 3. Time of day and date of the fall equinox, 1910 – 1915.

Year	GMT	Winnipeg Sidereal Time	Date
1910	22:25	16:03	23-Sep
1911	4:14	21:53	24-Sep
1912	10:02	3:41	23-Sep
1913	15:51	9:31	23-Sep
1914	12:39	6:16	23-Sep
1915	3:28	21:03	23-Sep

Table 4. Estimates of picture time and date relative to the fall equinox.

Year	Time	Date
1910	4:32	23-Sep
1911	5:28	24-Sep
1912	12:16	23-Sep
1913	18:06	23-Sep
1914	14:52	23-Sep
1915	5:39	23-Sep

Table 5. Estimates of picture time and date relative to the spring equinox.

Year	Time	Date
1910	14:52	27-Mar
1911	20:41	27-Mar
1912	2:30	26-Mar
1913	8:19	27-Mar
1914	14:08	27-Mar
1915	19:57	27-Mar

The next step is to add 6 days, 8 hours, and 36 minutes to the time of day and date of the equinoxes. The results are shown in Tables 4 and 5. Of all the possibilities, there are four that fall in the early to mid afternoon, March 27, 1910 (2:52 p.m.), March 27, 1914 (2:08 p.m.), September 23, 1912 (12:16 p.m.), and September 23, 1914 (2:52 p.m.). Considering the approximations we have made along the way, we should not rule out any of these possibilities yet.

There is still one remaining clue that could help us reduce the number of possible dates – the weather.

The Canadian Prairie Provinces, including Manitoba, experience extremes of climate, with differences between summer and winter temperatures greater than cities in any other parts of Canada.[3] Winnipeg is located in the continental climate region, and has one of the most severe climates of the Canadian prairie cities. According to Ref. 1, the average mean temperatures for Winnipeg over the time period 1895 through 1998 for March was −7.8°C (18°F) and for September was 12.4°C (54.3°F). While September is the wettest month, with 2.3" of precipitation, most of it is rain. In comparison, March has an average of 1.4" of precipitation, with about 80% of it falling as snow. Frost continues until early to mid May. On the average, the first frost free day is May 25. The summers in Winnipeg are short and cool, with frost usually returning by the middle of September.

The men in the picture are not dressed for severe weather. They certainly could not have posed for the picture in the sub-zero temperatures characteristic of Winnipeg in March. Since there is no snow on the ground, the temperature must have been high enough for it to melt. The men look like they are dressed for cool but not cold weather. For these reasons, we can rule out the two dates in March. Of the two remaining dates, one is associated with a time only ½ hour earlier than the time we found from measuring the lengths of the shadows. The photo was most likely taken on September 23, 1912 between 12:16 and 12:50 p.m. (The local time on the conductor's watch would have been between 12:36 and 1:10 p.m.)

WHY?

There is one last question to answer - *"Why?"*. The three men sitting in the front row holding papers might give some clues. Surely this was a special occasion.

These papers are the only other documents which appear in the picture besides those held by the conductors and the young telegraph operator. While it would not be unusual to see the conductors with the train schedules in their pockets, and the telegraph operator holding onto recent wire transmissions, these three other men seem to be regular yard workers. It would be unusual for them to be dealing with documents. The man in the center of the front row is presenting his paper directly to the camera (Figure 16). It appears to be a certificate of some sort, with a black mark on the upper left corner, perhaps a stamp or a seal. Hoping that it would give a clue to the occasion for the picture, I examined the paper under a microscope, trying to resolve some of the details of the writing. Unfortunately, the features of the stamp, as well as the writing on the certificate, were below the resolution of the film and were not recorded for posterity.

Figure 16.

In a second attempt to figure out the reason for the photograph, I sent an email to the Canadian Pacific Railroad (CPRR), inquiring about their photo archives and for information on the crews that worked the railyards. The CPRR might shed light on the occasion, whether it was the celebration of some event, or an annual photograph taken on a particular holiday. An employee of the railroad replied that unfortunately, due to budget cuts, the CPRR no longer supported its archives, but that she suspected that the photograph was taken upon the successful completion of some kind of apprenticeship. She had no further information.

The only way I can think of to confirm the date of the picture and find the reason it was taken is a meticulous search of Winnipeg newspapers for dates close to September 23, 1912 to see if the photograph was ever published and if the individuals were identified. However, the Winnipeg Tribune from those years is not available online nor is it available on microfilm through the Family History Library. Without a trip to Winnipeg, the occasion for the picture will remain a mystery.

FURTHER INVESTIGATION

Let's not forget that the real reason for this investigation was to find out more about Uncle Patrick Swords. So far, we have figured out quite a bit about him – that he lived at 951 Sherburn St. in Winnipeg, Manitoba, between 1910 and 1915. He died sometime between late 1914 to early 1915, after which time his widow Kate lived at that address.

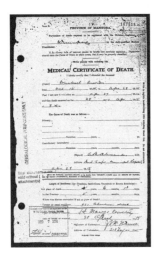

Figure 17.

This was a lot to go on. Simply knowing that he died between 1914 and 1915 provided enough information for the Manitoba Vital Records Office[40] in Winnipeg to find his death certificate (Figure 17). It revealed an astonishing amount of information. Not only did the death record give the date of Patrick's death, it also gave his birth date, his parents' names, his birth place, his place of death, his place of burial, his address (again on Sherburn St.), his occupation, and much more.

Michael Patrick Swords was born on August 5, 1878 in County Kildare, Ireland, the son of James Swords and Margaret Tranor, both natives of County Kildare. He had been in Manitoba for 5 years where he worked as a mechanic for the Canadian Pacific Railroad. He died at 8 a.m. on April 28, 1915, at King Edward Hospital (Figure 18), after having been ill for 6 months and 13 days. He was buried two days later, April 30, 1915 in St. Mary Cemetery in Winnipeg. The cause of death had been whited-out because of Canadian privacy laws. But the King Edward Hospital was founded in 1912 as a sanatorium for tuberculosis patients[4]. Voila! The cause of death. Short of making a trip to Winnipeg to study the local newspaper archives, this is the end of our investigation of the railroad picture.

Figure 18.

Ironically, in spite of all this successful digital detective work, the only thing we have not been able to figure out is which of the men in the picture is Uncle Patrick Swords.

---

[1] http://www.hermetic.ch/cal_sw/ve/ve.htm
[2] http://www.xylem.f2s.com/kepler/sidereal.htm
[3] Adaptability of Prairie Cities: The Role of Climate, Current and Future Impacts and Adaptation Strategies. Chapter 2, Changing City Climates. http://ims.parc.uregina.ca/publications/chapter2.pdf
[4] http://www.lung.ca/tb/tbhistory/sanatoriums/first.html

THE DATABASE DETECTIVE

INTRODUCTION

One reason the FBI is successful at catching criminals because it has an enormous amount of information organized into readily available databases. What works for the FBI can work for you. Thanks to the internet, there are now many databases available online that were not easily accessible in the past. As discussed in the chapter the Digital Detective, online catalogs of cars, cash registers, types of liquor, cameras, and other items are often the key element in determining the date and place where a picture was taken.

Online databases can also be used for researching a specific relative and for obtaining background information on the historical era or geographical area he lived in. Ancestry.com, familytreemaker.com, and familysearch.org, the web site of the Family History Library, are just a few of the many good sources of genealogical information available over the Internet. Many of the US, Canadian, and UK census records are now available through these web sites in searchable format. City directories are also becoming available online.

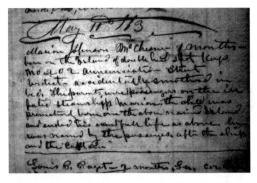

Coroner's Report, New Orleans, LA
May 11, 1863

Marion Johnson McChesny, 1 month – born on the Island of Double Head Shot Keys. No. 202 Annunciation Street. Verdict – accidentally smothered in bed. The parents were passengers on the ill fated steamship Marion. The child was prematurely born on the above Island and ended his eventful life as above. He was named by the passengers after the ship and the Captain.

There are also many useful databases in hard copy form available on microfilm through the Family History Library. Some of the more well known include the Index to Foreign-Born Voters, naturalization records, probate records, and court proceedings. Many others are interesting and unusual. Would you think to look for an ancestor in the coroner's reports? Admission records of an orphan asylum? Admissions to the city insane asylum? Be careful because there is always the danger that you will learn more about your relatives than you really want to know.

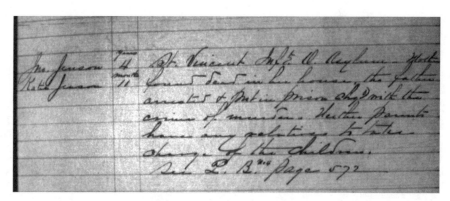

Record of Disposition of Destitute Orphans, New Orleans, LA
October 27, 1878
Jno. Jensen (4 yrs), Katie Jensen (11 mos)

St. Vincent Infant O. Asylum. Mother found dead in her house, the father arrested and put in prison, charged with crime of murder. Neither parent has any relatives to take charge of the children. See P.B. No 4, Page 572.

Databases can also be used for creating a profile of what is being sought. In this case, databases are not used to match one item with another. Rather, they are concerned with predicting characteristics of the unknown based on patterns derived from the data. For example, in criminal profiling this kind of database has been used successfully to predict the education level and the type of car used by people involved in certain types of crimes.

When used in genealogy, profiling databases can be used for similar reasons—to predict the area of a city where an ancestor might have lived, the age he might have been released from an orphan asylum, the port through which he entered the United States, who he might have chosen as the godparents for his children, and many other useful facts. Profiling databases are similar to those used by advertising agencies, political pollsters, and the health care and insurance industries for profiling the most likely customers or voters, or for constructing actuarial tables.

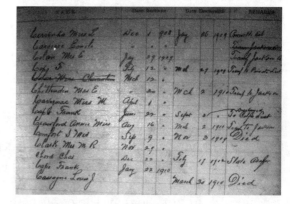

Page from the registry of
the Indigent Insane
New Orleans, 1888

The use of databases in genealogy is still in its infancy. While researching specific individuals or comparing a suspected relative with already known family members are staples of genealogical research, the use of databases for profiling unknown family members or for inferring family background is still largely unrecognized. A symptom of this is the lack of available software that can be used by a genealogist to create his own searchable database of family information. While there are several popular software packages on the market that can be used for organizing a family tree, they are only useful as storage places for facts and relationships that have already been established, that is, for entering names in their proper niches in the family structure. You must already know who a person is in order to enter his name in a genealogical software program. These programs are not usually searchable and cannot be reorganized. They are not very useful as research tools in themselves. Entering a family name into Family Tree Maker® is equivalent to the FBI entering a fingerprint into its system only after the criminal has been identified.

City Insane Asylum Record of Patients
New Orleans., LA, October 30, 1883

Michael Mullen, white, male, 53? [sic] years, native of Ireland, laborer, recommended his commitment to the S.- I.- A. [State Insane Asylum] at Jackson, La. on October 30th – 1883, finding him insane suffering from "Chronic Alcoholism."

Like all Irishmen, he is witty. He is gay & pleasant in his speech, at times rational, and then again he will wander off, and address imaginary persons or objects. He is a laborer, single, and has been a hard drinker for years. To use his own expression "I have been drinking every since before I was born; it runs through my nature."

Ideally, a genealogist needs software that not only stores information, but that can also manipulate this information to retrieve facts and recognize patterns that otherwise would not be noticed. Word processors such as Microsoft Word® have some capabilities in this direction, but spreadsheet programs such as Microsoft Excel® are much more versatile at managing genealogical information in these ways.

Record of Disposition of Destitute Orphans, New Orleans, LA
August 9, 1875
Edward Paul Schroeder

Sent to St. Vincent Inft Orphan Asylum. The mother of the child aged 21, deceived by a person under promise of marriage. She seems like a modest woman and being without friends is unable with the child to find employment. See Permit book No 4 page 554.

The important thing to emphasize here is the organization of information, and not the physical or electronic means by which it is accessed. The more versatile the tools you have for working with information, the more likely you are to reveal interesting relationships. You can actually organize all of your family information on index cards arranged in piles on your kitchen table. I would not recommend this, though, as it is not very efficient, and someone might open the door on a windy day.

Even if your index cards are very well organized and taped down to the table, the use of brainpower in searching the information is still highly inefficient and inaccurate compared to what can be accomplished with computers. Compiling xeroxed pages from census records or from city directories is another way to storing and organizing information for later use, but it is time consuming to work with material in this form. In my experience, the most useful means of compiling databases are computer spreadsheet programs such as Microsoft Excel® or Access® that can electronically reorganize information according to a variety of criteria.

The purpose of this chapter is to give you ideas on how to construct and manipulate your own databases to extract otherwise hidden information. It is not meant to provide a list of web sites or organizations you can go to for finding data in the first place. I will leave that to more conventional genealogy books. Many of the research techniques described here are based on research on my own Irish Catholic family living in New Orleans, Louisiana in the 1800s, but the same techniques are adaptable to other ethnic and religious groups, geographical areas, and time periods.

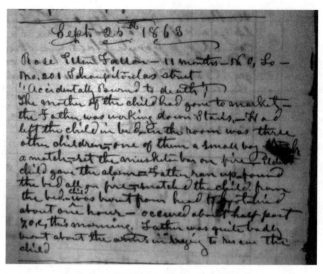

Coroner's Report, New Orleans, LA
Sept 25, 1863

Rose Ellen Fallon – 11 months – N.O., LA 0 No. 201 Tchoupitoulas Street. "Accidentally burned to death"
The mother of the child had gone to market – the father was working downstairs, had left the child in her bed. In the room was [sic] three other children. One of them a small boy struck a match – set the musketo [sic]bar on fire. Eldest child gave the alarm. Father ran up, found the bed all on fire, snatched the child from the bed. Child was burnt from head to foot. Did about one hour – occured [sic] about 7 o.c. this morning. Father was quite badly burnt about the arms in trying to rescue the child.

What to Look For

Professionals distinguish between data and information. Data are merely facts. They become information when meaning is attached to them. In working with databases, simply compiling facts is not enough. You should look for patterns that appear among names, dates, addresses, events and any other kind of element in the data. Did a couple have children every other year? What were the occupations of the men in the family? Did your relatives die young or live to be very old? Did your ancestors follow a traditional pattern in naming their children?

It is not only important to make a note of which patterns were followed when, it is just as important to notice when patterns were interrupted or when expected patterns were not followed at all. What is missing from the data can be just as revealing as what actually appears. Gaps and deviations from the usual can be very interesting. A simple example is the appearance of gaps in known birth records. During the 1800s, many couples had children at regular intervals, often less than two years apart. A deviation from this pattern, where there is a much wider gap than usual between two children in a family, can indicate a miscarriage or a child who died very young. Infant deaths were very common. Some parents were even known to delay the registration of a child for several months, not wanting to go through the trouble if the child died.

GETTING STARTED

The database most useful to your family research is the one you compile yourself, well worth the effort. Databases can be created from any sources that you might have access to such as a city directory, a collection of death certificates, hospital admission records transcribed directly from microfilm from the Family History Library, or a list of ancestors' birthdates given to you by elderly relatives. The more data you organize in your database, the greater the chance it will yield valuable information.

Preparing a database is easy, if you have the resources to draw from. When I compile a database, I usually use an Excel® spreadsheet to organize my information, using one row per entry, with each cell holding one piece of information.

Each row might represent a person, for example, and the cells along the row might be allocated in any convenient order to his age, sex, residence, and place of birth. In this case, the first column would carry the names, the second would carry the ages, the third would record the sex, and so on. Even if you are using another means of arranging your information, such as a handwritten table or a set of index cards, this method will still work.

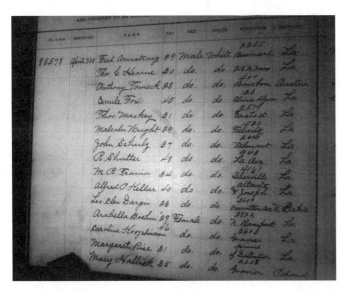

Figure 1. A page from the register of Persons Adjudged to Be Insane by the Civil District Court for the Parish of Orleans and Ordered to Be Conveyed by the Civil Sheriff of the Parish of Orleans to the State Insane Asylum at Jackson, La. See Table 1.

Table 1. Sample database of Persons Adjudged to be Insane and Sent to the State Asylum at Jackson, LA. See Figure 1.

Case No.	Date Rec'd	Name	Age	Color	Sex	Residence	Place of Birth
85578	April 7/08	Fred Armstrong	29	White	Male	2255 Brainard	La.
		Thos. G. Hearne	30	White	Male	218 N. Miro	La.
		Anthony Tomeck	28	White	Male	400 Bourbon	Austria
		Emile Fox	45	White	Male	123 Elmira, Algiers	La.
		Thos Mackey	31	White	Male	2519 Erato St.	La.
		Malcolm Wright	29	White	Male	1520 Felicity	La.
		John Schulz	37	White	Male	2000 Valmont	La.

Figure 1 is a digital photograph of a page from the Register of Persons Adjudged to Be Insane by the Civil District Court for the Parish of Orleans. (Not all of them are my relatives!)

The page is double, with the facing page on the right (not shown in the figure) listing each patient's occupation, martial status, disease, how long insane, cause of affliction, and remarks. The image was obtained from Family History Library microfilm No. 906706. Table 1 is the database of the names of the adjudged created from the register. Because of space limitations, the table shows only eight columns of a total of fourteen, and only the first few entries on the page. The database as shown is ordered chronologically. Since it was created using a computer spreadsheet, it can be reorganized according to other criteria such as last name or age. Each arrangement can reveal additional useful clues. You probably will not need to create a database of your relatives who were committed to the local insane asylum—your collection of birth, marriage, and death certificates can be organized using the same method.

As you accumulate more information in database form, you may want to create a database of databases. Don't laugh. This is a good method of keeping track of what information you already have and what information you still need to augment your collection. Table 2 gives an example of a database of surnames I extracted from city directories over of a range of years (a database of city directory databases). As I accumulate information on other surnames and from other directories, I keep track by checking off or coloring in boxes in the table.

Table 2. Database I have created to keep track of which surnames I have extracted from which city directories.

Year / Surname	1870	1871	1872	1873	1874	1875	1876	1877	1878
Bernard		X		X		X		X	
Brechtel		X							
Fitzpatrick	X	X	X	X	X	X	X	X	X
Flynn		X							
Hanlon	X	X	X	X	X		X		X
Lyons		X							
Martin		X	X	X		X		X	
Mullen		X							
Rice	X	X	X	X	X	X	X	X	X
Swords		X							
White		X		X		X		X	X

It is a loss to copy information from a source such as a city directory only on individuals you already know about in your family, if there are other individuals listed with the same surname. There can be other unknown family members lurking in the records. A list of all the Kellys or Schmidts from the city directories or census records has much more potential than a list of the few of whom you are already aware. What about that Great Great Uncle George who died in 1865 in his 30s? He is probably long gone from the memories of living descendents of the family, but he is still listed in the census records with other family members, waiting to be found. Unless you write down all the Kellys or Schmidts, Uncle George might remain an ink spot on an old paper. Your database has more potential if you have all the Kellys or Schmidts recorded for later reference.

There are two kinds of databases with data about people. The first kind is the periodical database, a collection of data such as census records or city directories that were compiled at specific times. Periodical databases are more or less inventories of people. This type of reference is a kind of 'snapshot' of a population at regular time intervals, and can be used to cross reference individuals each time they appear.

The second kind of database is the event database, containing records that were updated on a continuous basis, such as birth, marriage, and death registers and hospital admission records. The data contained in event databases usually do not involve the same individuals more than once or perhaps twice. You would not be surprised to see the same person appearing several times in city directories, but you would be very surprised to see him make regular appearances in death records.

PERIODICAL DATABASES–USING CITY DIRECTORIES

There are many genealogical reference materials that are used every day that are not recognized for the databases they are. The census records are probably the most well known, but city directories can be more informative and easier to work with since they are published ten times as frequently and cover a more limited population. Less recognized periodical databases are annual membership lists of social organizations, lists of benefactors to a church, and the Who's Who of a professional group.

A city directory is not just a list of names. It is a list of names organized alphabetically that belongs to a collection of similar lists compiled over a range of years. By comparing names or addresses within a single directory, or across a collection of directories, it is possible to observe patterns that are useful in reconstructing long forgotten family relationships.

Until recently a directory was usually compiled by hand over several months of the previous year. For example, the city directory for 1895 would have been assembled sometime during mid to late 1894. If someone is listed in 1895, it means he was living at that address through at least mid 1894. If an individual is listed in 1894 but not in 1895, he either died or moved away between late 1893 and late 1894, the months between the completion of the 1894 directory (where he appears) and the completion of the 1895 city directory (where he does not appear).

There are two important ways city directories can be used to investigate a family. The first is to focus your search on a single address to find out who was living at that address and when. This method is straightforward if a family stayed in one place over a period of time. Changes in the residents at the address reflect changes that occurred in the family. Noting the first and last appearance of someone at an address can be lead to his birth year, the year he was married, or the year he died.

The second way of using city directories is to track an ancestor through a variety of addresses, to determine who else lived there before, during, and after the ancestor was listed. Changes in his address can be give clues to changes in the ancestor's family – he could have needed a new home to accommodate a growing family, or his fortunes could have changed due to hard times or upward mobility.

1880 New Orleans City Directory

City directories usually provide at least four types of information about a resident: year, name, address, and often occupation. As telephones came into common usage in the late 1870s, directories began to include telephone numbers[1]. A normal city directory for a particular year is organized alphabetically by last name, then by first name, occupation and address. But there is nothing sacred about this arrangement, and the information can be resorted according to any type of information, in any order: [first name, last name, address, year, occupation], or [address, occupation, first name, last name, year], etc. Each different arrangement can provide clues to family structure.

Tracing a Family through a Single Address

Investigating a family who lived at the same address over a period to time can give insight into the chronology and structure of the family. Figure 2 gives simple suggestions for researching such a family. It is not meant to be an exhaustive list, but it is a good start.

Even today, it is usual for a man to first be listed in a city directory at 18 years old, about the time he starts his working life. In the 1800s and into the 1900s, he would likely live at home with his parents until he married and started his own family. Then he would usually move to a new location. When a male ancestor appeared at and disappeared from the address can give a hint about his birth year and the year he was married or he died.

If the family had more than one son, each should appear at the family's address in the approximate order of his birth. Since the directories of the 1800s were compiled by hand, a son could have been omitted from a directory due to human error, so that he might not appear on schedule. A son could also have started work at an earlier or later age than his brothers,

Figure 2. Simple Suggestions for Using City Directories

Record all the residents at the family address over the years of interest.

What year did each son first appear at his parents' address? → Calculate approximate birth year by subtracting 18. Also gives approximate birth order.

Are there gaps in the appearance of the sons? → Use other resources to identify daughters not listed in the directory and children who died before reaching adulthood.

What is the first year that each son appears at a new address? → He was probably married the year before, while this 'new' directory was being compiled.

---

[1] The list of telephone subscribers for the 1879 New Orleans Telephonic Exchange lists 100 names. The directory gave the following directions to subscribers:
To call the Exchange give a long ring with the bell crank and when the operator signals back, remove the telephone from the hook and give the name of the subscriber wanted. When called by the Exchange give a ring back, then remove the telephone from the hook and say Hello! Hello!

throwing off the calculation of his birth year. Even so, the chronological appearance of the sons in the directories should more or less reflect the chronological order of their births. It was not as common in the 1800s and early 1900s to list a daughter in a family, unless she had a specific skill as a midwife or a milliner, or unless she ran a boarding house. Yet the existence of daughters in a family can be indicated by gaps in the estimated ages of the sons in the family.

Peter Fitzpatrick lived at 628 Burgundy St. in New Orleans for nearly 40 years, from the time he was the father of young children in the early 1870s until he died at the age of 83 in 1909. He had many sons sharing this address with him during this time (Table 3). Let's see when these sons appeared and disappeared from the Fitzpatrick household to estimate their birth and marriage dates along with an approximate birth order. Any gaps we find in birth dates should indicate the presence of daughters or children who died young.

The match is pretty close between the sons' names and birth years shown in Table 4 calculated from the city directories and the correct birth dates shown in Table 5 obtained from civil birth records at the Louisiana State Archives. John is the only son out of order–he must have started work sooner in life than his brothers Michael and Peter Jr., since he is listed earlier in the directory than they are, although he is their younger brother. There is also no evidence in the birth records that the family had a son named George.

Even so, the predictions are accurate enough to reveal gaps in the birth order where other children might have been born. These could have been daughters or children who did not reach adulthood. (See Table 6.) In the case of the Fitzpatrick family, there are gaps of three years between William and John (1858-1861), five years between Peter Jr. and George (1865–1870), and three years between George and Edward (1871–1873). This assumes George is a son. If George is eliminated, the gap between Peter Jr. and Edward (1865-1873) is eight years.

The civil birth records show that the family had four additional children who fit in these gaps rather nicely. The birth of the oldest daughter Elizabeth, who died in childhood, is successfully predicted between William and John, but her birth was a year later than predicted. Two other children, Margaret and James, were born between Peter Jr. and George. (James died shortly after birth.) A child is predicted between George and Edward, but a daughter Catherine was not born until later. The final list of the Fitzpatrick children's birth dates is given in Table 7.

In many cases, knowing the first year of a man's absence from his parents' address can lead to the discovery of his marriage date. The process can be repeated to obtain information on the son's sons.

The match between the guesstimates provided through the city directory and the real marriage dates obtained from civil marriage records is very close. The predictions shown in Table 8 take into account that an estimated marriage year usually includes the latter months of the previous year because of the timetable on which the directories were often compiled. Each known marriage date in this example falls exactly into the time period predicted by the city directories.

Table 3. Residents of 628 Burgundy, New Orleans, LA

Year	Name	Occupation
1876	Peter	Screwman*
1877	Peter	Laborer
	William	Clerk
1878	Peter	Screwman
	William	Clerk
1879	Peter	Laborer
	William	Clerk
1880	Peter	Screwman
1881	Peter	Laborer
	William	Clerk
	John	Blacksmith
1882	Peter	Laborer
	William	Clerk
	Michael	Laborer
1883	Peter	Laborer
	William	Clerk
	Michael	Laborer
1884	Peter	Laborer
	William	Bookkeeper
	John	Blacksmith
	Peter Jr.	Laborer
1885	Peter	Laborer
	William	Cashier
	John	Horseshoer
1886	Peter	Laborer
	John	Horseshoer
1887	Peter	Laborer
	John	Horseshoer

*A screwman was a laborer who packed cotton into boxcars and ships with a screw-like device to compress the cotton into as small a volume as possible.

Table 3. Residents of 628 Burgundy, New Orleans, LA (cont'd)

Year	Name	Occupation
1888	Peter	Laborer
1889	Peter	Laborer
	George	Tinner
1890	Peter	Screwman
	George	Tinner
1891	Peter	Laborer
	John	Laborer
	Peter Jr.	Laborer
1892	Peter	Screwman
	John	Screwman
	Edward	Screwman
1893	Peter	Laborer
1894	Edward	Laborer
	Joseph	Laborer
1895	Peter	Screwman~
1896	Peter	Laborer^
1897	Peter	Laborer
	Edward	Laborer
	Joseph	Laborer
1898	Peter	Laborer
	Edward	Laborer
1899	Peter	Laborer
	Edward	Laborer
	Joseph	Laborer
1900	Peter	Laborer
	Edward	Laborer

~Listed in 1895 at Old 628 Burgundy
^Listed from 1896 forward at 2728 Burgundy

Table 4. Chronological order and birth year of Fitzpatrick sons derived from city directories*.

Sons in Order of Appearance	First Appears	Estimated Year of Birth
William	1877	1858
John	1881	1862
Michael	1883	1864
Peter Jr.	1884	1865
George	1889	1870
Edward	1892	1873
Joseph	1894	1875

* Assuming they appeared for the first time at 18 years old, and and that a directory for a specific year was compiled during the previous year.

Table 5. Actual chronological order and birth year of Fitzpatrick sons*.

Birth Order of Sons	Estimated Year of Birth	Actual Year of Birth
William	1858	1859
Michael	1864	1861
Peter Jr.	1865	1864
John	1862	1865
Edward	1873	1869
Joseph	1875	1872
George*	1870	-----

*There was no son named George.

Sons in Order of Directory Appearance	Yr of Birth Estimated from Directory
William	1858
Three Year Gap	
John	1861
Michael	1863
Peter Jr.	1865
Five Year Gap	
George	1870
Three Year Gap	
Edward	1873
Joseph	1875

Table 6. Comparison of the birth years of missing children with estimated positions in the order

Missing Children	Year of Birth
Elizabeth	1862
Margaret	1867
James	1868
Catherine	1875

Arrows indicate predicted position in birth order

Table 7. List of Fitzpatrick children and their birth dates.

Child	Date of Birth
William	Feb. 6, 1859
Michael	Jan. 18, 1861
Elizabeth	Mar. 1862
Peter, Jr.	Jan. 7, 1864
John	Feb. 10, 1865
Margaret	Mar. 10, 1867
James	Sep. 23, 1868
Edward	Oct. 26, 1869
Joseph	Jul. 25, 1872
Catherine	Feb. 9, 1875

Table 8. Estimated and actual marriage dates of Fitzpatrick sons*.

Son	First Yr at New Address	Est'd Date of Marriage	Actual Date of Marriage
William	1886	late 1884–late 1885	Aug. 8, 1885
Michael	1884	late 1882–late 1883	Nov. 25, 1882
Peter Jr.	1892	late 1890–late 1891	Jan. 3, 1891
John	1893	late 1891–late 1892	Dec. 19, 1891
Edward*	After 1900	After 1900	?
Joseph*	1900	late 1898–late 1899	?

*The marriage records of these two sons have not yet been located.

You might discover other patterns when you research the residents of a certain address. A young man might be listed at the family address for a while, and then show up elsewhere for a few years, only to reappear later at his original residence. This could indicate that his wife died and he moved back in with the family, that his fortunes changed and he could not afford to live anywhere else, or that his father died and he had to live with his mother to help support her and the rest of the family. The disappearance and later reappearance of the son at the address can be indications of important changes in his life that merit further investigation.

Tracing a Family through Multiple Addresses

You can also gain insight into a family by tracking an ancestor through multiple addresses. Tracking someone this way is a little more difficult than researching his life at only one address, since you might not find him in every directory. The ancestor might have changed occupations, or the city could have renumbered the street where he lived, leading to ambiguities in identifying him. He could also have left town. In some cases, reorganizing your information by other criteria such as occupation or place of employment can help to resolve such uncertainties.

The goal of tracking a relative through multiple addresses is to find other family members living with him through the years. The process of checking addresses can be repeated for these newly discovered family members to find out where else they might have resided when not living with your relative. These new family members could themselves have lived with other relatives before or after living with your ancestor, leading to the discovery of even more new family members. The process can be repeated on each new name that arises.

It is important not to jump to conclusions about the identity of someone with a common name. You could spend a lot of time researching the wrong person. I have stumbled across two men, both named John Hanlon, both Irish immigrants to New Orleans, both about the same age, both laborers married to women named Catherine, both with sons named John Hanlon Jr. born about the same time. (The Irish will never win prizes for the imagination they exhibit in naming their children.) Fortunately I discovered the duplication of names and was able to get back on track before too long. This is not the only time this has happened to me, so be careful in researching individuals with common names.

In tracking the family of Thomas Lyons through the New Orleans city directories, the best clues are not provided by Thomas Lyons, but by his wife. Thomas left Mary a widow before 1861, as that is the first year she appears in the directory as Mary Lyons, wid. Thomas. There were two other Lyons listed with her at 6 Constance St. that year – Patrick, a contractor, and Michael (no occupation). This was definitely the Mrs. Mary Lyons of interest; the Patrick living with her was already known to be her son, thanks to a birth certificate issued when he lost a child in 1863.

Mary Lyons far outlived most of the famine immigrants. She died in 1897 at the age of 94, so that she appeared in the New Orleans city directories for over thirty years. Although there could have been two or more Mary Lyons in New Orleans during this time, both widows of men named Thomas, they would almost surely have been listed in the same directory at least once. Yet this never happened.

Steps 1 through 10 in Figure 3 give detailed instructions on how to trace an individual through a series of addresses to observe where he was living when, and with whom. To do so it is necessary to reorganize directory entries in new ways, by first name, by address, or by occupation.

Resorting Directories By Name

To track an ancestor through multiple addresses, you must first identify which entries in the directories are that ancestor. The easiest way to do this is to compile a database of all the entries for a particular surname in all the directories, as shown in Table 9 (Step 1), and then to rearrange the data in one big list alphabetically by given name. See an excerpt in Table 10 (Step 2).

Sorting the database in this way causes all the Marys, Michaels, Patricks, and so on to appear together in individual name groups. Sorting chronologically within each name group can be helpful.

There will probably be a few ambiguous entries in your list. To rule them in or out, these names must be researched using other sources of information such as entries in the same directory, entries

Figure 3. Using City Directories—Method #2

Step 1. Record all the residents by the surname of interest listed in every directory. (Table 9.)

Step 2. Rearrange the entries according to first name. For each first name, rearrange the entries in chronological order.

⭐ Result is a database with all the Anns, Marys, Michaels, Patricks, etc. together in groups. Each group will show a chronological list of addresses for that first name. (Table 10.)

Step 3. Extract from the database only those entries you can positively identify as your ancestor.

Step 4. Make a list of ambiguous entries that cannot be positively identified as your ancestor, but that also cannot be ruled out. Search other sources such as birth, marriage, death records for reasons to accept or to reject each ambiguous entry. (Table 11.)

Step 5. Combine all entries for your ancestor from Step 3 and Step 4 into one list.

⭐ Result is a list of all the entries for your ancestor, including name, address, and occupation over the period of interest. (Table 12)

Step 6. Resort entries from the original database (Table 9) in alphabetical order by street name. For each address on a street, sort residents in alphabetical order by first name.

⭐ Result is a list of addresses, and for each address, a list of residents. (Table 13.)

Step 7. Extract the information for only your ancestor's addresses, listing street names in alphabetical order. Note the names of other people living at any of these address.

⭐ Result is a list of family members who lived at these addresses. (Table 14.)

Step 8. Summarize the individuals appearing at your ancestor's addresses, along with their possible relationships to your ancestor.

⭐ Result is a list of family members and possible family relationships—the beginnings of family structure. (Table 15.)

Step 9. Repeat Steps 2 through 8 for other members of the family, both those already known and those newly discovered. (Table 16 through Table 21.) Add new discoveries to Table 15 as you go along.

Step 10. Reorganize original alphabetical list (Table 9) by other key items such as occupation and place of work. Look for individuals with these items in common with known family members. (Table 22.)

⭐ Result is a final list of family members and possible family relationships as indicated by name, address, and occupation. (Table 23.)

Table 9. Database of New Orleans city directories for the surname Lyons. The actual list is larger, covering 1849 through 1889. Because of the size, only some of the entries for 1873, and 1874 are shown.

Year	Last Name	First Name	Occupation	Work Info	Home Address
1873	Lyons	Mary	wid. Thomas		r. 303 Marais
	Lyons	Mary E.	wid. Z. S.		r. 152 Jackson 4th dist.
	Lyons	Michael	cooper	124 St. Joseph	r. Girod c. Tchoupitoulas
	Lyons	Michael	saloon		111 Tchoupitoulas
	Lyons	M. T.	printer	N.O. Picayune	205 Euterpe
	Lyons	Patrick	engineer		205 St. Thomas
	Lyons	Patrick	finisher	Cronan's Foundry	
	Lyons	S.			194 Laurel
	Lyons	William	boot & shoemaker		70 Girod
	Lyons	W.	lab.		r. 172 Terpsichore
	Lyons	Zekiel	Ball & Lyons		r. 273 Camp
1874	Lyons	C. R.	wid. Louis W.		r. 498 St. Charles
	Lyons	David	cook		r. Burdette c. Pearl
	Lyons	David	driver	St Charles St R.R. Co	r.n.s. S. Basin b. 3rd & 4th
	Lyons	Duthel	collector	Mark H. Applegate	r. 314 Second
	Lyons	Elizabeth	wid. Nimrod		r. 166 Toulouse
	Lyons	Elizabeth	wid. Thomas		r. Josephine n.w.c. Willow
	Lyons	Isaac	druggist		r. 273 Camp
	Lyons	Jacob	clerk		bds. 273 Camp
	Lyons	James	apprentice	L. Daffy	r. 246 St. Louis
	Lyons	James		N.O.M. & T.R.R.	
	Lyons	Jeannette	wid. Stephen		r. 351 Customhouse
	Lyons	Jeremiah	grocer	Magnolia n.e.c. Erato	r. Same

Table 10. Results for the Mary Lyons who were widows, obtained from sorting the database of Table 9 by first name and then chronologically. Those names positively identified as 'the' Mrs. Mary Lyons, wid. Thomas, are shaded in and bolded.

Last Name	First Name	Occupation	Year	Work Info	Home Address
Lyons	Mary	wid. John	1880		r. 75 Spain
Lyons	Mary	wid. John	1886	furnished rooms	r. 79 Girod
Lyon	Mary	wid. Joseph	1873		r. 240 Dyrades
Lyon	Mary	wid. Joseph	1882		r. 237 Magazine
Lyon	Mary	wid. Joseph	1883		r. 237 Magazine
Lyon	Mary	wid. Joseph	1884		r. 237 Magazine
Lyons	Mary	wid. Joseph	1885	furnished rooms	1 Carroll
Lyons	Mary	wid. Joseph	1889		r. 339 S. Franklin
Lyons	Mary	wid. Leon	1888		r. 465 Burgundy
Lyons	Mary	wid. Louis	1874		r.s.s. N. Poydras b. Clara & S. Claiborne
Lyons	Mary	wid. Louis (col'd)	1871		r. S. Poydras b Claiborne & Clara
Lyons	Maria	wid. Stephen	1880		r. 601 Annunciation
Lyon	Maria	wid. Stephen	1881		r. 601 Annunciation
Lyon	Maria	wid. Stephen	1884		r. 328 St. Thomas
Lyon	Maria L.	wid. Stephen	1893		r. 392 Constance
Lyons	**Mary**	**wid. Thomas**	**1870**		**r. 61 Marigny**
Lyons	**Mary**	**wid. Thomas**	**1873**		**r. 303 Marais**
Lyons	**Mary**	**wid. Thomas**	**1875**		**r.n.s. Marais b. Spain & Washington**
Lyons	**Mary**	**wid. Thomas**	**1878**		**r. 171 Spain**
Lyons	**Mary**	**wid. Thomas**	**1879**		**r. 111 Tchoupitoulas**
Lyons	**Mary**	**wid. Thomas**	**1880**		**r. 111 Tchoupitoulas**
Lyons	**Mary**	**wid. Thomas**	**1884**		**r. 336 Conti**
Lyons	**Mary**	**wid. Thomas**	**1885**		**r. 336 Conti**
Lyons	**Mary**	**wid. Thomas**	**1889**		**r. 500 Royal**

in directories of other years, or civil birth, marriage, and death records. When these additional reference materials are used, four of the ambiguous entries for Mary Lyons can be ruled out, two can be positively identified, and one is still uncertain (Step 4). See Table 11. The final chronological list of the entries identified as Mrs. Mary Lyons, wid. Thomas is shown in Table 12 (Step 5). The entry for the address on Liberty St. (1887) has been omitted from the list because of its uncertainty; however, it can be restored later if necessary.

Resorting Directories By Address

By resorting your database by address you can find out who lived at the same residence as your ancestor over the time period of interest (Step 6, Table 13). Each of these new people will very likely be a family member, although it might not be possible to say for certain what the relationship is without further research. Note that family members do not have to appear at the same address in the same year that your ancestor was living there. The names of the individuals listed at any of the widow Lyons' addresses are shown in Table 14 (Step 7).

It's probably a good idea when you reach this point to summarize your results. Make a separate list of all the family members you have found so far, with the relationships you think they had to your ancestor. Note that in Table 15 (Step 8) there are two Patricks listed. It is likely that they are separate individuals, because of their different occupations. The names Thomas and William are marked with question marks. By the time Mary Lyons was living with these two family members at 336 Conti St. in 1884, she was 81 years old. Her siblings were probably dead, so that Thomas and William could be sons or just as well grandsons.

Caring for elderly relatives is not a modern problem. Families with aging members have always faced challenges. How the Lyons family coped with the widow as she aged becomes evident from patterns that emerge from the lists of names and addresses. Mary Lyons appears in many of the directories, but not in all of them. In general, she appears for a couple of years living with family members, she disappears for a couple of years, and when she reappears, she is living at a new address with other family members. This pattern suggests that during the missing years, she was living with relatives who did not live in New Orleans, or with married daughters who did not appear in the city directory under the name Lyons. Maybe she was in a hospital. It is unlikely that she was simply overlooked by the people compiling the directories.

Any of these possibilities could be true considering her age. In 1867, the earliest year she is missing from a directory, she was 64 years old, far beyond the life expectancy of about 40 years in the mid 1800s. In fact the census records indicate that she was living with her daughter Bridget (Mrs. Thomas Martin) in 1870.

Table 11. Ambiguous listings for Mary Lyons. Reasons for ruling entries in or out are given in the last column. Columns on occupation and work info are not shown. Entries with positive identification are shaded in and bolded.

Year	Last Name	First Name	Home Address	Notes
1885	Lyon	Maria L., Mrs.	r. 328 St. Thomas	Mary wid. Thomas already identified for 1875
1878	Lyon	Mary J., Mrs.	r. N. Roman b. Celestine & Aubry	Mary wid. Thomas already identified for 1878
1861	**Lyon**	**Mary, Mrs.**	**r. 6 Constance**	**Identified by the birth certificate of a stillborn child born at this address who belonged to her son Patrick**
1866	**Lyon**	**Mary, Mrs.**	**r. 6 Constance**	**Identified by the birth certificate of a stillborn child born at this address who belonged to her son Patrick**
1870	Lyons	Mary, Mrs.	r. 28 Liberty, 1st dist.	Mary wid. Thomas already identified for 1871
1874	Lyons	Mary, Mrs.	r. 75 Spain	Identified as wid. John by same entry at this address in 1880
1887	Lyons	Mary, Mrs.	r. 39 Liberty	Unknown

Table 12. Complete list of addresses for Mrs. Mary Lyons obtained from Tables 10 and 11.

Year	Last Name	First Name	Occupation	Home Address
1861	Lyon	Mary, Mrs.		r. 6 Constance
1866	Lyon	Mary, Mrs.		r. 6 Constance
1870	Lyons	Mary	wid. Thomas	r. 61 Marigny
1873	Lyons	Mary	wid. Thomas	r. 303 Marais
1875	Lyons	Mary	wid. Thomas	r.n.s. Marais b. Spain & Washington
1878	Lyons	Mary	wid. Thomas	r. 171 Spain
1879	Lyons	Mary	wid. Thomas	r. 111 Tchoupitoulas
1880	Lyons	Mary	wid. Thomas	r. 111 Tchoupitoulas
1884	Lyons	Mary	wid. Thomas	r. 336 Conti
1885	Lyons	Mary	wid. Thomas	r. 336 Conti
1889	Lyons	Mary	wid. Thomas	r. 500 Royal

Table 13. Results of resorting the database in Table 9 by address. Those names positively identified as 'the' Mrs. Mary Lyons, wid. Thomas, are shaded in and bolded. Because of the extensive size of this database, only a part of it is shown.

Address	Year	First Name	Occupation	Work Info
Magnolia c. Erato	1870	Jeremiah	grocery	Magnolia c. Erato
	1872	J.	grocery	
Magnolia n.e.c. Erato	1871	Jeremiah	grocer	
	1875	Jeremiah	grocer	
	1876	Jeremiah	grocer	Magnolia n.e.c. Erato
	1877	Jerry	grocer	
Magnolia s.w.c. Erato	1874	Jeremiah	grocer	Magnolia s.w.c. Erato
126 1/2 Mandeville	1889	William	sheet iron worker	Edwards & Haubtman
	1886	Mitchell	shoemaker	
	1893	Michel	shoemaker	
	1888	Mitchell	shoemaker	
Marais b. Spain & Washington	**1875**	**Mary**	**wid. Thomas**	
70 Marais	1887	Michael	lab.	
303 Marais	**1873**	**Mary**	**wid. Thomas**	
437 1/2 Marais	1893	John	lab.	
61 Marigny	**1870**	**Mary**	**wid. Thomas**	
220 1/2 Marigny	1889	William	clk.	
Marigny c. Prosper	1852	Patrick		
	1853	Patrick		
	1854	Patrick		
	1855	C.		
	1855	Patrick		
	1856	C.		
	1856	Patrick		

Table 14. All Lyons living at addresses associated with Mary Lyons wid. Thomas, obtained from Table 13.

Address	Year	Residents	Occup.	Address	Yr	Residents	Occup.
Constance St.	1861	Mary Mrs			1880	Mary	wid Thomas
		Michael				Eliza, Mrs	wid Michael
		Patrick	contractor			Patrick	lab.
	1866	Mary Mrs			1881	Eliza, Mrs	saloon
		Michael			1884	Eliza, Mrs	saloon
		Patrick	contractor		1885	Eliza, Mrs	saloon
					1886	Eliza, Mrs	saloon
61 Marigny St	1870	Mary	wid Thomas				
	1889	William	clk.	336 Conti	1881	Thomas	machinist
						William P	clk JH Grover
303 Marais St	1873	Mary	wid Thomas		1882	Thomas	tinsmith
						William P	clk.
171 Spain	1875	Mary	wid Thomas		1883	Thomas	tinsmith
						William P	clk.
111 Tchoupitoulas	1873	Michael	saloon		1884	Mary	wid Thomas
	1874	Michael	saloon			Thomas	tinsmith
	1875	Michael	saloon			William	clk.
	1876	Michael L	saloon & boarding		1885	Mary	wid Thomas
	1877	Michael L	saloon			Thomas	tinsmith
	1878	Michael	saloon			William	clk.
		Patrick	laborer		1885	Mary	wid Thomas
	1879	Mary	wid Thomas			Thomas	tinsmith
		Eliza	wid Michael, saloon			William	clk.
		Patrick	laborer	500 Royal	1889	Mary	wid Thomas
						Thomas	sheetiron wkr Edwards & Haubtman

Even a dry list of names and addresses can disclose poignant episodes in a family's history. In 1880, the widow was living with Eliza Lyons, wid. Michael. Eliza's deceased husband was probably the widow's son Michael who lived with her on Constance St. in 1866. Civil birth and death records and the 1880 census reveal the unfortunate situation Michael's death put her in. Eliza was left with three minor children to support, a 13-year-old daughter, an 8-year-old son, and a 2-year old toddler and was three months pregnant. She must have really needed her mother-in-law's help caring for her children while she eked out a living running the family saloon. At the same time, for economic or health reasons, Mary Lyons might not have been capable of living on her own any longer since she was 77 years old.

Table 15. Lyons family members and their probable relationships (so far).

Name	Relationship
Mary wid. Thomas	Mother
Michael L.	Son
Patrick (Contractor)	Son
Eliza	Daughter-in-Law
Patrick (Laborer)	Grandson?
Thomas	Son/Grandson?
William P.	Son/Grandson?

In 1880, a second Patrick Lyons appeared at the 111 Tchoupitoulas address. Could he have been an older son of Michael and Eliza, who had to go to work to replace the income the family had lost upon his father's death? Marriage records show that Michael and Eliza were married in February 1863, so that their oldest child could have been 16 years old by late 1879 when the 1880 directory was compiled. This was old enough to work and therefore to be listed in the city directory. He is listed as a laborer, so he is probably not the same Patrick Lyons who lost a child in the 1860s. The earlier Patrick was a contractor, implying that he was a businessman with some education and financial means. This new Patrick could have been a nephew or a cousin, but whoever he was, he almost certainly was a member of the extended family.

Once you have researched your ancestor's addresses and identified the family members he was living with, the next step is to repeat the process (Steps 2 through 8) for these new relatives (Table 15) to see where each one of them lived and with whom. If these family members are found at addresses other than the ones they shared with your ancestor, they might be listed with still other relatives. Because a new relative's name can be very common and hard to trace through other addresses, care must be taken to track the right person. When we were tracing Mary Lyons through the directories, this was not too difficult because she was listed as the widow of Thomas.

Since we know so much about him already, let's research Michael Lyons, the widow's son. Starting again with the alphabetical list in Table 10, we must figure out which Michael listings refer to the right person. (See Table 16.) Michael is a very common name, so that there are sometimes several listed in the same directory. (Refer to the earlier comment on the Irish

Table 16. List of Michael Lyons taken from the alphabetical database in Table 9.

Year	First Name	Occupation	Work Info	Home Address	
1861	Michael	lab.		63 St. James	(1)
	Michael			**6 Constance**	
1866	**Michael**			**6 Constance**	
1868	Michael Thos	printer		Chippewa b Washington & 4th	(2)
1869	Michael	printer		219 Chippewa	(2)
1870	Michael T Jr	printer	Picayune	294 Camp	(2)
1871	Michael	board'g house		79 Girod	(4)
	Michael	cooper	124 St Joseph	e.s. Girod b. Constance & Tchoupitoulas	(3)
1872	Michael	cooper	124 St Joseph	79 Girod	(3)
	M. T.	printer	Picayune	114 Thalia	
1873	Michael	cooper	124 St Joseph	Girod c. Tchoupitoulas	(3)
	Michael	**saloon**		**111 Tchoupitoulas**	
1874	Michael	cooper	124 St Joseph	79 Girod	(3)
	Michael	**saloon**	**Same**	**Tchoupitoulas n.w.c. Girod**	
	Michael T.	pressman	NO Picayune	116 Thalia	(1)
1875	**Michael**	**saloon**		**111 Tchoupitoulas**	
	Michael T.	printer		116 Thalia	(1)
1876	**Michael L.**	**saloon & boarding**		**111 Tchoupitoulas**	
	Michael T.	printer	NO Picayune	116 Thalia	(1)
1877	**Michael L.**	**saloon**		**111 Tchoupitoulas**	
	Michael T.	printer	N O Picayune	116 Thalia	(1)
1878	**Michael**	**saloon**		**111 Tchoupitoulas**	
	Michael T.	printer	N O Picayune	116 Thalia	(1)
1879	Michael T.	printer		115 1/2 Thalia	(2)

Table 16. (Continued)

Notes	
(1)	Eliminated because he appears in the same year as 'the' Michael Lyons.
(2)	Same individual working as a printer who was eliminated by reason (1).
(3)	Retained – same address as Michael Lyons, son of the widow.
(4)	Retained–same address identified as cooper in (3).

imagination in naming their children.) Besides the listings that can easily be identified as our Michael, there are entries for
- Michael the laborer living at 63 St. James St. (1861),
- Michael the printer living at 116 Thalia St. (1874, 1875, 1876, 1877, 1878 1879), and
- Michael the cooper living at 79 Girod (or Girod c. Tchoupitoulas) (1873, 1874).

Michael the laborer appearing in 1861 can be put aside for the time being. Since our Michael is already accounted for in 1861 living on Constance St., there is no reason to believe that Michael the laborer ties into the Lyons family. In the future, we might uncover information showing that he was a cousin or uncle, or that he was Mary Lyons' brother-in-law. But at least for now he can be ruled out as being Michael Lyons, the widow's son.

Michael the printer can also be quickly eliminated because he appears in the 1879 directory. We know that our Michael was dead by then, since his widow is listed at the saloon on Tchoupitoulas St. that year. However, it is worth noting that things could have happened differently. If our Michael had died on December 31, 1878, for example, he would still have been listed in the 1879 directory. In this case the printer would have to be

Figure 4. The corner of Girod and Tchoupitoulas, New Orleans, the location of Michael and Eliza Lyons' saloon in the 1870s.

eliminated because he appears in earlier directories at addresses different from those listed for the widow's son.

At first glance, Michael the cooper can be eliminated because he appears in several of the same directories as our Michael the saloonkeeper. The problem is that the cooper is listed in 1871 through 1874 at Girod b. Constance and Tchoupitoulas, Girod c. Tchoupitoulas, or 79 Girod. This can be interpreted as the same address as the saloonkeeper, who starting in 1873 is listed at Tchoupitoulas c. Girod or 111 Tchoupitoulas, located on the corner of Tchoupitoulas and Girod. It seems that the saloon owner is the correct man, because his widow was listed as running the saloon after he died. But the cooper seems to be the correct man, too–the 1870 census says that Eliza's husband Michael was a cooper and the city directories say that this cooper lived at Girod c. Tchoupitoulas. How could they both be the right man?

The answer is that they *are* both the right man. The reason for his double listing can be pieced together by supplementing the city directories with information provided by civil birth records.

In 1871 Michael Lyons the cooper lived near the corner of Girod and Tchoupitoulas, with a workshop located at 124 St. Joseph St. According to birth records, in mid-1870 Michael Lyons' wife gave birth to a set of twins. He began taking in boarders most likely to supplement his income, so that he was listed at his home address in 1871 as having a boarding house. Two years later, he opened a saloon in time to be listed in the 1873 directory. It was intended to be a family-run business, evidenced by the listing of his widow Eliza at this address long after his death. He was able to get two listings – one for his cooperage and the other for either his boarding house or his saloon, so that he was listed twice at the same address (though stated a little differently in each case to disguise the double listing). Note that being a cooper and owning a saloon are compatible occupations. His wife could run the saloon during the day, and he could take care of it in the evenings after he got home from making barrels in his workshop on St. Joseph St. A picture of the location of the saloon on the corner of Girod and Tchoupitoulas as it appears today is shown in Figure 4.

The final list of the Michaels positively identified as the widow Lyons' son is given in Table 17. There are Michaels who appear as early as 1852, but because of lack of information prior to 1861, none of them can be ruled in or out. These Michaels can always be added back into the final list if they are ever identified as relatives. Table 17 can now be reorganized by address to see if Michael ever lived with any other Lyons that are not already among known family members. The results of resorting by address are shown in Table 18 in chronological order. The table also gives the names of all the individuals who ever appeared at any of his addresses.

The only new Lyons who appears in this second go around is Mary Lyons, wid. John. Without further investigation, it is not possible to identify how this new Mary Lyons fits into the family, but the best guess is that she could be Michael's aunt, sister-in-law to Mary, wid. Thomas. Table 19 gives a summary of how the Lyons found during the second iteration could be related to Michael. When

Table 17. City directory listings for Michael Lyons, the Widow Lyons' son.

Yr	First Name	Occupation	Work Info	Home Address
1861	Michael			6 Constance
1866	Michael			6 Constance
1871	Michael	board'g house		79 Girod
1871	Michael	cooper	124 St. Joseph	e.s. Girod b. Constance & Tchoupitoulas
1872	Michael	cooper	124 St. Joseph	79 Girod
1873	Michael	cooper	124 St. Joseph	Girod c. Tchoupitoulas
1873	Michael	saloon		111 Tchoupitoulas
1874	Michael	cooper	124 St. Joseph	79 Girod
1874	Michael	saloon	Same	Tchoupitoulas n.w.c. Girod
1875	Michael	saloon		111 Tchoupitoulas
1876	Michael L.	saloon & boarding		111 Tchoupitoulas
1877	Michael L.	saloon		111 Tchoupitoulas
1878	Michael	saloon		111 Tchoupitoulas

the process is repeated a third time for Mary, wid. John, the only additional family member identified is a John who lived on Spain St. in 1875.

Resorting Directories By Occupation

The remaining possibility is to organize directory information by occupation or place of work. In the earlier examples, there was no reason to do so, since there was only one Mary Lyons wid. Thomas listed through the years, and there was already sufficient information to identify Michael by his address.

The starting point is the same as before – to identify entries for a particular family member in the alphabetical database of names in Table 10. Based on the occupations of this family member, the original list of Lyons (Table 9) can be rearranged by occupation (instead of address as before), to find family members with similar occupations or places of work.

This is a good exercise to leave for the reader. The list of all Lyons family members derived from tracing Mary Lyons, wid. Thomas (and her assumed relatives) through the city directories by name, address, and occupation is shown in Table 20.

Table 18. Listing of all Lyons living at addresses associated with Michael the son of the Widow Lyons.

Address	Year	Residents	Occupation
6 Constance St.	1861	Mary, Mrs	
		Michael	
		Patrick	contractor
	1866	Mary, Mrs	
		Michael	
		Patrick	contractor
79 Girod or Girod b. Constance & Tchoupitoulas or Girod c. Tchoupitoulas	1871	Michael	boarding house
	1872	Michael	cooper, 124 St Joseph
	1873	Michael	cooper, 124 St Joseph
	1874	Michael	cooper, 124 St Joseph
	1886	Mary	wid. John, furnished rooms
111 Tchoupitoulas	1873	Michael	saloon
	1874	Michael	saloon
	1875	Michael	saloon
	1876	Michael L.	saloon & boarding
	1877	Michael L.	saloon
	1878	Michael	saloon
		Patrick	laborer
	1879	Mary	wid. Thomas
		Eliza	wid. Michael, saloon
		Patrick	Laborer
	1880	Mary	wid. Thomas
		Eliza, Mrs.	wid. Michael
		Patrick	lab.
	1881	Eliza, Mrs.	saloon
	1884	Eliza, Mrs.	saloon
	1885	Eliza, Mrs.	saloon
	1886	Eliza, Mrs.	saloon

Table 19. Lyons family members associated with Michael Lyons.

Name	Relation
Michael L.	
Mary, wid. Thomas	Mother
Patrick (Contractor)	Brother
Eliza	Wife
Patrick (Laborer)	Son?
Mary, wid. John	Aunt?

Table 20. Possible members of the Lyons family of New Orleans, identified by common addresses and occupations.

Individual	Relationship	Reason Included
Mary wid. Thomas	Mother	-----
Mary, wid. John	Sister-in-Law?	Address
Eliza	Daughter-in-Law	Listed as Wid. Michael
John	Son/Grandson?	Address/Occupation
Michael L.	Son	Address
Patrick (Contractor)	Son	Address
Patrick (Laborer and/or Foreman)	Grandson?	Address/Occupation
Thomas – 1881 (Machinist)	Son/Grandson?	Address
Thomas – 1881 (Sheetiron Worker)	Son/Grandson?	Address/Occupation
William (Sheetiron Worker)	Son?	Occupation & Place of Work
William P. (Clerk)	Grandson?	Address

Widow Tracking

A few more words about widows. The directory in which a woman is first listed as a widow can indicate when her husband died. The example of Eliza Lyons, wid. Michael showed how useful knowing this can be in piecing together a family's history. A second example is that of Maurice (Morris) Ivory and his wife Mary Swords, who appeared in the New Orleans city directories in the mid 1880s. (See Table 21.) It is clear that Maurice died in 1882 or 1883 because after this his wife is listed as a widow. Narrowing down the date of death to a year or two is very helpful when requesting a search for a death certificate.

On the other hand, when a widow disappears from the city

Table 21. Widow tracking.

Year	Name	Address
1881	Maurice Ivory	227 Clara St.
1882	Morris Ivory	181 1/2 S. Derbigny
1883	Morris Ivory	181 1/2 S. Derbigny
1884	Mary Ivory, wid Maurice	226 Clara St.

directory, there are several possible reasons, assuming she did not moved away from the area. The first reason is that she died. The second reason is that she moved in with another family member and had no reason to be listed. This is probably why Mary, wid. Thomas Lyons was missing from some of the directories. The third reason is that she remarried. For instance, Amelia Gauthreaux, the widow of Justillien, disappeared from the New Orleans city directory under the name Gauthreaux because she married John Charles Controwinski in June 1889.

An illustration of how much information about a man can be revealed by the appearance of his widow in the city directories appears in the chapter A Case Study in Digital Detective Work. Michael Patrick Swords was listed in the Winnipeg, Manitoba city directories from 1910 through 1914. (Note that this gives a latest date for his arrival in Winnipeg.) The appearance of his widow Kate at the same address in 1915 gave his approximate date of the death as 1914 to 1915. This was enough information to obtain Michael Sword's death certificate from the Manitoba Vital Records Office. The certificate was a source of a great deal of additional information: his birth date and place, his parents' names, when he died, and where he was buried. Knowledge of his birthplace and birth date led to his baptismal records in Ireland, as well as those of all his siblings, complete with their baptismal sponsors.

EVENT DATABASES

Birth, Marriage, and Death Records

The second kind of database that can be used as a source of genealogical information is the event database. This kind of database includes birth, marriage, and death records, civil court records, hospital admission records, naturalization records, and any other database that was constantly updated to keep track of certain events as they occurred. Although finding an individual in this kind of database can be hit and miss, if you are lucky to spot a relative in an events database, you may find out a great deal of information that other sources do not provide.

The most researched of all event databases are civil birth, marriage, and death records. The dates of birth, marriage, and death are the most essential pieces of information you can have about someone. Birth records almost always give the name of at least one parent, a birth date, a birthplace, and perhaps information about another member of the family who reported the birth. A marriage record might have the names of relatives and friends of the bride and groom who acted as witnesses. A death certificate might give an address, the name of a spouse, the cause of death, and an occupation that will allow you to recognize the person in the city directories. Since births, marriages and deaths are usually accompanied by religious rites, knowledge gleaned from them can lead to church records.

Birth, marriage and death records can reveal far more than just cold facts. A collection of births, marriages, and deaths can reveal the structure and history of a family that are not readily apparent from a single record. For example, comparing birth and death dates of family members might explain why Uncle Joe was raised by his grandparents, or why Aunt Mary could not possibly be the mother of Cousin William because Aunt Mary was only 5 years old when William was born.

In an earlier section on city directories, we found that when his wife Eliza gave birth to twins in 1870, Michael Lyons began to take in boarders and then opened a saloon. When he died several years later, his mother wid. Mary Lyons, moved in with Eliza, who was three months pregnant and had three minor children to care for. This information was gleaned in part from the civil birth and death records of New Orleans and is an excellent example of the kind of picture they can paint of a family's history.

There is value not only in noting what appears in databases, but also in noting what is absent. Gaps in information become apparent only when you are working with a collection of records. For example, chronological gaps in the birth dates and gaps in traditional naming patterns of the known children in a family can point to missing children and give insight into the previous generation.

Even if a couple had children regularly every two or three years, they might have skipped names that should have appeared in their naming scheme. These absences can point to information about the aunts, uncles, grandparents or other relatives whose names should have appeared in the lineup but did not. If the name of the mother's sister was skipped, for example, it might mean that this sister died as an infant, was disowned by the family, or that she was much older than the mother so that the mother never knew her. If the name of a grandfather is skipped in favor of an uncle, it could mean that this uncle acted as a father figure in that family or that he was wealthy and the family were playing up to him hoping for an inheritance.

Significant clues offered by patterns found in birth records are summed up in Figure 5, and illustrated below by the example of the Rice and Swords families, who emigrated from Ireland to New Orleans in the 1850s.

Bernard Rice and Catherine Swords evidently followed the traditional Irish naming pattern for naming their offspring where the first son is named after his paternal grandfather, the second son after his maternal grandfather, the third son after his father, the fourth son after his father's oldest brother, the fifth son after his mother's oldest brother, and so on until all the names of the parents' immediate male relatives have been exhausted. The daughters are named similarly, with the first daughter named after her maternal grandmother, the second daughter after her paternal grandmother, the third daughter after her mother, the fourth daughter after her mother's oldest sister, the fifth daughter after her father's oldest sister, and so on until all the names of the parents' immediate female relatives have been exhausted. If one side of the family runs out of male or female names, the parents continue with the remaining names on the other side of the family. For example, if the mother does not have any brothers, the sons in the family are named after their grandparents, their father, and the father's brothers in chronological order. If all the names on both sides of the family are used up but there are still more children to be named, the parents usually continue with

Figure 5. Clues from Gaps in the Chronology and Naming Patterns of Children

1) Do the names of the sons and daughters follow a regular pattern when compared to the known male and female names found in the parents' birth families?

    Yes: Naming patterns can be used to predict as yet undiscovered names in the parents' birth families.

2) Are there chronological gaps in the known births in a family?

    Yes: Good indication of miscarriages or children who died young.

3) Do chronological gaps in the children's birth correspond to gaps in the naming pattern?

    Yes: Indication of a child who died after it was registered. Search birth records during this gap for a child with the missing name who died young.

4) Are there gaps or exceptions in the naming pattern used by the parents that do not correspond to chronological gaps in births?

    Yes: A name missing from the lineup without a corresponding chronological gap can indicate a disruption of the relationship of the parent to the relative whose name is missing.

    Ex 1:   The name of an older brother who acted as a father figure might be used rather than that of the name of a father who died very young;

    Ex 2:   The name of an older sibling of a parent might be missed if that sibling died and was never known by the parent.

5) Are there disruptions in the family occurring at the same time as gaps in the births?

    Yes: Could give an estimate of the date of death of one parent and the remarriage of the other.

6) Do multiple children appear with the same name?

    Yes: Birth year of the second child is likely the latest date the first child died. The repetition of a name also indicates the importance of that name to the parents and could lead to the names of their own parents (the grandparents of the child).

names of family friends or more distant relatives. Names that repeat in the traditional pattern are dealt with in various creative ways.

The names and dates of baptism of Bernard Rice and Catherine Swords' children are shown in Table 22. See Tables 23 and 24 for the names of their parents and siblings, obtained from Armagh Ancestry, Armagh City, County Armagh, and The Kildare Heritage and Genealogical Center, Newbridge, County Kildare. (Civil birth records are not available.) Comparing the Rice sons' names to those expected from the naming tradition reveals two anomalies. See Table 25. The name of the maternal grandfather Matthew was not chosen for the second son. Maybe Grandfather Matthew

Table 22. The names and dates of the children of Bernard C. Rice and Catherine Swords.

Child	Date of Bapt
John Charles	Nov. 4, 1861
Thomas J.	Sep. 1, 1863
Bernard J.	Sep. 29, 1865
Marie	Nov. 13, 1867
Catherine	Aug. 11, 1869
Julia	Sep. 7, 1871
Elizabeth N.	Jul. 22, 1875
Mary Ellen	1877
Matthew Adam	Apr. 17, 1879

Table 23. The children of John Rice and Ann Byrnes, Co. Armagh, Ireland.

Name	Bapt Date
James	1831
Mary Ann	Jul. 13, 1835
Bernard*	Sep. 4, 1837
Bridget	Jan. 31, 1840
Felix	Jun. 23, 1842
Catharine	Apr. 16, 1845

*Married Catharine Swords.

Table 24. The children of Matthew Swords and (1) Mary Nolan and (2) Mary Farrell.

Children of Mary Nolan	Bapt Date
Mary	Feb. 2, 1822
Patrick	Mar. 27, 1824
Thomas	Apr. 15, 1826
Matthew	Mar. 22, 1828
Catharine	Feb. 10, 1833
Patrick	Jan. 1, 1835
Darby	Sep. 27, 1837

Children of Mary Farrell	Bapt Date
Catharine*	Jul. 7, 1839
Maria	Feb. 27, 1842
Bridget	Oct. 6, 1844
Julia	May 23, 1847
Eliza	Jul. 16, 1854

*Married Bernard C. Rice.

Table 25. Bernard Rice's sons' names compared to the Irish naming tradition.

Tradition	Names on Father's Side	Names on Mother's Side	Status	Sons' Names
Paternal Grandfather	John		Used	John
Maternal Grandfather		Matthew	Skipped	Thomas
Father	Bernard Jr.		Used	Bernard Jr.
Father's Oldest Brother	James		Used	James*
Mother's Oldest Brother		Thomas	Moved Up	Matthew
Father's Second Brother	Felix		Not Used	
Mother's Second Brother		Matthew	Moved Up	
Mother's Third Brother		Patrick	Not Used	
Mother's Fourth Brother		Darby	Not Used	

*If the missing child was a son.

Table 26. Bernard Rice's daughters' names compared to the Irish Naming Tradition.

Tradition	Names on Mother's Side	Names on Father's Side	Status	Daughters' Names
Maternal Grandmother	Mary			Marie
Paternal Grandmother		Ann	Skipped	
Mother	Catherine			Catherine
Mother's Oldest Sister	Marie		Already Used	
Father's Oldest Sister		Mary Ann	Already Used	
Mother's Second Sister	Bridget		Skipped	
Father's Second Sister		Bridget	Skipped	
Mother's Third Sister	Julia			Julia
Father's Third Sister		Catherine	Already Used	
Mother's Fourth Sister	Eliza (Elizabeth)			Elizabeth**
Mother's Fourth Sister				Elizabeth
Family Friend				Mary Ellen

**If missing child was a daughter.

did not want a child named after him, or perhaps Catherine hated her father. Also, the name James should have appeared where a gap in the birth order occurs.

It is curious that there is no daughter named after her maternal grandmother Ann. Ann Rice immigrated with the family and did not die until 1866, after the three oldest Rice sons were born. Perhaps this tells us something about her personality. The name Bridget is also conspicuously absent even though both the mother and the father had sisters by this name. One possibility is that both of these Bridgets died at birth or as young children. There is no evidence that either one of them immigrated to the U.S. with the rest of her family. (See Table 26.)

To sum up, if the missing child were a son, his name would be James. If the missing child were a daughter, her name would be Eliza or Elizabeth. The first possibility is correct, as the birth records reveal a son James born on September 12, 1873 between the daughters Julia and Elizabeth. He lived only a few days.

The final lineup of the all the children of Bernard C. Rice and Catherine Swords is shown in Table 27.

Table 27. Complete list of Bernard C. Rice's children, including the missing son James.

Child	Date of Bapt
John Charles	Nov. 4, 1861
Thomas J.	Sep. 1, 1863
Bernard J.	Sep. 29, 1865
Marie	Nov. 13, 1867
Catherine	Aug. 11, 1869
Julia	Sep. 7, 1871
James	Sep. 12, 1873
Elizabeth N.	Jul. 22, 1875
Mary Ellen	1877
Matthew Adam	Apr. 17, 1879

Hospital Admission Records

An extremely valuable but often overlooked events database is hospital admission records. See Figure 6 for an excerpt from a page from the Charity Hospital records, New Orleans, LA. Hospital records have many characteristics in common with census records; indeed, they are census records to some extent. But hospital records are also unlike census records. Census records are taken once every ten years, but hospital admissions are updated daily. Census records offer a picture of the more stable elements of a population, whereas hospital admission records show its more transient aspects. An immigrant who was sick upon his

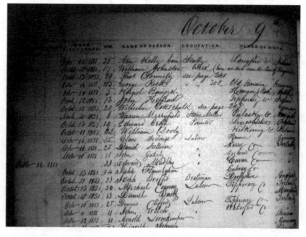

Figure 6. Excerpt from Charity Hospital admission records, October 9, 1851.

arrival in the U.S. and who was taken to the hospital immediately from the boat would appear in the admission records, even if he were in the hospital for only a few hours. This same immigrant would probably not appear in the census records of that town unless he settled there.

Hospital records are usually more accurate and comprehensive than census records, as each patient was admitted by a hospital clerk who was an educated person with legible handwriting. Since the clerk who entered a name into the register normally recorded it a second time in an alphabetical or chronological index, names that are uncertain in the register can be cross checked with the index. Important information was typically collected on the patient as he was admitted, including his occupation, age, place of birth, last place from, how long in town, marital status, how long he had been sick, and his illness. Sometimes more than one family member were admitted at the same time. When the same name does appear more than once in the records, there is plenty of information to cross check entries to see if they refer to the same person, or to different people with the same name, and to verify the overall reliability of the information.

This abundance of data in hospital admission records can given leads to the discovery of other kinds of genealogical information. For example, if you were researching the ships records for an ancestor named John Hanlon from County Wexford, Ireland, you might be able to obtain information from the hospital records that would point to the approximate date of his arrival. From the list of all the Hanlons who were admitted to the hospital during the 1850s, Hanlons from County Wexford show up only during 1851 and 1852. There was none admitted for the rest of the 1850s. (Table 28.) The dates of admission and the lengths of time each of these patients had been in New Orleans can be used to determine that the Wexford Hanlons all arrived in late 1850 through early 1851. Although the hospital lists probably do not account for all the Hanlons from Wexford who settled in New Orleans, they probably give a reasonable cross section that can serve as a starting point for researching the date and the ship John Hanlon arrived on.

Table 28. Hanlons from Co. Wexford appearing in the Charity Hospital admissions from 1851 through 1858.

Yr	Date Adm	Date Disch	Name	Place of Birth	Age	Last From	Time in NO	Mar Stat	Long Sick	Disease
1851	4 Feb	10 Mar	Hanlon or Handley, Ann	Wexford Co.	19	Liverpool	3 mos	S	1 wk	Int Fever
1851	14 Feb	10 Mar	Handley, Mary	Wexford Co.	20	Liverpool	1 mo	S	1 wk	Typhus Fever
1851	2 Aug	4 Aug	Hanlan, Ann	Wexford Co.	25	Ireland	1 yr	S	1 wk	Bilious Fever
1851	9 Aug	22 Aug	Handlan, Elizabeth, born Collaton	Wexford Co.	50	Liverpool	8 mos	W	4 dys	Int Fever
1851	4 Sep	7 Sep	Hanlan, John	Wexford Co.	19	Ireland	10 mos	S	4 dys	Int Fever
1852	28 Jan	29 Jan	Handlan, John	Wexford Co.	19	Liverpool	12 mos	S	5 mos	Int Fever
1852	12 Oct	16 Oct	Hanlon, Bernard	Wexford Co.	22	Ireland	2 yrs	S	1 wk	Bilious Fever

UNUSUAL REFERENCE MATERIALS

There are many unusual and interesting reference materials available that are prime ancestor hunting grounds. If you have lost track of an ancestor, he just didn't fall off the face of the earth. Most people leave a paper trail as they go through life. Even obscure episodes are probably documented somewhere. The job is to find out where.

Some interesting possibilities are seaman's protection certificates, physician's records, police reports and coroner's records. Sometimes several of these unconventional sources can be combined to construct an incident in an ancestor's life. For example, if an ancestor was shot dead in a drunken barroom brawl, there was probably a police report issued about the incident accompanied by a coroner's report and a newspaper article. There might even be a request from a funeral home to take possession of the body for burial services.

Here are a few examples of unconventional references and what they can reveal about an ancestor's life:

- List of Fire Victims and Their Losses

The fourth name on this list is that of Gustave Potier, f.m.c. [free man of color]. The records state that he was married, lost about $25 or $30 in the fire, and was apportioned $10.10 by the city in compensation.

This record gives a clue to the latest date that Gustave could have been married. It also states that he was a free man of color (either a free Negro or an emancipated slave).

List of Fire Victims and Their Losses
New Orleans, LA 1844

- Seaman's Protection Certificates

The website of the National Archives and Records Administration, Northeast Region at Boston http://www.mysticseaport.org/library/initiative/protectionindex.cfm[1] gives the history of Seaman's Protection Certificates:

"In response to the impressment of American seamen by British ships, Congress passed an *Act for the Relief and Protection of American Seamen* in 1796. The Act required customs collectors to maintain a record of all United States citizens serving on United States vessels. Each seaman, once registered with the customs collector, was given a Seaman's Protection Certificate. These certificates vouched for the citizenship of the individual and included identifying information such as age, height, complexion, place of birth, and in some cases eye and hair color. The intention of these certificates was to discourage impressments."

Seaman's Protection Certificate
Philadelphia, 23 February 1852

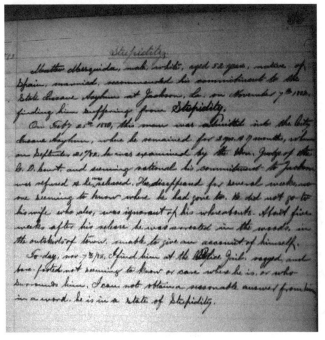

- Insane Asylum Admission Records and Physician's Exams

Stupidity – Mathew Mesquida, male, white, 52 years old, native of Spain, married, recommended his commitment to the State Insane Asylum at Jackson, La. on November 7th, 1882, finding him suffering from Stupidity.

On February 25th, 1880, this man was admitted into the City Insane Asylum, where he remained for 2 yrs & 7 mos, when on September 21st/82, he was examined by the Hon. Judge of the [Circuit District] Court, and seeming rational, his commitment to Jackson was refused and he was released. He disappeared for several weeks, no one seeming to know where he had gone to. He did not go to his wife who also, was ignorant of his whereabouts. About five weeks after his release he was arrested in the woods, in the outskirts of town, unable to give an account of himself.

Today, Nov. 7th/82, I find him at the Police Jail ragged and bare-footed, not seeming to know or care where he is, or who surrounds him. I cannot obtain a reasonable answer from him; in a word he is in the state of stupidity.

- Coroner's Reports

    State of Louisiana, City of Jefferson, Mayor's Office
    I the undersigned Mayor of the City of Jefferson do hereby testify that Pierre Paul Gugni, aged three years & three months, died this morning at about 7 oclock [sic] of a relapse of measles and that no physician was attending him.
    In testimony whereof I have set my hand at the City of Jefferson this 29th day of April 1857.

    J. Saize
Mayor

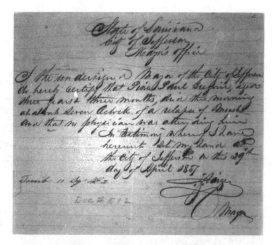

- Records of the Disposition of Destitute Orphans, Office of the Mayor, New Orleans, LA

    Lizzie Duggan, 16 years of age. The mother cannot control her & takes this step to try to reclaim her. She is now in parish prison and this request is to be made at exhaustion of time for which she was committed.

    This is done at earnest request of mother. [Signed] Sarah Duggan. Permit Book #4, page 588.

- Registry of Free Persons of Color

    I do hereby certify that Mary T. Mount a free woman of color has been registered at the Parish Court on the 18th April 1843 and has complied with the provisions of an Act of the Legislature approved 22d March 1843 by furnishing Surety Bond at the Recorder's office of Municipality No. 3, for the faithful observance of said Mary T. Mount of the laws now ____ which may hereafter be created for the regulation and government of free persons of color who are allowed to remain in the State of Louisiana.

    New Orleans, 27th Septr 1843
    Recorder's Office of Municipality No. 3

    [Signed] J. R. Viame
Secretary of the Recorder

112

USING MULTIPLE SOURCES TO CONSTRUCT A FAMILY STORY

Combining information from several sources often reveals complementary facts that can be pieced together to create an interesting picture of how an ancestor lived. Several good examples of this are given in this chapter. The efforts of Michael Lyons to support his growing family with a double income from his cooperage and the family saloon would never have come to light without supplementing the city directories with census records and city maps. How the old widow Mary Lyons and the young pregnant widow Eliza came to each other's aid after Michael's untimely death in 1878 would not have been discovered without using city directories, census records, and birth and death records to complete the story.

In researching multiple sources, be on the lookout for unusual reference material such as insane asylum admissions and orphan records. They are among many unconventional places to look for relatives who seemed to have vanished. Discovering an ancestor in an unusual place often provides a key piece of information that solves a mystery and fills a hole in a family's story.

The descendents of Heloise Ragondet Pall Devuyst believed that she was widowed in the early 1840s by the death of her first husband, Louis Michael Pauly. Her three children, Eugenie Marie (b. 1844), Jean Armand (b. 1846), and Victor Henry (b. 1849) were recorded in the New Orleans civil birth records as the legitimate children of her second husband Isidore Devuyst.

The admission records of the lunatic asylum tell a different story. On March 1, 1847, Heloise's first husband Louis Michel Palle was admitted to the insane asylum suffering from delirium tremens – the advanced stage of alcoholism. He was released March 4, 1847, only to be readmitted the same day for three additional days. Nothing more is known about Louis, but the website http://www.obwy.com/la/m/md194008.htm[2] gives a clue to his fate:

"[The] eastern Louisiana State Mental Hospital has provided acute and long-term care inpatient mental health services for more than 150 years. On November 21, 1848, the entire mentally ill population of CHNO [Charity Hospital, New Orleans] was transported by steamboat up the Mississippi River to Bayou Sara and from there, by oxcart to the insane Asylum of Louisiana (ELSH). It is one of the oldest landmarks in the [Parishes of East and West Feliciana]."

Whatever his destiny, Louis was almost certainly dead by 1852. That is the year that Isidore and Heloise (the Widow Palle) were married in St. Augustine's Church in New Orleans. Their sacramental marriage record states that by the act of marriage, the Devuyst children were made legitimate.

Was this a class love triangle among Heloise, Louis and Isidore? Did Heloise lie to Isidore about Louis? Did she assume that since her husband had been 'put away' in a mental institution that she could get away with calling herself a widow? Perhaps she thought he was dead, only to discover that he was still alive in the insane asylum. (Imagine how shocked Isidore much have been if he found out!) Or did Heloise obtain a civil divorce from Louis that allowed her to have a civil marriage to Isidore though it was not sanctioned by the Catholic Church? Even after Louis was admitted to

Charity Hospital in 1847, Heloise and Isidore continued their liaison. Perhaps they were unaware that he was still alive. Their last child Victor Henri Devuyst was born in 1849.

The 1850 census answers some of these questions. In that year, Isidore, Heloise, and their two children Eugenie and Victor were living in New Orleans. There were others in their household: Heloise Pale, 11 years old, and Pierre Palle, 28 years old. Their relationship to Heloise is uncertain – perhaps the younger Heloise was her daughter by Louis or her niece, and perhaps Pierre was her brother-in-law. By this time Isidore must certainly have known about Heloise's first husband, although we can never be sure what she told him about Louis.

Isidore disappeared from the city directory after 1854. Family legend has it that Isidore died from drinking a glass of ice water in the middle of July after leading a parade. When Heloise Ragondet Palle Devuyst died from 'hydropsie' in 1860 (according to her sacramental burial record), she was listed as the Widow Devuyst.

Maybe the victim of this saga is Louis Michel Palle. Perhaps he found that on his wages as a coal dealer he could not support his wife Heloise in the style to which she had become accustomed. In anguish over his wife's attentions to his rival Isidore, he could have been driven into alcoholism, especially if he discovered she was pregnant with Louis' child.

This fascinating account of the Devuyst/Palle family could never have been constructed without consulting several different sources:

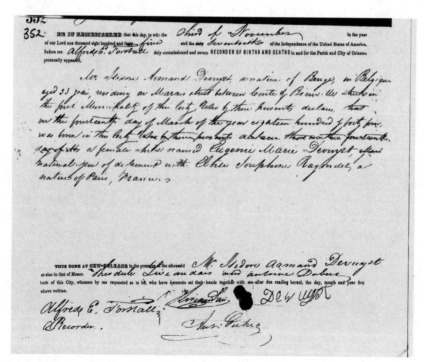

New Orleans Civil Birth Certificate of Eugenie Marie Devuyst, March 14, 1844

Catholic Archdiocese
Sacramental Marriage Records

Isidore Devuyst, a native of Brugge, Belgium, married Heloise Josephine Fragonet [sic], widow of Louis Michel Pauly, a native of Paris, France, July 31, 1852 in New Orleans, LA. (The record is in French).

1850 Census Records

Isidore (38 yrs), Heloise (41), Eugenie (6 1/2), Victor (7/12) Devuyst, and Heloise (12), and Pierre Pale (28)

1854 New Orleans City Directory
Devuyst, G. *[sic]*, shoemaker, St. Phillip n. Johnson

Admission records to the Lunatic Asylum, Charity Hospital, New Orleans

Louis Palle was admitted March 1, 1847 suffering from delirium tremens and discharged March 4, 1847. He was a coal dealer, 48 years old, a native of Paris, France. He had been in New Orleans for eight years. The record states he was a widower, although other records indicate that his wife Heloise Ragondet Pauly was still alive. (He was registered as Louis Michel Pauly on the first line of this page of admissions.)

New Orleans Civil Death Certificate of Mrs. Widow Devuyst, April 16, 1856

CULTURAL PROFILING

Event databases are valuable in revealing patterns of living that give a feel for the way of life of the times. I refer to this as cultural profiling, equivalent to the FBI's criminal profiling mentioned at the beginning of this chapter. This kind of research is based on general observations of a large amount of data collected over an extended period of time. It is not data that are gathered all at once, but that often come along for the ride during research into other topics.

This type of research cannot provide you with specific information on an individual, but it can give you valuable insight into patterns of living your relative might have followed, so that you can second guess where else he might turn up. Information on the ethnic composition of a city, the life expectancy, the typical year of marriage, the typical year of birth of the first child, and how quickly a widow or a widower married again after the death of his or her spouse, can tell you a lot about the culture in which your ancestor was born, lived, and died. Such knowledge of the cultural background of your ancestor might lead you to use common resources in unconventional ways. For example, knowledge of family customs in the 1800s such as the circumstances under which a man would first appear in a city directory (when he started his working life), and when he would typically move out of his family's home (when he got married), led to the use of city directories to locate children who died at birth.

The key to cultural profiling is to recognize patterns in large amounts of data. Public hospital admission records are an excellent source of information for this type of research. Because of the very large number of entries, many interesting observations can be made from them that provide an idea of the living conditions and culture of the times. For example, weather conditions can be deduced from the number of admissions, since severe hot or severe cold weather can cause an increase in the number of hospitalizations. The immigration profile of a town can be derived from the countries of birth of patients, their ages, and the amounts of time they had been in the city. The effects of historical events such as wars or famines can be seen as a rise in the number of immigrants from a certain country. A general profile of the commerce of a town can be deduced from the occupations given at admission.

Data are not only useful in tabular or spreadsheet form. Data can also be plotted as a visual tool for cultural profiling. Figure 7 is a plot of the number of patients admitted on each day in 1851 to Charity Hospital, the public hospital in New Orleans. These data were accumulated as I transcribed the 1851 register for our New Orleans web site. Counting the number of patients admitted each day was not difficult, as there are 50 lines on a page, and the number of admissions could be found on a certain day by noticing how many empty lines were present at the bottom of a page. An average of 65% of the hospital admissions during this time were Irish, mostly admitted with some type of fever. The two most common diagnoses were intermittent fever, where a patient's temperature cycled up and down in the course of the day, returning to normal in between, and remittent fever, where the fever cycled, yet never returned to normal.

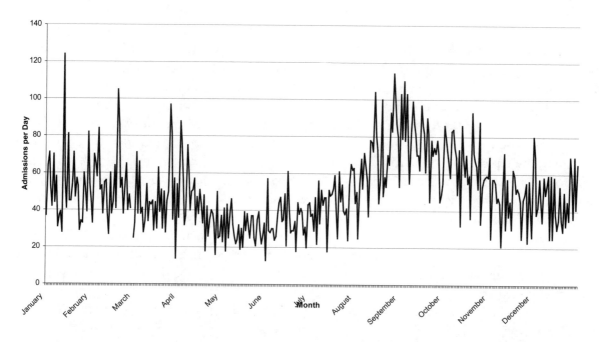

Figure 7. The number of admissions to Charity Hospital in New Orleans for each day in 1851.

Important questions to ask are: What patterns show up in the data? Are there any unusual features or interesting characteristics? Are there any striking exceptions to a general trend?

The number of admissions in 1851 is a curve that rolls up and down in the course of the year. The maximum of the curve occurs at the end of August. There are also positive and negative spikes superimposed on this smooth curve throughout the year. The largest positive spikes occur on certain days–January 13, February 19, March 26, and April 2, when the number of admissions suddenly increased well above the average, and then quickly died away over the next day or two. The negative spikes seem periodic. The increases and decreases in the number of admissions were caused by something – they were reactions of the population to some phenomenon that caused people to get sick, especially the Irish.

Whatever was responsible for the general ups and downs in these numbers had to be something that changed in a more or less continuous fashion throughout the year. The number of admissions increased and decreased as whatever it was increased or decreased on an annual basis. A big hint comes the fact that the peak of the curve occurred at the end of August. This is usually the hottest and wettest part of the year in New Orleans – prime breeding conditions for mosquitoes carrying yellow fever.

The mosquito takes two to four weeks to breed in stagnant water, depending on the temperature. The hotter the weather, the less time required for the eggs to hatch. If there is a correlation between hospital admissions and the mosquito population, a change in the number of new patients should lag high and low rainfalls on the average by three weeks. A large rainfall in July, for example, should show up at the end of the month, perhaps into the earlier parts of August. Table 29 shows the monthly rainfall for the city of New Orleans for 1851 and can be compared to Figure 7 of the 1851 admission records. This information was obtained from Elizabeth Mons, at the Louisiana Office of State Climatology in Baton Rouge, Louisiana[3]. The State has rainfall data going back to 1836, but temperature records only as far back as 1871. While a comparison here must be made on the basis of rainfall records alone, the effects should be the most pronounced in the summer months, when the weather is usually the hottest. The relationship between the mosquito population and the number of hospital admissions is confirmed by the figure since the minimum and maximum number of admissions track the minimum and maximum rainfall, with the expected offset of two to four weeks.

Table 29. Annual rainfall in inches per month for New Orleans for 1851 through 1853.

	J	F	M	A	M	J	J	A	S	O	N	D
1851	4.26	3.75	1.57	4.56	2.73	1.42	4.23	8.39	3.9	3.86	8.3	3.15
1852	0.83	1.53	4.47	4.96	6.39	1.58	5.52	2.46	0.64	3.51	6.84	5.1
1853	3.2	4.4	7.12	1.85	3.32	1.78	11.51	6.28	4.95	5.84	7.03	4.56

Were the Irish involved in an activity that exposed them to mosquitoes?

This question can be answered by looking at Irish American history. In the late 1840s, Ireland experienced a devastating famine due to the failure of the potato crop. Although the population of Ireland had seen an enormous increase of 172% between 1791 and 1844, the failure of the potato crop in 1846 through 1849 leading to the Great Famine caused Ireland to lose one third of its population to death and emigration over the next thirty years. The effects of the famine persisted well into the 20th century; the population of the country continued to decline until the 1960's, when it reached a minimum of just over 4 million[4], including both Northern Ireland and the Republic of Ireland. A comprehensive and fascinating account of the effect of the Famine on the population of Ireland is given by Liam Kennedy, Paul S. Ell, E. M. Crawford, and L. A. Clarkson in their book *Mapping the Great Irish Famine*[5].

At the same time, during the first half of the 1800s New Orleans experienced a tremendous growth. During the 1830's, the population more than doubled to 102,193, making New Orleans the third largest city in the United States. Sixty percent of this population was Negro, either slaves or freemen of color[6].

But by 1850, this had changed. The population had already increased somewhat to 116,375, but now it was 80% white, due to immigration from Europe. Even so, the city was not prepared for the tidal wave of over a quarter of a million additional immigrants who arrived in the early 1850s, over half of whom were Irish escaping the Great Famine. These destitute Irish offered a ready source of cheap labor, suitable for menial and often dangerous jobs. A steamboat captain explained that slaves were not used as stokers on the boats because "every time a boiler burst, they would lose so-many-dollars-worth of slaves; whereas getting Irishmen at a dollar a day they pay for the article as they get it, and if it is blown up, they get another"[7].

An important factor that drew Irish immigrants to New Orleans over other ports of entry was the cotton industry. When cotton was shipped

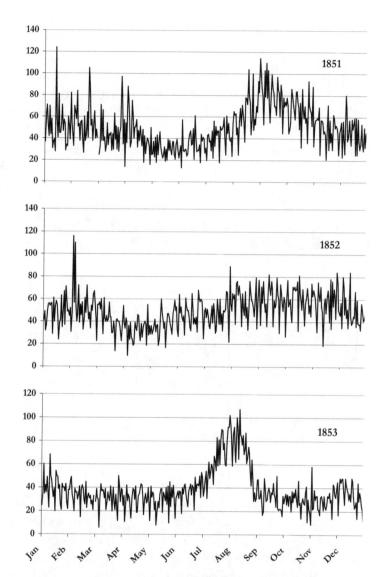

Figure 8. The number of admissions to Charity Hospital in New Orleans for each day in 1851, 1852, and 1853.

via the Port of New Orleans to the textile mills in England, it was not economical for the ships to return empty, so they were packed Irish ballast, immigrants eager to find a better life in the New World. These ships were known as 'coffin ships', since as high as 50% of the passengers would die in transit to the New World[8,9]. Often passengers arrived too weak to leave the docks. Although many of these Irish were in transit to points farther up the Mississippi, Missouri, and Ohio Rivers, to destinations such as St. Louis, Louisville, and Cincinnati, many remained in New Orleans. As pressure mounted on the city to drain more land to accommodate its dramatic increase in population, the fair-skinned Irish were put to work in the subtropical sun by the thousands, building railroads, canals, and streets, often standing knee deep in stagnant pools of mosquito-infested water.

If the cause in the swell in hospital admissions was infection by mosquitoes carrying yellow fever, other years must exhibit the same pattern. Figure 8 shows the number of admissions for each day of 1851, 1852 and 1853. Each of these years follows the same general pattern, with the maximum number of admissions occurring during the summer months, lagging heavy rainfall by about three weeks. One interesting feature is that the curve for 1853 rises to a maximum in July, and then bottoms out in October to a minimum level, well below that of other years.

In 1853, New Orleans experienced its worst yellow fever epidemic, taking the lives of over 12,000 people during the summer months, over half of whom were Irish. The unusually high rainfall in July of just over 11.5", coupled with the unsanitary and crowded living conditions of the Irish, was the epidemic equivalent to a match on a dry forest. The mosquito population must have soared, as reflected in the increased hospital admissions for late July through early August 1853. A possible reason why the number of admissions was so low after the epidemic had passed is shown in Figure 9, the number of deaths in the hospital per day for 1852 and 1853. Of the 50 patients

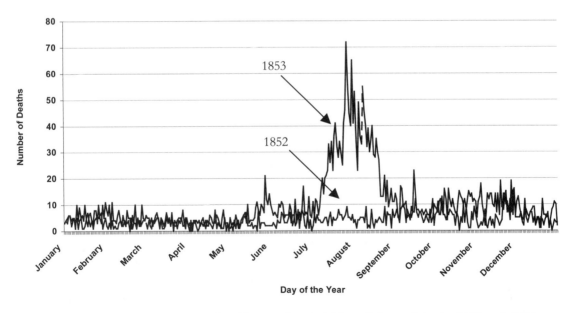

Figure 9. Daily death totals for Charity Hospital, New Orleans, LA, for 1852 and 1853.

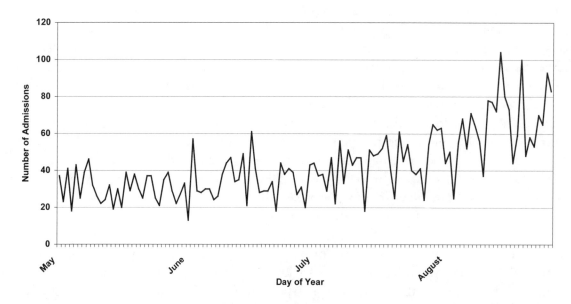

Figure 10. Enlarged portion of Figure 5 showing admissions to the Charity Hospital for May through August 1851. Negative spikes occur every seven days, always on a Sunday.

admitted on an average day during a 'normal' year, about five would die sometime during their stay in Charity Hospital. But in the summer of 1853, at the height of the epidemic, this number reached a maximum of 72 deaths out of 103 admissions on July 27. The reason why there were so few admissions during the last few months of 1853 is that most of people who would normally carry the fever were already dead.

A question still remains about the sharp positive spikes in the admission records for January 13, February 19, March 26, and April 2, 1851. What were the events occurring on these days that caused the number of people admitted to the hospital to increase so sharply and so briefly?

Ships records give a good hint. While the smooth trends in the curve represent the infection of Irish already living in New Orleans, the spikes represent Irish *just arriving* in New Orleans. Because of the crowded and confined environment of a ship, it was not uncommon for epidemics to break out during voyages to the New World. Many times, when a boat arrived infected with typhus or another infectious disease, its sick passengers were immediately brought to the public hospital while the ship was being registered in the Port, a process that could take a couple of days. The first four peaks in the admission records correspond to the arrival of the ships Springfield and Onward (January 13), Eudocia (February 19), Blanche (March 26), and Ottillia (April 2), all originating from Liverpool, and all carrying typhus epidemics. There are other smaller spikes that are somewhat obscured by noisy data. The peak on October 2 corresponds to a group of patients afflicted with typhus offloaded from the Ship Olympus. However, the Olympus does not appear in the list of arrivals, probably reflecting the occasional practice of refusing landing to infected ships, which were then rerouted to other ports. It is also possible that the original destination of the Olympus was further up the river, but she was forced to make a stop in New Orleans to offload her sick.

The final mystery is the presence of the periodic negative spikes in the admission numbers. Figure 10 is an enlarged portion of the plot from Figure 7. The dates where the negative spikes occur in July are July 6, 13, 20, and 27 – every seven days. The perpetual calendar found on the web site http://www.wiskit.com/calendar.html[10] shows that they were all Sundays. The Irish Catholics who worked so hard building the city during the week honored Sunday as a day of rest, even if it meant putting off bringing their sick to the hospital until the next day.

One last comment about cultural profiling. Although large databases are valuable in deducing general trends in the way of life during certain eras, you should also be alert to interesting nuggets that lie hidden underneath tons of facts.

In researching the Charity Hospital records described above, I have come across a few interesting individuals who were admitted to the hospital. Antonio Oliva, a 44-year-old laborer from Buenos Aires, was admitted on February 23, 1851 suffering from intermittent fever, and discharged the next day. He was single and had been living in New Orleans for 10 years at that time. His last place of residence was China. Of the tens of thousands of people who appear in the records for 1851, he is the only person originally from South America, and one of perhaps two people who indicated they had lived most recently in the Far East. Even today it is rare to find an individual who has experienced life on three continents. A novel could probably be written about this man – growing up in Argentina in the early years of the 1800s, his experiences while working the ships across the Pacific Ocean and back, his stay in China in the mid 19th century, and his time in what is arguably still one of the most colorful cities in the United States. Yet this obscure hospital record is probably all that remains of what must have been a fascinating life.

---

[1] http://www.mysticseaport.org/library/initiative/protectionindex.cfm

[2] http://www.obwy.com/la/m/md194008.htm

[3] Elizabeth Mons, Louisiana Office of State Climatology, E327 Howe-Russell Geoscience Complex, Louisiana State University, Baton Rouge, LA 70803-4105, private communication.

[4] http://www.wesleyjohnston.com/users/ireland/past/famine/demographics_pre.html

[5] Liam Kennedy, Paul S. Ell, E. M. Crawford, and L. A. Clarkson, *Mapping the Great Irish Famine*, Four Courts Press, 1999.

[6] Earl F. Niehaus, *The Irish in New Orleans 1800–1860*, Ayer Publishers, Inc., p. 23.

[7] Edward R. Sullivan, *Rambles and Scrambles in North and South America* (London, 1852), p. 216. See also Berger, *The British Traveler*, p. 168, as quoted by Neihaus, p. 49, Ref. 54.

[8] http://freepages.genealogy.rootsweb.com/~emeraldidyll/Ireland/Famine--Liverpool_and_Coffin_Ships.htm

[9] http://205.213.162.11/project_write/PW_2002/handouts/sampleppt/tsld008.htm

[10] http://www.wiskit.com/calendar.html

CASE STUDY IN DATABASE DETECTIVE WORK THE HISTORY OF THE ULMER FAMILY

In 1648, Michael Ulmer, his wife Anna, and six of their children joined the stream of Catholic refugees fleeing Germany to France as a result of the Thirty Years War. Little did they realize that three and a half centuries later, their many-times-great granddaughter would reach back across the Rhine to reconnect them with their German origins and to document their struggle for survival using tools inconceivable to those so many generations in the past. The key to unraveling the mystery of the Ulmers was not so much what the records of those times included. It was insight into what was missing.

THE ORIGINS OF THIS RESEARCH

As a preface to this case study in cultural profiling, it is necessary to provide a brief background on my research into the Ulmer family. My interest in the Ulmers began in the late 1960s with the discovery of an iron box that had remained unopened in my maternal grandmother's closet for over forty years. It had belonged to her maternal grandmother Rose Ulmer, who died in 1919. Miraculously, we found the key, and discovered inside a beautiful old marriage contract between Rose's parents Joseph Ulmer and his second wife Louisa Hentz, written in French and dated January 17, 1853 in Reichshoffen, France (Figure 1). The contract outlined the legal agreement between the couple, what each brought to the marriage, and what would happen to community property if one of them died or deserted the other. It was the equivalent of a modern prenuptial agreement.

The document had an identification number in the upper left corner of its cover, which I used to request further information from France. In a short time, the corresponding marriage license arrived, which listed the bride and groom's parents and dates and places of birth, along with many other important facts. The parents of the bride and groom were my grandmother's grandmother's grandparents, that is, my great great great great grandparents. After sending further inquiries to the city halls of the various little towns in Alsace where the Ulmers lived, I requested the death record from Sigolsheim of an Ulmer relative named Jean Hentz from the late 1700s. The reply came back with not only the requested

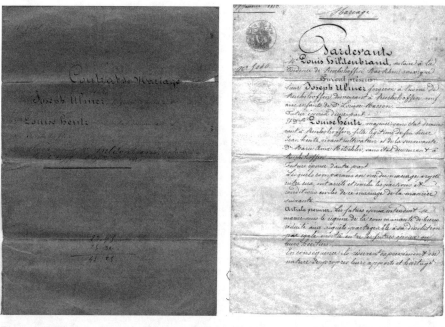

Figure 1. The cover and first page of marriage contract between Joseph Ulmer, blacksmith, and his second wife Louise Hentz, 17 Jan 1853, Reichshoffen, France.

death record, but also with the birth record of this ancestor (Figure 2).

The birth certificate was a five-line record of poorly written Latin, with Jean Hentz' name and date of baptism, along with the names of his parents and his godparents. There were a few signatures below this, including a cross between the two words 'Signum Matrina' (signature of the godmother), indicating she could not write her own name. The envelope also contained a polite note from the French authorities advising me there was no further information to be found. My search had temporarily come to an end.

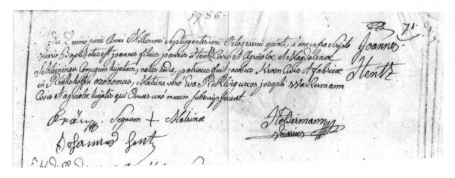

Figure 2. Birth record of Jean Hentz, June 10, 1785, Sigolsheim, France.

BIRTH, MARRIAGE, AND DEATH DATABASES

This is how things remained for about twenty years, until the internet opened many new avenues of research for genealogists. I also learned about the resources of the Family History Library, and found it had microfilms of the civil records and the church records for Sigolsheim back to 1664. Figure 3 is a digital photo taken of the microfilm record of the death certificate from 1679 of my tenth great grandfather Michael Ulmer, who at that time was the patriarch of the family.

There is a rule in genealogy that no matter how far back you have been able to trace your family, you immediately want to go back even farther. Although I had all the hard facts about the Sigolsheim community that the microfilm could provide, I became curious about the Ulmers before the records began in 1664. To learn more about the Ulmers and the world they lived in, I created databases from the baptismal, marriage, and burial records of the community, in the hope of second guessing the prior history of the family through cultural profiling. It was worth the effort to transcribe all of the earliest records, as the community was small, and any information the records provided on the history of other Sigolsheim families could shed light on the origin of the Ulmers.

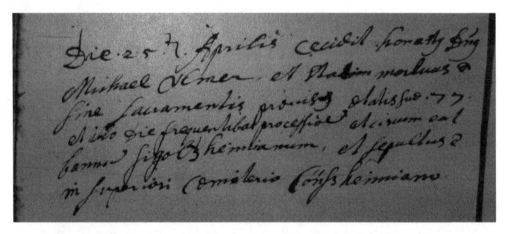

Figure 3. Death certificate of Michael Ulmer d. April 25, 1679, Sigolsheim, France.

Although most of the records were in good condition, the handwriting was illegible in places. A good way to work with records that are hard to read is to copy exactly what the word looks like, even if it does not make sense, carefully copying the short letters and the tall letters in their proper positions to preserve the shape of the word. Later, the same word might appear written more legibly in other records, for example, in the baptismal record of another child by the same parents. It is often possible to match an unreadable name with a clearer version just by matching the shape of the illegible version with a readable one. In all transcriptions, it is very important to copy things exactly as you see them, and to make a note of something that you are not sure of or find confusing.

The first page of the Sigolsheim baptismal records from 1664 shows the condition of the records. (See Figure 4.) Tables 1, 2, and 3 are excerpts of the databases of the earliest Catholic baptismal, marriage, and burial records of Sigolsheim, France, transcribed from microfilm obtained from my local Family History Center. In total, my databases cover the baptismal (1664 - 1765), the marriage (1665 - 1780), and the burial records (1665 - 1740) of the Sigolsheim community. There are question marks next to some of the names in the tables that are hard to read. These tables show only part of the several hundred records that comprise each database that relate to the whole village.

INTERESTING PATTERNS EMERGE

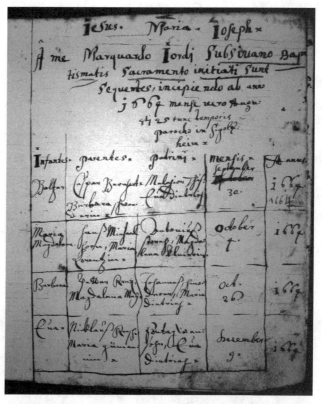

Figure 4. First page of the Sigolsheim baptismal records, 1664.

Close examination of this collection of baptisms, marriages, and burials revealed important cultural clues to the lives of Sigolsheim families. Patterns began to emerge on the relationships of the various community members to each other. For example, the witnesses to a marriage often were equivalent to modern justices of the peace rather than friends of the marrying couple, sometimes drawn from neighboring communities such as Kientzheim or Kaysersberg. These individuals were referred to as 'magister', 'senator', or 'consulis', which I found from online dictionaries to be the equivalents of the titles 'magistrate', 'senator' and 'counsel member'. It seems that couples rarely married for the first time later than their mid twenties. If a man's wife died, he was likely to marry again within a few months. Children were born shortly after a couple were married, and the wife typically bore a child every year and a half to two years until she was in her forties. Deaths of women in childbirth were not as common as I expected, although the mortality rate among infants was very high. These facts fit the general profile of a rural farming community even today.

The Ulmers were unusual for a farm family. Sigolsheim farm wives usually had their first child in their early to mid twenties, but from the birth years of the family members derived from their ages and dates of death, Anna Ulmer's children were not born until she was in her early 30s, or at least not the children who were with the family in Sigolsheim (Table 4). One way this makes sense is that older children existed, but they were not with their parents. So where could they be? If the Ulmers came to Sigolsheim before 1664, could they have left their older children behind somewhere else? Judging from the ages of the Ulmer children, the family would have settled in the area in the early to mid 1650s, assuming they were accompanied by children in their mid teens and younger.

What was happening in Europe in the mid 1600s that could have caused the Ulmers to immigrate to Sigolsheim?

The year 1648 coincided with the end of the Thirty Years War in Germany. This conflict was a complex collection of shorter territorial, dynastic, and religious conflicts among European powers. The War began in 1618 with a revolt in Prague of the Protestant nobility of Bohemia against their overlord Matthias II, Holy Roman Emperor and leader of the Hapsburg House of Austria[1]. The War ended in 1648 with the Peace of Westphalia, also known as the Peace of Exhaustion. During the Thirty Years War, the House of Austria, the Hapsburg Holy Roman Emperors Ferdinand II and Ferdinand III, and their Spanish cousin Philip IV were opposed by various nations including Denmark, the Netherlands, France, and Sweden.

The web site http://www.encyclopedia.com/html/section/ThirtyYe_TheAftermath.asp[2] provides an interesting description of the war's aftermath in Germany:

"The general results of the war may be said to have been a tremendous decrease in German population; devastation of German agriculture; ruin of German commerce and industry; the breakup of the Holy Roman Empire, which was a mere shell in the succeeding centuries; and the decline of Hapsburg greatness. The war ended the era of conflicts inspired by religious passion, and the Peace of Westphalia was an important step toward religious toleration. The incredible sufferings of the German peasantry were remembered for centuries. The political settlements of the peace were to the disadvantage of Germany as well as the Hapsburgs. The estrangement of N. Germany from Austria, then begun, was to continue for more than two centuries."

The web site http://www.genealogienetz.de/reg/ELS-LOT/als-hist.html[3] describes the War's effects on Alsace:

"The Thirty Years War (1618-1648) had been one of the worst periods in the history of Alsace. It caused large numbers of the population (mainly in the countryside) to die or to flee away, because the land was successively invaded and devastated by many armies (Imperials, Swedes, French, etc.).

After 1648 and until the mid-18th century, numerous immigrants arrived from Switzerland, Germany, Austria, Lorraine, Savoy and other areas."

These and other websites[4] provide descriptions of the population upheavals in the mid 1600s resulting from the Thirty Years War that support the theory that the Ulmers, perhaps with other members of the early Sigolsheim community, were forced to leave their homes in Germany and reestablish their lives in Alsace, recently ceded to France as a condition to the Peace of Exhaustion.

Table 1. Baptismal records from Sigolsheim, France for 1664, transcribed from Family History Library microfilm No. 747568.

Yr	Date	Child	Father	Mother	Godmother	Godmother	Notes
1664	30 Sep	Balthar?	Caspar Burgartin	Barbara Schmoderin	Melchior Tis	Catharina Dietrichin	
	5 Oct	Maria Magdalena	Johannes Michael Horn	Maria Lorentzin	Antonius Sonnis	Magdalena Blumerin	
	26 Oct	Barbara	Grttes? Roex	Magdalena Meyer	Joannes Huisderan?	Maria Dietrichin	
	9 Dec	Eva	Niklaus Krauss	Maria Guesanin?	Sontag Lisnuhofn?	Eva Dietrichin	

Table 2. Marriage records from Sigolsheim, France for 1666, transcribed from Family History Library microfilm No. 747568.

Yr	Date	Groom	Bride	Witnesses	Notes on Groom	Notes on Bride
1666	20 Jan	Joannes Jacobus Kock	Ursula Schmidt	Jacob Schnohorn? Keispergers, Antonio Liberman, Sigolsheimis	Sigolsheimis	ex Amerschwier
	16 Feb	Georgium Umbhoffer	Magdalena Ulmerin	Joannes Dietrich Magister and Jacob Guelgengrantz		
	20 Jun	Joannes Georg Keller	Catharina Koeckin	Joannes Jodoso Temp and Antonio Liberman		Buegtanea? ex Jarinanea? Sorfhaus?
	16 Jan	Jacobus Kuneberger	Barbara Libermannin	Marco Richenback and Christiano Allgaewer ex Kienheim	*ambo Sigolzheimensis	
	24 Nov	Nicholas Schmoderer	Susanna Kunepergerin	Sebastian Maurer and Joannes Kraus	Sigolzheimis	
	16 Nov	Joannes Locher*	Maria Francisca Mangoldin*	Joannes Hrietrick and Georgio Guelgeranz	*ambo Sigolzheimerses	Caparimon-ranensis?

Table 3. Death records from Sigolsheim, France for 1665, transcribed from Family History Library microfilm No. 747568.

Year	Date	Name	Age	Comment
1665	23 Jan	Margaretha Maentzlerin		
	28 Jan	Infans Benedict Naegelin		
	2 Mar	Sontag Kleinhauss Zuedleig	7 yrs	
	8 Mar	Petri Rex	3 wks	trium hebtomatarus
	15 Feb	Georgius Manz		Senator in homino pie defunctus est
	8 Apr	Nicolas Resch		
	13 Apr	Alde? Saltzmann	7 yrs	
	16 Jul	Caspari Bernhart	3 wks	
	20 Jul	Casparus Brodbacher		

Table 4. Ulmer birth, marriage, and death years.

Name	Year of Marriage	Year of Birth First Child	Year of Birth Last Child	Year of Death	Age at Death	Calc'd Year of Birth
Michael Ulmer	--	--	--	1679	Abt 77	1602
Anna Wissin Ulmer	--	--	--	1680	Abt 72	1608
Magdaline Ulmer	1666	1665	1681	1709	70	Abt 1639
Antonius Ulmer	1683	1684	1700	1704	64	1640
Anna Ulmer*	--	--	--	--	--	--
Jacob Ulmer	1672	1673	1692	1691	46	Abt 1645
Anna Margaritha Ulmer	1681	1682	1688	1688**	35	Abt 1653
Michael Ulmer, Jr.	1673	1674	1687	Aft 1687	---	Bef 1655

*Anna Ulmer appears in the records only as a baptismal sponsor. She is probably not Anna Wissin Ulmer, wife of Michael Ulmer, because married women usually appeared under their maiden names in the records.
**Died seven days after giving birth to her fourth child.

REFUGEES FROM THE WAR

What route would the Ulmers have used to traveled to Alsace? What would their journey be like?

Travel at that time was dangerous and slow, especially with small children. A family could not travel a long distance alone. For protection and to share daily responsibilities, a family would need to travel in a group of other families. An average adult walks about three miles an hour, but the pace of these refugees would be much slower. Considering the families could only travel during daylight hours, they probably covered as little as a mile a day.

To enter France, the families had to cross the Rhine River. Undoubtedly, they paid a high price for transit, as boats needed to ferry the large number of refugees escaping southern Germany were subject to the laws of supply and demand. The most likely place they crossed the river was at Strasbourg, which had been a political and economic center of the region since the 1200s, as well as a stop on the Paris-Vienna-Orient trade route, and a port on the Rhine route linking southern Germany and Switzerland to the Netherlands, England and Scandinavia[5].

Figure 5[6] shows a map of the region around the Rhine River, with Wurttemberg, Germany to the east and Alsace, France to the west. Sigolsheim is about 30 miles south-southeast of Strasbourg. It is about six miles west of the Rhine River across from the southern German towns of Ehrenstetten, Eschbach, and Hockwald. Because Strasbourg is about 30 miles north northwest of these German towns, in total the refugee party would have had to travel about 60 miles if they came from this region in Germany and crossed the Rhine at Strasbourg. At their slow pace, the trip would have required as much as several months, including time needed for repairs, to search for food, and to take care of the sick. Since many modern highways were built along well known travel routes sometimes dating back to Roman times, the Ulmers and their entourage would likely have walked along what are now highways N83 and A35 to reach their final destination.

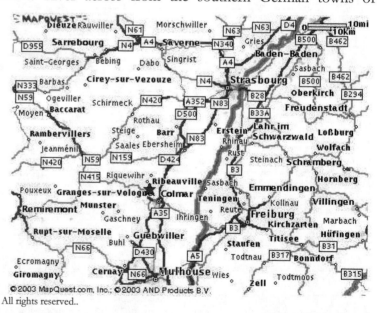

Figure 5. Map of the regions of Alsace and Wurttemberg, to the west and to the east of the Rhine River, respectively[6]. The location of Sigolsheim is marked with a star. The Rhine River appears down the center of the map.

Is there any evidence that the Ulmers were members of such a refugee party? How can their relationships to other members in the party be confirmed?

The group of refugees who escaped the aftermath of the Thirty Years War must have included several leaders who were responsible for the group's welfare. Upon arrival in France, these men might have retained their position to become the leaders of the newly established community. The families of these leaders would have forge bonds during the trip which lasted through subsequent generations, forming a characteristically tight-knit refugee group. Even if Sigolsheim was already populated when they arrived, the refugee families would typically marry among themselves for the first couple of generations.

A way of confirming the existence of the refugee group would be to examine the families with the oldest surnames in the community. Which families intermarried with the Ulmers? What was the structure of these families? Can family members be sorted into their correct generations? Did the earliest community leaders belong to these families?

To identify the oldest families in Sigolsheim, the database of Sigolsheim *deaths* can be organized according to the years of *birth* estimated from the ages at death, so that the person born furthest back in time appears at the top of the list. The burial records include all community members, even those who were adults at the start of the records and whose baptisms and marriages did not appear. Of course, because there is a lot of information that is missing, it is not possible to calculate a birth year for everyone, but sometimes it can be estimated from the year of birth of a spouse, the year of marriage, or the year of birth of the first and last child. The results are shown in Table 5.

The family names at the top of this chronological birth list include Umbhoffer, Horn, Krauss, Dietrich, and Maurer, which are the surnames of the spouses of the Ulmer children. See Table 6.

At the start of the church and civil records in 1664, there was a single Ulmer family in Sigolsheim. Of the eight Ulmers in this family, it is clear by their estimated dates of birth which individuals were parents, and which were their children. If the Ulmers had traveled to Alsace as part of a larger group, other families in their entourage should show a similar structure. There would be one, two or at most three individuals representing the 'older' generation born between the end of the 1500s and the beginning of the 1600s, their children born between twenty and thirty years later towards the middle years of the century, and then grandchildren born twenty to thirty years after that, later in the 1600s.

The exact years are not important. Each family would have its own chronology. This 'clumping' of birth years into generational clusters would occur only if a family were a new arrival in town, and the group did not include more than one or two families with the same surname. At

Table 5. The years of birth calculated from the ages and years of death of Sigolsheimers born through 1611.

Calc'd Yr of Birth	Yr of Death	Date of Death	Name	Approx Age at Death	Notes
1596	1682	7 Jul	Casparus Better?	86	
1599	1679	8 Jul	Adam Salzmann	80	
1601	1675	21 May	Egidin Maurer	74	Sigolsheimensis
1602	1679	25 Apr	Michael Ulmer	77	buried in Coenssheimian
1602	1687	7 Apr	Margaritha Ruffin	85	relicta vidua Georgi Umbhoffer
1603	1686	29 Jun	Anna Locherin	83	
1605	1685	4 Jan	Dominicus Salus	80	fuit miles
1606	1676	29 Jun	Antonius Liebermann	70	civis huig pagi
1607	1687	17 Aug	Samson Offinger	80	fuit parnes parochi huius loci
1608	1680	19 Jun	Anna Wessin	72	relicta vidua Michael Ulmer
1611	1676	10 May	Catharina Koer	65	uxor honesti viri Georgi Keller, textor hagi payi
1611	1695	17 Jan	Anna Grisin?	84	

Table 6. Children of Michael Ulmer, their spouses, and their spouses parents.

Child of Michael Ulmer	Spouse	Spouse's Father	Spouse's Mother
Magdaline Ulmer	George Umbhoffer	George Umhoffer	Margaritha Ruffin
Antonius Ulmer	Anna Maria Hornin	Unknown	Unknown
Anna Ulmer*	N/A	N/A	N/A
Jacob Ulmer	Anna Catharina Kraussin	Andreas Krauss	Unknown
Anna Margaritha Ulmer	Jacob Dietrich	Heinrich Dietrich	Unknown
Michael Ulmer, Jr.	Apolonia Maurerin	Edigin Maurer	Unknown

*Anna Ulmer appears in the records only as a baptismal sponsor. She is probably not Anna Wissin Ulmer, wife of Michael Ulmer, because married women usually appeared under their maiden names in the records.

Table 7. Three generations of the Umbhoffer family.

Name	Yr of Birth	Yr of Death	Notes
George Umbhoffer	1602	1673	Magistrate
Margaretha Ruffin	Abt. 1602	1687	Widow of George Umbhoffer Year of birth estimated from husband's
George	Abt. 1638	1688	Husband of Magdalena Ulmerin, m. 16 Feb 1666
Margaritha	1645	1700	Wife of Joannes Rundi, m. 21 Aug 1670
Jacob	1646	1717	Husband of Margaretha Huberin, m. abt. 1670
Infant of George Umb.	1665	1666	George Umbhoffer & Magdalena Ulmerin
Jacob	Abt.1666	1687	Prob George Umbhoffer & Magdalena Ulmerin
George	1666	1667	George Umbhoffer & Magdalena Ulmerin
Maria	1670	---	George Umbhoffer & Magdalena Ulmerin
Maria Francisca	1671	1672	Jacobus Umbhoffer & Margaretha Huberin
Joannes Jacobus	1672	1673	Jacobus Umbhoffer & Magdalena Huberin
Maria Magaritha	1672	1675	George Umbhoffer & Magdalena Ulmerin
Maria Francisca	1673	1679	Jacobus Umbhoffer & Magdalena Ulmerin
Josephus Rundi	1673	---	Joannes Rundi and Margaretha Umbhofferin
Joannes	1674	1674	George Umbhoffer & Magdalena Ulmerin
Jacob	1676	1701	Jacobus Umbhoffer & Magdalena Huberin
Marthana	1677	1680	George Umbhoffer & Magdalena Ulmerin
Joannes Michael	1678	---	Jacobus Umbhoffer & Magdalena Huberin
George	1679	1730	George Umbhoffer & Magdalena Ulmerin
Anna	1680	1687	Jacobus Umbhoffer & Magdalena Huberin
Anna	1681	---	George Umbhoffer & Magdalena Ulmerin
Maria Francesca	1682	1736	Jacobus Umbhoffer & Margaretha Huberin
Phillipus	1684	---	Jacobus Umbhoffer & Margaretha Huberin
Joannes Georgius Rondi	1684	1703	Joannes Rundi and Margaretha Umbhofferin
Anna Maria	1686	1743	Jacobus Umbhoffer & Margaretha Huberin

Note: My database of burial records is incomplete after 1725.

that time, parents had children when they were in their twenties, thirties and early forties. Their children were usually born at reasonably regular intervals, within a span of about twenty years. However, the marriages of these children did not normally occur at regular intervals, so that the births of grandchildren happened more or less continually, sometimes several in one year. Over the next three or four generations, the chronological distinction between generations would be completely lost, with the disappearance of any 'clumps' in age.

Of course, there were very large families that were exceptions to this pattern, such as a couple who had so many children that their youngest child was born after their oldest child was already married and having his own children, or parents with a daughter or son who married and had children at an exceptionally young age. In these large families, the gaps between the generations disappear earlier, during the parents' and their children's generations. Typically, however, it can be easy to determine which individuals belonged to which generation by noting during which cluster of birth years they were born. The birth years of the Umbhoffer, Horn, Krauss, Dietrich, and Maurer families who married into the Ulmers show such a clumping pattern. The example of the Umbhoffer family is shown in Table 7.

George Umbhoffer (b. 1602) and his wife Margaretha Ruffin represent the first, or oldest generation, George (b. 1638), Margaretha, and Jacob Umbhoffer were their children, and George Umbhoffer (b. 1685) was the first of their twenty grandchildren. Other families in the community show a similar three-generation pattern.

More evidence that the early Sigolsheimers were members of a refugee group is given by the list of baptismal sponsors. The dates that specific family members served as sponsors show the same clustering pattern as that displayed by their birth years. This is to be expected, since a baptismal sponsor is typically a person of child-bearing age. See Table 8.

Table 8. The generations of the Umbhoffer family derived from the list of baptismal sponsors.

Name	Years Chosen as Baptismal Sponsor
George Umbhoffer	1665, 1667, 1670
Margaritha Umbhoffer	1669, 1670
Joannes Umbhoffer*	1671
Anna Maria Umbhoffer	1685, 1689, 1690, 1692, 1695, 1698, 1701, 1706, 1709
Jacob Umbhoffer	1686
Jacob Georgius Umbhoffer	1690, 1695, 1697, 1701, 1705, 1706, 1707, 1711, 1712, 1713, 1714, 1717, 1718, 1720, 1722
Francisca Umbhoffer	1698, 1701
Jacob Umbhoffer	1700

*This was probably Joannes Jacobus Umbhoffer.

WHAT'S WRONG WITH THIS PICTURE?

Through my spreadsheets, the history and growth of the families in the Sigolsheim community could be reconstructed beginning in 1664. Parents could be linked to children, grandchildren and so on down the line, creating family trees spanning several centuries. The Ulmers were prolific compared to other families in the community, so that by the end of the 1600s, there were countless Ulmers living in Sigolsheim and the surrounding communities.

Some families were not so fortunate and nearly became extinct. A prominent case of a family that nearly disappeared was that of Bernard Naegler, his wife and nine children. The family had already lost one child in 1665, and a second one in July 1674. Then the parents and six of their seven remaining children were wiped out by a mysterious epidemic between late December 1674 and mid

Table 9. Members of the Benedict Naegler family in order of death. Victims of the epidemic are in bold and shaded.

Name	Date of Death	Age	Date of Birth	Notes
Infans Benedict	Jan. 28, 1665	N/A	N/A	Born before start of records
Margaretha	Jul. 29, 1674	1 yr	Jun. 14, 1673	--
Son of Benedict	**Dec. 29, 1674**	**11 yrs**	**1663**	**Born before start of records**
Son of Benedict	**Dec. 30, 1674**	**10 yrs**	**1664**	**Born before start of records**
Anna Magdalena	**Dec. 30, 1674**	**3 yrs**	**Jun. 12, 1671**	**--**
Joannes Michael	**Jan. 5, 1675**	**9 yrs**	**1665**	**Did not have birthday yet in 1665. Buried in Kiensheim cemetery.**
Joannes Jacob	**Jan. 24, 1675**	**6 yrs**	**Jun. 16, 1669**	**Buried in Kiensheim cemetery.**
Benedict	**Jan. 27, 1675**	**N/A**	**N/A**	**Father**
Magdalena Burhardt	**Feb. 6, 1675**	**N/A**	**N/A**	**Mother**
Joseph	**Mar. 14, 1675**	**8 yrs**	**Aug. 31, 1666**	**--**
Christopher	Dec. 28, 1727	70 yrs	1657	Born before start of records

March 1675. Within the first few days of this period, the family lost four children, ages 3, 9, 10, and 11. The family seemed to have tried to save itself from doom, since two of the sons were apparently relocated to the neighboring community of Kientzheim, about 1 mile away. But these two children were possibly affected before they moved, since they died too. Only the oldest son, 17-year-old Christopher survived to carry on the name. The dates of death of the Naegler family members are listed in chronological order in Table 9, along with their dates of birth and ages at death.

The Naegler family was not the only family that was nearly destroyed by the epidemic. The list of the burials in the town reveals several other families that suffered the same fate. Of the seven members of the William This family, only two survived, 9 year old Anna and 5 year old Joannes. Joannes Locherer lost his wife Maria Francesca Mangoldin, his three children, ages two through seven, his sister-in-law Elizabetha and one of his two nieces. The Weber, Lieberman, Tempe, and Flugauf families were affected to a lesser extent.

The characteristics of this epidemic provides an insight into the life of the Sigolsheim community. Figure 6 is a plot of the baptisms and burials for Sigolsheim from the beginning of the records in 1664 through the turn of the century in 1700. Apparently, the community was growing steadily until the plague struck. The death and birth rate were characteristic of a growing community, both growing steadily until late 1674, when the death rate soared and the birth rate plummeted. The death rate was very low for the next couple of years, probably because the people who would normally contract the disease were already gone. By 1678, the number of deaths more or less recovered, and resumed its pattern of highs and low that would last past the turn of the century.

The birth rate shows a different pattern. The dramatically low number of births that occurred in 1674 continued for the next ten years until 1684, when the birth rate suddenly jumped back to normal levels. This extended period of low birth rate cannot be explained by the loss of women of childbearing age. While the death rate partially recovered in 1679, the number of births remained disproportionately low, indicating that the cause of initial affliction was also responsible for the suppression of the birth rate over the next decade.

An important clue to the cause of the epidemic is the sudden recovery of the birth rate in 1684, when the number of births jumped to the level it would have increased to, had there been no interruption. It is as if whatever happened to cause the low birthrate suddenly 'unhappened', restoring the community to normal. This abrupt recovery is another indication that the reduction in the number of childbearers was not the problem. If this were the case, the number of births would have gradually recovered as children surviving the epidemic matured. The evidence indicates that the problem was that the fertility of the women of childbearing age was reduced and not the population.

There are still other clues. Some families were almost wiped out, while others remained unharmed. The number of babies who died in infancy remained constant, in spite of the disproportionate number of children and elderly who died. Another clue is that the epidemic happened during the colder months, December 1674 through April 1675. These clues rule out contaminated water that presumably would have been shared year round by the whole community.

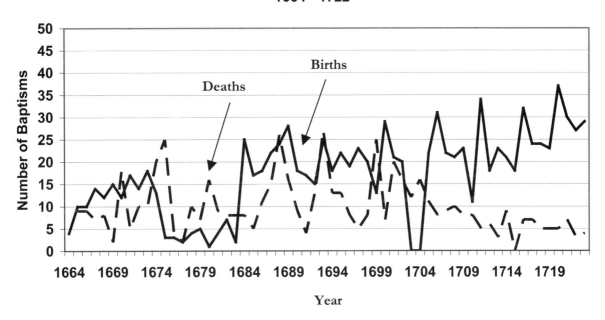

Figure 6. Sigolsheim baptisms and burials, 1664 – 1700.

They also eliminate a contagious disease such as smallpox or measles, that would have quickly spread through the whole population, exhausting itself within at most a year.

THE MYSTERY IS SOLVED

The answer may be *ergot of rye*, a plant disease that is caused by the fungus *Claviceps purpurea*. The so-called ergot replaces the grain of rye with a dark, purplish sclerotium, which is an inert stage of the fungus occurring in winter. It contains a number of poisonous alkaloids. (See Figures 7 and 8.) Although ergot is far different in appearance from the grain, its occurrence was so common that it was thought to be part of the rye plant until the 1850's, when the true nature of ergot was understood. It is the ergot stage of the fungus that contains a storehouse of compounds that have been useful as pharmaceutical drugs and of mycotoxins that can be fatal when consumed. Ergot is also the source from which LSD was first isolated. It is believed that symptoms of ergotism have been recorded since the middle ages and possibly even as far back as ancient Greece[7].

The web site http://www.genealogienetz.de/reg/ELS-LOT/als-hist.html[8] provides more information:

"What is now France was the center of many .... severe ergot epidemics because rye was the staple crop of the poor, and the cool, wet climate was conducive for the development of ergot. Ergot infection of rye was more likely during these wet periods because the rye flower remained opened longer, which provided more opportunity for the fungus to infect the flower. The regular rye grain and the hard, purplish black, grain-like ergot produced by the fungus were harvested and ground together during milling. The flour produced was then contaminated with the toxic alkaloids of the fungus. In 944 AD, in southern France, 40,000 people died of ergotism. Peasants sometimes lived on bread alone, consuming several pounds a day." [8]

Figure 7. A stalk of rye grain infected with ergot[8]

Figure 8. The poisonous dormant stage of ergot[8].

Could the Sigolsheimers have been victims of an ergot epidemic?

Egotism as the cause of the epidemic that struck Sigolsheim in the mid to late 1670s would explain the containment of the illness to specific families who probably shared stored food and ate meals together. It would also explain why the epidemic occurred in winter, when families ate contaminated grain stockpiled from the harvest in the fall, and when the ergot was in its poisonous dormant stage. The affect of the epidemic on different age groups could also be explained by the ingestion of ergot. Infants young enough to eat porridge could avoid infection since porridge is made with water boiled long enough to destroy alkaloids. Teens and children old enough to eat bread would be especially vulnerable because they consume more food per unit of body weight than adults. When that food is poisoned, they take in more poison per unit of body weight than adults[9]. The elderly would also be more open to ergotism, as they are presumably the most feeble members of a community.

Research on historical climatic conditions supports the idea that the weather was favorable for an ergotism epidemic in Sigolsheim in the late 1600s. While few official weather records exist from medieval times, climatic conditions over more than the last thousand years have been reconstructed from proxy data, that is, data obtained from objects that are sensitive to climatic phenomena. Some examples are tree ring widths, ice cores, pollen deposits, glacier lengths, deep sea sediments, lengths of time that waterways were frozen, and ratios of certain radioisotopes. Analyses of such data can be used to provide estimates of past climate conditions, such as temperature, precipitation, or wind speed[10,11,12]. Reconstruction of weather patterns indicate that between the 16th and 19th centuries, global temperatures were about 1.0°C cooler than present, gripping the Earth in a climatic regime that has universally been acknowledged as the *Little Ice Age*[13].

Mary Kilbourne Matossian in her book *Poisons of the Past*[9], discusses ergotism in England during the 17th century. The weather conditions she describes could also apply to France during the same period of time. She writes:

"During the period 1647 - 1699, a time of low fertility [in England], the mean winter temperature was 1.5°C, as compared with 2.1°C for the period 1700 - 1799. This sets off the second half of the seventeenth century as a time for colder winters. Summers tended to be warm enough, however, for ergot alkaloid production. Weather annals during 1645 - 1658 reported five hot summers…out of fourteen. During the period 1659 -1680 fourteen out of twenty-one summers had the minimum July temperature, 16°C, necessary for alkaloid production. But during 1681 - 1699, a time of increasing fertility, only three out of nineteen summers were warm enough for alkaloid production. If one selects from the period 1645 - 1699 those years in which cold winters were followed by summers warm enough for alkaloid production, one finds a total of nine, and all nine fell within the period of English fertility depression: 1641 - 1685."

There are three types of ergotism: gangrenous, convulsive, and hallucinogenic. In *gangrenous ergotism*, people experience nausea and pains in the limbs. Quite often bodily extremities turn black, dry and become mummified, making it possible for infected limbs to spontaneously break off at the joints[14]. The initial burning sensation caused by gangrenous ergotism led to the Latin name *ignis sacer*, which means holy fire. This human malady was so horrible that in 1093 a religious order was founded in southern France to help those afflicted. St. Anthony was the patron saint, so the malady, now called ergotism, was then named St. Anthony's fire[15]. In *convulsive ergotism*, people experience epileptic seizures, ravenous hunger, violent retching, tongue biting or unusual breathing patterns. Because of this, various parts of the body become grossly deformed. This results in permanent nerve damage and long recovery periods[14].

In *hallucinogenic ergotism*, people often experience symptoms of one of the other forms of ergotism along with vivid hallucinations. The other symptoms are very much like those of modern psychedelic drugs, including nervousness, physical and mental excitement, insomnia and disorientation. People with this form of ergotism have been observed to perform strange dances with wild, jerky movements accompanied by hopping, leaping and screaming. They often dance compulsively until exhaustion causes them to collapse unconscious[14]. It is believed that many of the reports of witchcraft, including those during the Salem witch trials, were caused by ergotism[16,17,18].

There are reports as far back as 1582 of European and Chinese midwives using ergot to reduce hemorrhage following childbirth. Ergot can also cause spontaneous abortions, explaining the suppressed birth rate in Sigolsheim during the mid 1670s to mid 1680s[19]. The sudden recovery in birth rate in 1684 was probably due to the elimination of ergot-tainted grain, as awareness of the cause of the disease finally reached Sigolsheim, over a decade after the source was discovered in 1670 by Dr. Thuilliers[20].

To learn more about this fascinating disease and the key role it played in other historical events such as the spread of the Bubonic Plague[21] and the defeat of Peter the Great in the Dardenelles[17], see References 7, 8, 19, and 20. In *Poisons of the Past* (Ref. 9), Mary Kilbourne Matossian gives an interesting analysis of the long term effect that ergotism has had on European civilization.

SO WHAT ABOUT THE ULMERS?

We will never know why the Ulmers were spared from the ergot epidemic. Maybe it was something as incidental as having a barn facing the sun kept their grain from infection. Perhaps Michael Ulmer was the leader of the convoy the day the group discovered the site where they would build Sigolsheim and he got first choice of location for his house. Maybe his barn was higher up in the village. Since hot air rises, maybe those few degrees of warmth afforded by his higher elevation made the difference between life and death for his family.

Or perhaps it was the opposite. Maybe he was last in the convoy that day because he broke his ankle or stopped to help deliver a baby, so that he was forced to take the least desirable property on the edge of town on a hill away from the village stream. His misfortune became his family's salvation. Who knows? The meager records left by the immigrants over three hundred years ago leave few clues to why some families faced tragedy while other were spared.

What is certain is that the Ulmers watched as their neighbors hallucinated to their deaths, while their neighbors' limbs fell off, and while nearly every pregnancy in the village resulted in either a miscarriage or a stillbirth for over ten years. Even if someone suspected infected grain as the cause, the village had few options for food - it was either hallucinate or starve to death. Maybe the Sigolsheimers, ignorant of the poison that was systematically killing clusters of villagers, believed it was a supernatural power or witchcraft causing the tragedy.

Yet the Ulmers survived, and their children survived, and their children's children survived. The number of Ulmer descendents three and a half centuries later is in the thousands. Yet no one alive today can tell their story. All we know about their lives is what can be deduced from the slim volume of church records that has persisted through weather, pestilence, war, politics, and most importantly, the passage of time.

---

[1] http://www.pipeline.com/~cwa/Bohemian_Phase.htm
[2] http://www.encyclopedia.com/html/section/ThirtyYe_TheAftermath.asp
[3] http://www.genealogienetz.de/reg/ELS-LOT/als-hist.html
[4] For example http://www.historylearningsite.co.uk/peace_of_westphalia.htm, mars.acnet.wnec.edu/~grempel/courses/ wc2/lectures/30yearswar.html, and www.worldwideschool.org/library/books/hst/european/TheHistoryoftheThirtyYearsWar/toc.html, and http://www.fortunecity.com/victorian/riley/787/30/
[5] http://www.genealogienetz.de/reg/ELS-LOT/als-hist.html
[6] http://www.mapquest.com
[7] http://www.botany.hawaii.edu/faculty/wong/BOT135/LECT12.HTM
[8] http://www.genealogienetz.de/reg/ELS-LOT/als-hist.html
[9] Mary Kilbourne Matossian, *Poisons of the Past, Molds, Epidemics, and History*, p. 12.

[10] H. M. van den Dool et al, "Average winter temperatures at de Bilt (the Netherlands), 1634-1977," *Climatic Change* I, (1978), p. 319-330, as quoted by Mary Kilbourne Matossian in *Poisons of the Past*, p. 66.

[11] H. H. Lamb, *Climate: present, past and future*, (London, 1977), John H. Brazell, *London Weather*, (London, 1968); D. Justin Schove, "Summer temperature and tree rings in Scandinavia, a.d. 1461 – 1950", *Geografiska Analler* 36, nos. 1-2 (1954), pp. 40 – 80, as quoted by Mary Kilbourne Matossian in *Poisons of the Past*, p. 66.

[12] http://www.co2science.org/dictionary/define_p.htm#Proxy

[13] http://www.co2science.org/subject/other/clim_hist_1thousand.htm and the references contained therein.

[14] http://web.utk.edu/~kstclair/221/ergotism.html

[15] http://botit.botany.wisc.edu/toms_fungi/oct99.html

[16] http://web.utk.edu/~kstclair/221/ergotism.html

[17] http://botit.botany.wisc.edu/toms_fungi/oct99.html

[18] Matossian, Chapter 9, "Ergotism and the Salem Witchcraft Affair", p. 113.

[19] http://www.uic.edu/classes/osci/osci590/6_3Plague.htm

[20] http://www.plant.uga.edu/labrat/ergot.htm

[21] http://www.uic.edu/classes/osci/osci590/6_3Plague.htm

THE DNA DETECTIVE

INTRODUCTION

In the course of the last few centuries the means of criminal investigation have advanced from the highly subjective to the extremely technical. Investigative tools have evolved from eyewitness accounts and circumstantial evidence to modern forensic techniques that depend on fingerprints and DNA analysis. Genealogical research methods have experienced a parallel development. While gathering personal memories will always be an important part of genealogical research, DNA analysis has recently become a useful tool for genealogists to obtain specific information on family relationships.

In this chapter, you will find much information for researchers of all levels of interest. For those of you who don't sweat the details, there is an introduction to the basics of DNA-based genealogy. For those with intermediate or advanced interests, there is more detailed information later in this chapter.

The Basics:
- A short DNA background
- Mutations and why they are important in genetic genealogy
- How DNA is used in genealogy, including the types of markers studied
- Single-name DNA studies, what they are and how to join one

Intermediate Level:
- How to start a single-name DNA study
- Connecting your family with important historical events through a DNA study

- Non-paternity events
- A description of the major genetic genealogy testing companies
- Online databases

In-Depth:
- DNA markers, haplogroups, and clades
- Cladograms, what they are, how they are used, and how to create your own
- Pairwise mismatches

For Everybody:
- Remaining mysteries

The discussion on Most Recent Common Ancestor (MRCA) analysis spans all levels. For those interested only in knowing an estimate for their MRCA, there are lookup tables available. For those interested in performing their own calculations, instructions for building spreadsheets are provided that can be used for exploring various possibilities not covered by the lookup tables. Electronic versions of these spreadsheets that are ready to use are included on the Forensic Genealogy CD and on the web site www.forensicgenealogy.info. For the more mathematically inclined, there is a section on the mathematical derivation of the formulas used for MRCA calculations.

In many cases, I give examples from my own Fitzpatrick DNA study, which I have marked with a star. Table 1 gives the definitions of many important DNA terms that will be used in this chapter.

ABOUT DNA

DNA, or deoxyribonucleic acid was first isolated in 1869 by Johann Friedrich Miescher in the nucleus of human white blood cells. But it was not until 1953 that the molecular structure of DNA was characterized by James Watson, Francis Crick, and Rosalind Franklin[1]. DNA is regarded as the blueprint of life, the arrangement of chemicals that defines each human being as unique, with the exception of identical twins who share an identical genetic makeup.

In recent years, DNA analysis has become a key factor in criminal, political, historical, and archeological investigations. The DNA profiles of humans, animals[2], and plants[3] are used as evidence to both convict and exonerate criminals in court. The Innocence Project started in 1992 by Barry C. Scheck and Peter J. Neufeld works to exonerate death row inmates through post-conviction DNA testing[4]. DNA was critical in the identification of the charred remains of the Tsar Nicholas Romanov and his family who were executed in 1917 during the Russian Revolution[5] and to prove that the son of King Louis XIV and Marie Antoinette died as a child in a Paris prison in

1795[6]. DNA is also being used by the U.S. Department of Wildlife and Fisheries to create genetic databases of endangered animals[7], and to track illegal trade in wildlife or animal parts[8]. DNA was even used by the 2000 Summer Olympic Games Committee to mark genuine artwork and one-of-a-kind sports souvenirs[9].

Figure 1. DNA double helix

DNA is a ladder-shaped double helix molecule (Figure 1). Information is stored in the rungs between spirals, specifically in chemical bases (adenine, thymine, guanine and cytosine, commonly labeled A, T, G and C) called nucleotides that pair up to form the rungs of the ladder. A gene is a particular sequence of bases that provides a blueprint for the production of a specific protein. Only about 3% of human DNA is organized into genes. The rest is so-called 'junk–DNA', that until recently was regarded as uninteresting because it does not express itself as the proteins that are related to physical characteristics such as brown hair or a tendency towards diabetes.

Recent studies have challenged these early notions about junk-DNA. It has been found that large segments of junk-DNA are 'ultraconserved', that is, identical junk-DNA appears in otherwise genetically diverse species such as humans, rats, mice, dogs, chicken, and fish[10]. Because junk-DNA has apparently resisted change since these species shared a common ancestor 400 million years ago, scientists now believe that junk-DNA plays a vital role in the survival of a species. Research has indicated that nearly 1/3 of junk-DNA is involved in the development of a fertilized egg into an embryo, in the role of controlling gene expression. In other words, junk-DNA seems to act to program genes in a fertilized egg to produce proteins required for normal embryonic development[11].

Having an analysis done based on junk-DNA does not compromise your privacy. Since junk-DNA is not directly associated with genetic disorders, it is not interesting to insurance companies. You can participate in a DNA study without concerns over implications to healthcare coverage.

Human DNA is organized in each cell into 23 pairs of chromosomes (Figure 2). Upon conception, each individual receives one member of each pair from his mother's egg and the other member from his father's sperm. Each pair is a matched set, except for the pair that determines the sex of the child. In this pair the mother donates one of her X chromosomes to all of her children, but the father donates either a second X to create a daughter or a Y to create a son. As an aside, this is why the sex of a child can be chosen during in vitro fertilization; sperms carrying X chromosomes are slightly heavier than those carrying Ys, allowing them to be separated.

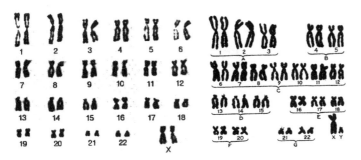

Figure 2. The 23 pairs of human chromosomes. All pairs are a matched set except for the last pair that determines the sex of the child. Females have a matched XX pair (bottom left) but males carry an XY pair (bottom right).

Table 1. Important DNA terminology.

Term	Definition
Locus (plural loci)	Position on DNA
Short Tandem Repeat (STR)	Stretches of DNA where a short sequence of the chemical bases A, G, C, T, repeats itself
Allele Value	The number of times an STR repeats
DYS number	An identification number assigned to a locus by HUGO
HUGO	Human Gene Nomenclature Committee
Haplotype	An individual's set of STR values
SNP (or UEP) (Often referred to as 'snips')	Single Nucleotide Polymorphism (Unique Event Polymorphism), a very slowly mutating Y-chromosome locus that is used to define specific segments of the population, not necessarily cultural groups.
Haplogroup	A population defined by specific SNP mutations. Haplogroups are not cultural groups, although a haplogroup can be strongly represented by a cultural population such as the Vikings, American Indians, etc.
Mitochondrial DNA (mtDNA)	DNA found outside the cell nucleus in small organelles called mitochondria. Except in extremely rare circumstances mtDNA is inherited only from the mother.
Mutation	A change in one or more locations on DNA when DNA is replicated during cell division.
Most Recent Common Ancestor (MRCA)	The most recent ancestor shared by two people.
Transmission Event	The transmission of a DNA marker from a parent to a child upon conception.
Nonrecombinant	Sections of DNA that remain intact as they are transmitted to offspring, that are not recombined with other DNA to form new genetic material of a child. mtDNA and most of the DNA on the Y-chromosome are nonrecombinant.

The members of matched pairs of chromosomes can carry different genes that serve the same purpose. For example, an individual can inherit a gene for brown eyes from one parent and a gene for blue eyes from the other parent. In this case, the dominant gene on one chromosome will override the corresponding version (known as the recessive gene) on the other. (The brown-eye gene is dominant.)

The only way that a recessive gene can manifest itself is if it appears on both members of a pair of chromosomes so that there is no dominant gene to override it. This can happen for all 23 pairs of chromosomes in the female, but in a male, an extra 'leg' of the 23rd chromosome is missing. If there is a gene that is recessive on the mother-donated X chromosome of this pair that is absent on the father-donated Y chromosome because of this missing leg, that recessive gene cannot be overridden. The associated physical characteristic, which could be a disease such as hemophilia, is transmitted from a mother to her son. Women suffer from diseases caused by these same recessive genes, but only rarely, since the probability of an uncommon recessive gene appearing on both of her X chromosomes is very low. Half of the sons of a woman 'carrier' will suffer from the disease with a negligible chance that any of her daughters will manifest symptoms, although half of them will be carriers.

Different types of DNA analyses are used in forensic science, medicine, and genealogy. Forensic science is concerned with uniquely identifying an individual by DNA associated with a crime, or to prove an immediate biological relationship such as paternity. Polymerase Chain Reaction/Restriction Fragment Length Polymorphism (PCR/RFLP) techniques used by criminal investigators chemically amplify and cut all DNA (both genetic material and junk DNA) into smaller pieces whose lengths are determined by the locations of certain chemicals along the strands[12]. This type of DNA analysis has been popularized by such TV programs as *CSI*, *Forensic Files*, and *Medical Detectives*. Everyone who is familiar with these programs has seen RFLP results in the form of a series of dark bands on a strip of X-ray paper (called an autorad), each band representing a different size segment of DNA.

Identification of the source of unknown DNA can be made in two ways. The DNA taken from a known person can be matched with the profile of the unknown DNA if that person is available for testing. If he is missing, or refuses to give a sample, his DNA profile can be deduced from that of his parents, or in the case of paternity testing, from the DNA profiles of a woman and their alleged child. To a lesser degree of certainty, DNA matches can also be made by avuncular testing that involves more distant relatives such as aunts, uncles, grandparents, and first cousins.

In RFLP testing, the actual genetic content of the DNA is unimportant. Results depend only on the sizes of the fragments produced.

Criminal investigation also analyzes specific DNA markers called Short Tandem Repeats (STRs), places on DNA that repeat the same sequence of chemical bases a characteristic number of times. These markers are also important for genealogy (as discussed below), but forensic science uses a set of STRs that appear on many chromosomes, with an emphasis on STRs that mutate or change rapidly, so that a particular STR combination will to a high degree of probability narrow down the identity of the source of the DNA to a specific individual[13]. In some criminal cases, such as rape, analysis of DNA markers appearing only on the male chromosome can be useful in situations when there is difficulty separating male and female DNA, but this has the disadvantage that the analysis can only narrow down the investigation to a group of men with a common male ancestor, and not to a specific individual[14].

Forensic DNA analysis examines all chromosomal DNA (both genetic and junk DNA) and uses it to determine the identity of an individual or the identity of members of his immediate family[15].

Medical research is concerned with locating specific genes associated with a given physical characteristic that can be a disease such as diabetes or Huntington's disease. By identifying the genes responsible for these diseases, it is hoped that the affliction can be identified and treated even before symptoms appear. It is also the basis for gene therapy, where healthy sections of DNA are inserted in place of defective segments carrying genetic disorders. DNA analysis used for medical purposes involves a search for limited regions of genetic material associated with an abnormality.

Genealogical DNA analysis is similar to forensic analysis in that it uses DNA to establish kinship between individuals. It is also similar to medical analysis in that it uses only restricted regions of DNA and is used to identify individuals as belonging to certain hereditary groups. But genealogical analysis has major differences from both the other types. Unlike medical analysis, genealogical analysis uses only pre-determined segments of junk DNA, with no interest in how or whether this DNA has any physical influence. Unlike forensic analysis, genealogical analysis uses DNA only from the Y-chromosome or from a second type of DNA called mitochondrial DNA found outside the cell nucleus. Because of the moderate to slow mutation rates of these types of DNA, the biological relationships derived are not necessarily immediate, and could go back hundreds, or even thousands of years.

An easy way to understand the differences among forensic, medical, and genealogical analyses is to consider the significance of DNA left at the scene of a crime. A medical analysis of the sample might narrow the unknown criminal down to a population of people with black hair or the tendency towards diabetes. A genealogical analysis might identify whether a suspect had a common ancestor with the person who left the DNA sample. But only forensic analysis can confirm to a reasonable degree of certainty the identity of the criminal[16].

The main aspects of these three types of DNA analysis are summarized in Table 2.

TYPES OF DNA MARKERS AND MUTATIONS

There are two kinds of DNA, chromosomal DNA and mitochondrial DNA (mtDNA). Both carry markers that are useful for genealogical studies.

Table 2. Applications of DNA analysis.

	Type of DNA Used	Purpose	Analysis Determines
Forensic Science	All DNA	To determine identity or immediate biological relationships	Lengths of DNA fragments
Medicine	DNA found in genes	To identify genes causing disease	Presence or absence of specific genes in people with particular physical characteristics
Genealogy	Junk DNA	To determine genealogical relationships	Matching DNA profiles (haplotypes) among study participants

Chromosomal DNA is present only in the cell nucleus. It is the type of DNA referred to in the preceding sections that is inherited by a person from both his father and his mother. The Y chromosome is inherited along the exclusively male line of the family in the same way a family name is usually passed down from father to son in western cultures. For this reason, studying markers found only on the Y chromosome is a convenient way of studying the history of the paternal line of a family.

The Y chromosome markers used for genealogy are:
- Short Tandem Repeats (STRs) that mutate or change at a rate compatible with the time period of surname usage, and
- Single Nucleotide Polymorphisms (SNPs, often called 'snips') that mutate much more slowly and are used for long-term population studies along the exclusively male line.

Mitochondrial DNA (mtDNA) is found only outside the cell nucleus in small organelles in the cell called mitochondria, and is inherited by an individual almost always through his mother[17]. SNPs are also found on mtDNA. Because of their slow mutation rate, they are useful for long-term population studies along the exclusively female line. This is the type of DNA discussed in the best selling book *The Seven Daughters of Eve* in which Bryan Sykes uses mtDNA to show that nearly all modern Europeans are descendants of one of seven 'clan mothers' who lived sometime in the last 50,000 years[18]

When a cell divides, its DNA replicates so that the two resulting daughter cells are normally identical. To do this, the DNA double helix 'unzips' itself down the center, and each of the resulting single strands attracts the chemicals needed to reform its missing half. (See Figure 3[19].) In most cases, the reconstructed DNA is identical to the original, but occasionally a mistake or mutation occurs, causing the copied DNA to be different from the original. Mutations are natural phenomena that occur in all types of DNA. Mutations occur with a statistical frequency, that is, only the probability of a mutation can be predicted. Most mutations have no effect, but occasionally a mutation can cause physical benefits or disabilities.

WHY SURNAME STUDIES USE CERTAIN MARKERS

Figure 3. DNA replication

For DNA surname studies, between twelve and forty-three Y-chromosome STR loci are tested, with the probability of a mutation estimated at 0.002 to 0.009 (two to nine tenths of one percent or 2/10% to 9/10%) per locus per generation. Out of 1000 male offspring, on the average between two and four will experience a mutation on a specific Y locus. If the 1000 sons are tested on forty-two markers, on the average there will be about forty-two times this number, or eighty-four to one hundred sixty-eight offspring who have DNA profiles (also called a *haplotypes*) different from those of their fathers. (In comparison, the Hypervariable Region 1 (**HVR1**) of mtDNA mutates at the rate of 7.96×10^{-6} or 0.00000769 per locus per generation.)

The average mutation rate of 0.002 to 0.009 is used for all STR loci commonly tested in single name studies. It is based on several scientific studies[20], one of the largest by *Dupuy et al*[21] involving 1767 father-son pairs. There are some STRs that mutate more quickly, and some that mutate hardly at all. The STR loci analyzed for genealogical purposes have been chosen because they have mutation rates that make sense within the time period interesting to genealogists. A marker that changes very frequently would show so much variation even among closely related people that it would be useless. If a marker changed very slowly, there would a large number of people with the same allele (numerical value of a marker) who were not related within the time period of written history. In either case, the results of the study would be meaningless to single-name studies that are usually concerned with relationships over the last few hundred years. Much research is going on to obtain better estimates for the mutation rates of the individual markers used for Y-chromosome studies to increase the accuracy of Most Recent Common Ancestor (MRCA) predictions.

GENEALOGICAL DNA ANALYSIS

Because of their moderate mutation rates, Short Tandem Repeat (STR) markers that exist on the Y-chromosome are useful for establishing if two people might have a common ancestor over the last few hundred years through their exclusively male lines. Single Nucleotide Polymorphisms (SNPs) found on both the male Y-chromosome and the male and female mtDNA mutate much more slowly so that they are useful for defining deep pedigrees going back thousands of years either along the exclusively male or the exclusively female line of a family. SNPs are not as useful as STRs for identifying how two families might be related. All they can tell you is what broad population groups you belong to.

Short Tandem Repeats (STRs)

A Short Tandem Repeat (STR), also called a microsatellite, is a short sequence of nucleotides that repeats itself several times. The number of repetitions is called the value of the allele for that locus, with each locus having a characteristic range of allele values (alleles for short). Most loci are assigned DYS numbers (D = DNA, Y = Y chromosome, S = Single copy sequence) as defined by an international standards body called HUGO - Human Gene Nomenclature Committee - based at University College, London[22]. For example, at the STR locus **DYS391**, the base sequence may read TCTA TCTA TCTA TCTA TCTA TCTA TCTA TCTA where TCTA is repeated eight times, giving the locus an allele value of 8. A person's haplotype is his set of alleles for a specified set of STR markers. Some loci, such as **Y-GATA-H4**, still carry an older nonstandardized name invented by their discoverers characterizing the repeat motif exhibited by the marker or designating its location on the genome.

Closely related individuals have similar haplotypes. From the STR loci identified to date, a core set of loci defining the minimal haplotype for forensic applications has been designated by the Y-STR User's Group to include **DYS19, DYS385, DYS389I, DYS389II, DSY390, DYS391, DYS392,** and **DYS393**. It is based on established molecular locus characteristics, the amount of worldwide population data available, locus specific mutation rates, forensic validation, and successful application to forensic case work. The extended haplotype consists of these same loci with the addition of the double locus **YCAII**[23]. These loci are those most often used in population and forensic studies[24] and are included in the list of markers tested by the major genetic genealogy laboratories.

Single Nucleotide Polymorphisms (SNPs)

Single Nucleotide Polymorphisms (SNPs) are found on both the Y-chromosome and in mtDNA. SNPs are chosen as markers that exhibit one of only two values, so that they have mutated only once in human history. They are also known as 'Unique Event Polymorphisms' (UEPs). They are useful in mapping the demographic history of human populations. Each SNP is called 'biallelic' because it has one of two values, either the 'original' value or the mutated value.

By observing which populations have how many and which SNP mutations, a timeline can be created to indicate when and where a population appeared and how it was derived from pre-existing groups. The most widely shared SNPs are regarded as the oldest, while less frequently observed ones are considered to characterize later populations. A group of people who share the same set of SNPs is known as a *haplogroup*. The term *clade* is more commonly used to describe a female mitochondrial haplogroup. An organization of haplogroups or clades showing the relationship among their characteristic mutations is called a *phylogenetic tree*.

Y-Chromosome SNPs and Haplogroups

SNPs occur every 200 to 300 bases along the 3-billion-base genome. An SNP involves the alteration of a single nucleotide, usually a substitution of C (cytosine) for T (thymine). SNPs on all the chromosomes account for about 90% of the mutations found in human DNA. For a mutation to be considered a useful SNP, it must occur in more than 1% of the population[25].

Populations have been organized into 18 major haplogroups based on Y-chromosome SNPs. They are designated by upper case letters of the alphabet, with names of nested haplogroups alternating alpha and numeric characters[26]. For example, haplogroup R1b, also known as the Atlantic Modal Haplotype (AMH) is the most common haplogroup present in European populations. It is believed to have expanded into and recolonized Europe 10 to 12 thousand years ago after the last glacial maximum 18,000 years ago[27]. Results of SNP analysis are usually reported as either a positive or negative match to a certain haplogroup, based on the SNP mutations observed. Because SNPs are expensive to test, yet yield valuable historical and geographical information, there has been much research into predicting SNP haplogroups using STR marker values so that the probability that an individual belongs to a haplogroup can be estimated from his haplotype without SNP testing. There is an online haplogroup predictor at[28] https://home.comcast.net/~whitathey/hapest.htm.

Mitochondrial (mtDNA) SNPs and Clades

Since Brian Sykes first popularized mtDNA testing in *The Seven Daughters of Eve*, mtDNA has become a popular method of tracing deep female ancestry. In his book Sykes shows that about 98% of all people of Western Europe descend from only seven women who lived in Europe within the last 50,000 years. This does not mean there were only seven women contributing to the current European population. Some women might have had only sons, causing their mtDNA profiles to become extinct. Further research has shown that these 'clan mothers' themselves descend from a common ancestor 'Mitochondrial Eve' who lived in Africa about 200,000 years ago[29].

Mitochondria are small organelles found in all cells that have membrane-bound nuclei. These cells are common to animals, plants, and fungi. They carry their own DNA, different and separate from the DNA found in chromosomes. A mitochondrion acts as the power plant of a cell – accepting nutrients from the cell for the production of ATP, the indispensable source of the cell's energy. Any disruption in this energy production can be a disaster for a cell, so that mutations in mtDNA have been investigated as risk factors for Alzheimer's Disease, Parkinson's disease, cancer, and adult-onset diabetes[30]. It is generally believed that mitochondria were once independent bacteria that colonized the precursors of the complex cells found in present day animal and plant species, forming the symbiotic relationship we observe today.

With rare exceptions, the mtDNA carried in the tail of the sperm is lost when the sperm discharges its nucleus into the egg. The mtDNA found in the lining of the egg walls is nonrecombinant, meaning that is does not combine with any other DNA so that it is passed down virtually unchanged along the female line[31]. For these reasons, mtDNA is inherited by both men and women normally through the mother alone. I share the mtDNA of my brothers and sisters since we all have the same mother. We all share the same mtDNA with the daughters of my sister, but not with the daughters of my brothers, who have inherited mtDNA from their own mothers, my sisters-in-law.

Dr. Sykes' book is a popular representation of a body of scientific research that has identified a total of 36 major clades according to their characteristic mtDNA mutations. Of these, the seven clades identified by Dr. Sykes as H (Helena), J (Jasmine), U (Ursula), T (Tara), K (Katrina), X (Xenia), and V (Velda) (in order of largest to smallest) originated in different parts of Eurasia at different times. Each of them accounts for a different fraction of the current European population, as shown in Table 3. An additional Clade I (Iris) with origins in the Ukraine accounts for most of the remaining 2% of Europeans not covered by the others[32]. Other current human populations are grouped into other major clades – American Indians have four (A, B, C, and D), for example. A diagram of the population flows of the major world clades is found in Figure 4[33].

Table 3. Major European mtDNA haplogroups or clades[32].

Haplogroup	% Europeans	YBP* (kiloyears)	Origin	Notes
H	47	20	South France	Largest
J	17	10	Middle East	Second Largest
U	11	45	Greece	Oldest
T	9	17	Tuscany	---
K	6	15	N. Italy	---
X	6	25	Rep. of Georgia, Asia	---
J	5	17	Northern Spain	---
I	2	26	Ukraine	Smallest, Second Oldest

*Years before the present.

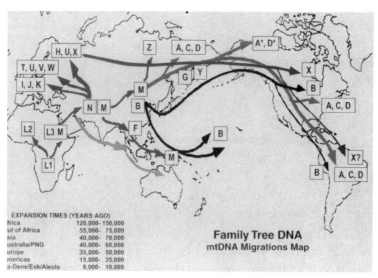

Figure 4. Diagram of major population flows as indicated by mtDNA analysis[33].

mtDNA is a powerful tool for studying important aspects of population growth and geographical expansion. Through comparison of the mutations in the mtDNA of a large number of people, a chronology for the expansion of humans into different parts of the world can be derived and coordinated with such influences as climatic changes and shifts from hunter-gathering to farming. mtDNA chronology can be adjusted to agree with archeological evidence for population expansions, such as a greater number of settlements, higher rates of refuse deposition, and more colonization of areas that were previously unoccupied[34]. The absence of mtDNA evidence of population growth can be used to indicate population distress caused by such influences as unfavorable weather conditions, disease, or pressure from other populations[35]. Such distress might create a population bottleneck where the number of individuals is greatly reduced, erasing genetic evidence of earlier growth and expansion.

SINGLE NAME DNA STUDIES

Since STR markers on the Y-chromosome are handed down virtually intact along the exclusively male line of a family in the same way that a family name is usually inherited, STR analysis is a useful tool for studying the structure and origin of a surname.

Single-name studies compare the genetic profiles of group members to establish family relationships, to verify information on family lines from conventional genealogical sources, and to place a family in an historical context. The information provided by DNA is complementary to what can be provided through written documentation. While DNA analysis can show kinship even when conventional sources of information are unreliable or nonexistent, documentation can give specific information on family ties that DNA can only estimate.

The characteristics of a study depend on the families involved, but a general feature is that as it develops, its participants usually fall into clusters with the same or similar haplotypes. Studies involving common surnames are usually large, and often reveal several unrelated haplotypes indicating multiple origins for the name. Studies on rare surnames are usually smaller, and tend to be genetically homogeneous. Groups of participants who descend from a single male generally manifest a more densely populated core group related to smaller groups of participants through one or two mutations. Nonpaternity events such as adoptions, name changes, and illegitimacies can become evident through individuals who have profiles that are very different from the major haplotypes exhibited by the majority of participants in the group.

One of the most widely publicized surname studies was that of the descendents of Thomas Jefferson. There had always been rumors supported by historical evidence that Jefferson had fathered several children with his quadroon house slave Sally Hemmings. It was known that all of Sally's proven children were conceived while Jefferson was at his home Monticello in Virginia, and that when Jefferson died, these children were released and Sally was allowed to live as a free woman of color[36]. Analysis performed by *E. A. Foster et al*[37] found an exact match between Y-chromosome DNA of a descendent of Jefferson's uncle Field Jefferson, and that of Eston Hemmings, a direct descendent of Sally's youngest son. While this only showed that Eston was descended from a Jefferson through an exclusively male link, considering the circumstantial evidence, it is obvious that the connection was to Thomas Jefferson himself.

The analysis disproved two other claims, that Sally's children were offspring of Jefferson's brother-in-law Peter Carr (husband of Jefferson's sister), and the claim made by the descendents of Thomas Woodson that he was the oldest of Sally's sons by Jefferson. Both the Carr and the Woodson DNA profiles were very different from that of Jefferson, ruling out these possible connections[38].

Starting a Single-Name Study

Collecting participants for a single-name DNA study is not as hard as it used to be. There are about 1,400 single-name DNA studies going on in the world now, some with several hundred participants and some with only a few. A searchable database of all the single-name DNA studies currently being conducted can be found at http://www.worldfamilies.net[39]. This site also gives a list of the studies with more than 50 participants. Sometimes surnames do not have their own study, but are part of another study representing a group of closely related names. The McDonald study for example also includes the related names Alexander, Allan, Balloch, Beaton, Blue, Buie, Cochrane, Connell, Currie, Darrough, Donald, Donaldson, Donnell, Gillis, Houston, Hughston, Hutchinson, MacAlistair, MacCain, MacIan, MacBride, MacCall, MacColl, MacConnell, MacCutcheon,

MacDaniel, MacDonald, MacDonell, MacDonnell, MacEachan, MacEachern, MacGill, MacIlraith, MacInnis, MacIvor, MacKeithan, MacKillop, MacKissick, MacLarty, MacQuiston, MacRanald, MacReynolds, MacRury, MacShennoch, MacSporran, MacSwain, McConnell, McDaniel, McDonald, McReynolds, Murchison, Murdoch, Rannie, Rodger, Ronaldson, Sanders, Sanderson, Wilkie, Wilkinson[40]. If you spot your own name on the list, don't hesitate to contact the study coordinator. If you cannot find your name in the database, you might consider starting your own group study.

Even large studies had to start somewhere. The group coordinator will usually be among the first participants, with other participants recruited from his genealogy community. Common sources of participants are genealogical societies, internet mailing lists, family reunions, and vital records. If you are female, you can still participate by coercing a brother, uncle, or other male relative to join.

I learned about the possibility of researching a family name using DNA, from an in-flight magazine highlighting the DNA study of the Irish clans sponsored by the Royal Irish Academy. Since I was then on my way home from the Fitzpatrick 2000 Clan Gathering, I had an immediate pool of Fitzpatricks that I could draw from as potential participants for my study. At that time DNA studies were not as popular as they are today, and the DNA companies conducting surname studies were still in their early stages. Our Fitzpatrick study took a year to organize, but in October 2001 we kicked off the project with the first 13 participants. They came from the U.S., England, Ireland, Australia, and Scotland. Many participants enrolled themselves, while others volunteered their fathers, brothers, nephews, or male cousins. Several participants paid for their tests out of their own pockets while others shared the cost among the genealogists in their families.

In gathering participants for your study, it is important to include other surnames that might have connections to your own. Our Fitzpatrick study has grown to include the Patricks, Moores, Sheras, and Stanleys, each group with a plausible reason (and a fascinating story) for believing they descend from Fitzpatricks. For example, the Patricks descend from Edward (Fitz)Patrick, kidnapped as a young boy with his brother from a beach in Ireland. He was brought to North Carolina where he was sold as a servant or a slave. He never saw his brother again. Though he tried later in life to find his family back in Ireland, he was never successful. The Patricks in the study have matched a Fitzpatrick from County Cavan, confirming the connection between the two surnames and providing a direction for further research. The Butlers are also of high interest to our Fitzpatrick study, as for many centuries they lived in Upper Ossory near the Fitzpatricks. A match between Fitzpatrick and Butler DNA would be an exciting development for both Clans.

In my own experience, initial reluctance to participate in a study is usually based on the cost. Until recently it has been difficult to recruit participants from Australia and New Zealand because of the unfavorable exchange rate these countries have had with the U.S. dollar. As of year 2000 the relative cost of testing was about double for Australians. But recently the exchange rate has improved for both the Australian dollar and the Euro, making the test less expensive for participants from outside the United States.

As a study grows larger and becomes well known it often becomes possible to find sponsors for new participants who otherwise could not afford to be tested. The Barton Historical Society (BHS) sponsors one of the largest DNA studies in the world; as of August 2004 it had enrolled 125 participants. To help reduce the cost of participation, the BHS has set up a sponsorship committee to collect donations and to screen potential sponsorship candidates. (See http://www.bartonsite.org/ie_index.html[41].) Sponsorships for $25 to $100 are granted on the basis of depth of pedigree to fill gaps in the known Barton family structure and to trace descendents of as yet unrepresented family lines.

A second reason people hesitate to participate in a surname study is based on a concern over the implications of giving a DNA sample for analysis. Part of this involves a misunderstanding of the nature of the junk DNA used for the study. It cannot be used for medical or insurance purposes. Another part is a concern over privacy issues. Who is going to see the results? How is privacy safeguarded?

These issues can usually be addressed through education about the DNA testing process. All DNA testing companies keep results strictly confidential and follow security procedures for all the tests they conduct. As a sample is submitted for analysis, it is immediately assigned an identification number that is used throughout the testing process. The identity of its owner is not known except to a limited number of people. Individual results are not shared even within the group unless permission is granted by the testee to do so. Matches within a study or with those participating in other studies are brokered either by the company doing the testing or by the study coordinator, who normally has access to his list of participants and their test results. Testing companies do not share results with any other organizations - the industry is highly competitive, and any release of otherwise confidential information could destroy a company's position within the community. For more information on privacy policies and procedures, visit http://www.duerinck.com/privacy.html[42].

CONNECTING WITH HISTORY THROUGH SINGLE NAME STUDIES

There are many reasons why people move from one place to another – famines, plagues, wars, better prospects elsewhere. By including participants in a study from unusual locations it may be possible to place a family in an interesting historical context. If your family background is French try searching in Africa or southeast Asia for people with your surname. If your ancestors were Irish don't forget that many Irish emigrated to Argentina during the Great Famine.

Every family has played a role in history. A family member could have been one of the porters Marco Polo used to carry spaghetti back from China, he could have been imprisoned by the Pope because he agreed with Galileo that the earth went around the sun, or he could have been the preacher who baptized Chief Red Cloud. It is only a matter of making the right connections with history, and DNA can help.

In this respect, Fitzpatrick is a good name to study. Its origins are confined to Ireland. It is not a rare name, nor is it very common. The main group of Fitzpatricks originated in County Laois, where many members of the family still live today. The Fitzpatrick Clan has a well-documented history starting with Bryan MacGiollaPhadraig (the name was later changed to Fitzpatrick), who took the oath of allegiance to King Henry VIII on October 8, 1537 and consequently was created First Baron of Upper Ossory[43] on June 11, 1541. The Fitzpatricks provide a good example of how a DNA study can be used to investigate a family's place in history.

On July 1, 1689, James II of England, a Catholic, was defeated at the Battle of the Boyne on the east coast of Ireland by his Protestant son-in-law William of Orange. During his reign James had returned control of Ireland to the Catholics, and after being ousted from the English throne by William in 1687, he saw the island as an area for staging an invasion of England and a return to power. James' loss at the Boyne resulted in the eventual return of control of Ireland to Protestant forces.

Within days of his defeat James returned to France, where he had been in exile as a guest of his ally the Catholic King Louis XIV. He was accompanied by his loyal Irish Brigade. As a term of its surrender to William after the Siege of Limerick in 1691, the remaining Catholic regular army was allowed to stay intact under the condition that troops still supporting James II leave the Kingdom, including England, Ireland, and Scotland. They were deported to France under the sentence of death should they ever return[44]. These soldiers came to be known as the Wild Geese. In France, the Wild Geese earned a reputation for bravery, with their descendents continuing to fight for France long after the deaths of both James and Louis XIV. Although the Wild Geese attempted on several occasions to return to their homeland, they never saw Ireland again.

What role did the Fitzpatricks play in the Battle of the Boyne? Is it possible to use DNA analysis to find out? If the Fitzpatricks were Catholics supporting James II, there should be descendents of the Irish Brigade and the Wild Geese still living in France today. If the DNA results of Fitzpatricks living in France are found to match the haplotype of the noble line from County Laois, it is possible that some of the Fitzpatrick clan supported James II at the Boyne and that these French Fitzpatricks are descendents of the Irish Brigade or the Wild Geese. This connection would need to be confirmed by written documentation such as family genealogies and church records, but a DNA match between French Fitzpatricks and known descendents of Bryan of Ossory would give strong evidence that Fitzpatricks were involved on the losing side of the conflict.

What is the chance that the Clan played both sides and that some of the Fitzpatricks supported the Protestants at the Boyne?

William Fitzpatrick and his wife Sarah Breckinridge arrived in America in about 1720 and settled in Virginia. They were evidently wealthy - their great grandson Benjamin was the owner of a large plantation and served as the governor of the State of Alabama from 1841 to 1845. Results of DNA tests on their descendents indicate that William was part of the noble line of Fitzpatricks from County Laois, although documentation is still lacking to provide a paper trail to explain this link.

The name William was more common in Ireland after William of Orange's victory at the Boyne. Because William of Ulster was born between 1690 and 1700, his first name indicates his father could have been a Protestant sympathizer. The Fitzpatrick family had been wealthy even before Brian MacGiollaPhadraig received his title in the mid 1500s. Because of their prominent position, it is likely they had a great interest in the outcome of the conflict and backed the English King in order to retain the lands that James might have confiscated had he prevailed.

William Fitzpatrick's wife Sarah Breckenridge was born in Breadalbane, Fifeshire, Scotland, where the Breckenridge clan had taken refuge in Campbell territory during the wars following the English Restoration in about 1660. The Breckenridges were members of a Protestant sect known as the Covenanters, who resisted interference by the government in private religious practices. In the early 1700s, many younger Breckenridges left Scotland for Ulster, perhaps to distance themselves even further from government harassment[45].

Considering his wealth, his Protestant wife, his origins in Ulster, his having the DNA of the noble line of Fitzpatricks from County Laois, his approximate birth year, and given the name William, it seems highly likely that William of Ulster came from a family of high profile Protestant supporters of William of Orange, and that his father might have been an officer in the Orange army at Boyne.

Research into the DNA profiles of the Fitzpatricks currently living in France and into documentation supporting William Fitzpatrick's connections to the Protestant military could strongly support the theory that Fitzpatricks played a historical role on both sides of the Battle of the Boyne. The noble line of Fitzpatricks were able to retain their lands apparently independent of which side was in control of Ireland possibly because there were family members on both sides of the conflict – not only members supporting the winning side as Protestant sympathizers of William of Orange, but also members sharing defeat with James II and being banished to France with the Irish Brigade and the Wild Geese.

NONPATERNITY EVENTS

One of the eventualities of every surname DNA study is the appearance of someone whose haplotype is completely different from all the others in the group. This is referred to as a non-paternity event, a situation where through adoption, a name change, illegitimacy, or any combination of these, an ancestor did not have the genetic profile of his alleged father. Sometimes the reason for the discrepancy is buried long in the past, going unnoticed for generations. Sometimes it is more recent and can be tracked down through testing others who, at least on paper, belong to the same family line. The famous study of the descendents of Thomas Jefferson and his house slave Sally Hemmings is a good example of a situation where verifying a non-paternity event was the focus of a study and not an exception to expected results.

There are many complications in figuring out the cause of a non-paternity event. Before the mid-1900s adoptions were often informal; that is, if a child was orphaned he would go live with the next door neighbors or with his maternal uncle Fred and nothing more would be said about it. Often adoption was considered a 'family secret', so that even a child who was adopted legally would not be told about it.

Immigration is one of the most frequent occasions where a name change can occur. Before the creation of the Ellis Island immigration station in 1906, there were many reasons why an immigrant was admitted into the U.S. under a name different from the one he had in his old country. Surname changes were common, especially among immigrants when a change in language was involved. Often, an immigration official did not understand the accent of an immigrant and recorded what he thought he heard (Burdo for Bordeaux), or the immigrant gave a translation of his name (Ash for Lafreniere, Bird for Loiseau)[46]. Occasionally, an immigrant would be escaping legal problems or religious persecution and gave an assumed name.

After Ellis Island was opened in 1906, immigration name changes became far less common. According to Marian L. Smith, an historian for the Immigration and Nationalization Service (INS) in her article "American Names/Declaring Independence"[47], passenger lists were created at the point of departure, and immigration officials worked from the ships manifests while processing arrivals. While these manifests could contain misspellings, officials were also under strict regulations that forbade them to change a name unless there was an obvious error or unless requested to do so by the immigrant himself.

Ms. Smith's article adds that, contrary to popular folklore, family name changes did not occur because of any language barrier at Ellis Island. "One third of all immigrant inspectors at Ellis Island early this century were themselves foreign-born, and all immigrant inspectors spoke at least three languages. They were assigned to inspect immigrant groups based on the languages they spoke. If the inspector could not communicate, Ellis Island employed an army of interpreters full time, and would call in temporary interpreters under contract to translate for immigrants speaking the most obscure tongues"[48].

There are other situations where a surname could change, for example, a family could have changed its name when it moved to another part of the country. Mark Haacke, the coordinator of the Haacke family study, found a branch of his family changed their name to Hickey when they moved to Oklahoma. What was originally a rare German surname was transformed into a common Irish surname, considerably complicating his family research[49].

The rate of illegitimacy has been studied extensively and found to vary considerably with nationality, culture, and time period. By 'rate of illegitimacy' is meant the number of illegitimate births divided by the total number of women capable of having children. The illegitimacy rate is different from the illegitimacy ratio, which is the number of illegitimate births divided by the total number of births over the same period of time. For a small number of births occurring in a large population of fertile women, the illegitimacy rate can be low at the same time the illegitimacy ratio can be very high.

In Catholic and Islamic societies illegitimacy rates are extremely low, but in Great Britain and Western Europe one in three children is born out of wedlock. Illegitimacy rates have been found to vary in time for Great Britain and Western Europe from 4.4% in 1540 down to about 1% in the 1600s, and in the 20th century alone, from 4% at the beginning of the century to 30% near the end. Illegitimate births are found to be higher among the uneducated and in situations where marriage occurs at an early age[50].

Non-paternity events are especially noticeable in family studies that involve a rare surname or a group descending from only a few known ancestors. These studies involve only one or at most several related haplotypes, so that wide variations are obvious. Non-paternity events can be harder to spot for studies that have multiple sources for a surname; for example, a surname that was related to a geographical location (Hill, Rivers, Lake), a profession (Miller, Smith, Wright), or that was a patronymic (Johnson, Williamson, Jackson). In the case of the surname of a wealthy family that existed when surnames were becoming common, a nearby group could have adopted the name for economic reasons or for protection. These studies might include so many different haplotypes that the occurrence of a non-paternity event is lost in the noise.

Nonpaternity events can also be hard to spot for families that have lived in the same geographical area for many generations. In this case, a high percentage of inhabitants of the area might descend from a single common ancestor so far in the past that familial relationships have long been forgotten. If a woman has an illegitimate child, chances are significant that the genetic father of that child is a relative of her husband. If their relationship is close, for example, if the two men are brothers or close cousins, her son will have a DNA profile probably identical to both men and the nonpaternity event will be genetically undetectable. If the relationship is distant, the DNA profile of the child will match the biological father, but differ somewhat from that of the woman's husband. Although the child will still have a common ancestor with his 'brother' (son of the woman and her husband), the ancestor will not be the husband as assumed, but someone from the more distant past. While DNA analysis may give a suspicion of a nonpaternity event of this type, there is no certainty because of the statistical nature of the mutation process.

Nevertheless, even in a group with a complicated variety of haplotypes, some results can turn up that are considerably off-the-wall by even the most liberal standards. Since such results indicate that someone of considerably different genetic makeup was involved with a family, they can provide a interesting opportunity for investigating a family's past historical or political connections.

Although the haplotypes in our Fitzpatrick study are relatively diverse, most of the participants match on 20 or so alleles out of 26. This is true even for other surnames included in our study, Moore, Stanley, and Shera. While this level of mismatch is not useful in Most Recent Common Ancestor (MRCA) calculations, (see below) it does show that most of us come from an ancient common background. Aside from this homogeneity, there are three people in our study who match on as few as six alleles out of 26 with some of the rest of the group.

Two of these unusual haplotypes are an exact match. One of them is a Catholic priest from New Jersey, and the other a retired engineer from New South Wales, Australia. These two men trace their families back to two small towns only 10 miles apart in County Clare on the west coast of Ireland. The American Fitzpatrick family emigrated to the U.S. during the Great Famine, and the family of the man in New South Wales arrived in Australia in the early 1900s. My investigation of why these men could match each other almost exactly, yet be so different from the rest of the group, led me to an interesting possible family tie with the history of western Ireland.

In 1588, the Spanish Armada (also called the Invincible Armada) was launched by Philip II of Spain in an attempt to overthrow the Protestant Queen Elizabeth I and gain the throne of England for himself. After several skirmishes in the English Channel, the Armada was finally shattered when the English set fire to several of their own ships and sent them into the Armada's anchorage off Calais, causing it to break formation and scatter. The Armada was subsequently defeated by a close range attack at Gravelines. Thanks to a change in wind the Duke of Medina was able to lead the Armada north around Scotland and along the west coast of Ireland in his escape. But the terrible weather he encountered was too much for the fleet; many of the Spanish ships were destroyed and many sailors drowned[51].

But is it possible that of the few survivors, a sailor made it to shore in County Clare? Is it possible that this sailor changed his name to mask his identity and settled for the rest of his life in this area of western Ireland? Is it possible that he married and had a son whose descendents include the two Fitzpatricks in our study who are so different from the rest of us that their male lines are not even Irish?

As online databases grow to include a more diverse collection of haplotypes it might be possible to find a match between these two Spanish(?) Fitzpatricks and members of another surname study. Until then the story about the Spanish survivor of the wreck of the Armada is much more entertaining than the theory that the non-paternity event resulted from an immigrant who worked as a milkman in a neighborhood of the Fitzpatricks.

GENETIC GENEALOGY TESTING COMPANIES AND TESTING OPTIONS

Major Testing Companies

The three main companies that specialize in genetic genealogy are Relative Genetics (RG), Family Tree DNA (FTDNA), and DNA Heritage (DNAH). RG and FTDNA offer a variety of products for Y-chromosome and mtDNA testing. DNAH only offers Y-testing. A summary of the testing options offered by the three major companies can be found in Table 4, with a list of the STR markers they test in Table 5. More information can be found on their websites.

Table 4. Comparison of testing options offered by the three major genetic genealogy testing laboratories~

	Relative Genetics			Family Tree DNA				DNA Heritage*		
Y-chromosome Paternal Line Analysis No. Markers/Alleles	15/17	24/26	37/43	-/12	-/25	-/37	-/59	23 alleles	Each add'l	43 allele panel
Cost~	$95	$155	$195	$99	$159	$189	$269	$137.8	---	$199
$/Allele	$5.59	$5.96	$4.53	$8.25	$6.36	$5.11	$4.41	$5.99	$5.99	$4.62
Native American Patrilineage Testing^	Based on 3 SNPs - Results compared to STR database of Native American haplotypes		$245	Estimated from STR results – SNP confirmation tests available for $100			---	N/A		
Native American Matrilineage Testing^	Based on HVR1 region of mtDNA		$245	Based on mtDNA HVR1 region – price depends on level of test refinement			$149/ $199	N/A		
African American Patrilineage Testing^	Based on 9 SNPs - Haplogroup derived from large database of current African populations		$349	Estimated from STR results – SNP confirmation tests available for $65			---	N/A		
African American Matrilineage Testing^	Based HVR1 mtDNA region - Haplogroup derived from large database of current African populations		$349	Based on mtDNA HVR1 region – price depends on level of test refinement			$149/ $199	N/A		
Extended Family Testing	Six different tests available		$195-$595	N/A				N/A		

~Prices current March 2006. *DNA Heritage allows a choice of alleles for a fixed price per allele, with a 23 allele minimum. A 23% discount is offered for a full panel test of 43 alleles. ^If an African (Native American) male and a European woman produced offspring, testing Y-chromosome SNP markers would confirm African (Native American) heritage only among males who descend along the exclusively male line, and would show no link with their European heritage. The matrilineal European descent could only be revealed by testing the mitochondrial SNPs of male or females who descend along the exclusive female line, and would show no indication of their African (Native American) heritage. If the male ancestor was European but the female ancestor was African (Native American), the reverse would be true. The test does not apply to descendents along mixed male and female lines.

Table 5. Loci tested by the leading DNA testing companies.

Locus	RG	FTDNA	DNAH	Locus	RG	FTDNA	DNAH
DYS385a	√	√	√	Y-GATA-C4	√		√
DYS385b	√	√	√	Y-GATA-H4	√	√	√
DYS388	√	√	√	DYS441	√		√
DYS389I	√	√	√	DYS442	√	√	√
DYS389II	√	√	√	DYS444	√		√
DYS390	√	√	√	DYS445	√		√
DYS391	√	√	√	DYS446	√	√	√
DYS392	√	√	√	DYS448	√	√	√
DYS393 or DYS395	√	√	√	DYS449	√	√	√
DYS394 or DYS19	√	√	√	DYS452	√		√
DYS426	√	√	√	DYS456	√	√	√
DYS437	√	√	√	DYS458	√	√	√
DYS438	√		√	DYS459a	√	√	√
DYS439 or Y-GATA-A4	√	√	√	DYS459b	√	√	√
DYS447	√	√	√	DYS463	√		√
DYS454	√	√	√	DYS464a	√	√	√
DYS455	√	√	√	DYS464b	√	√	√
DYS460	√	√	√	DYS464c	√	√	√
DYS461	√		√	DYS464d	√	√	√
DYS462	√		√	DYS607		√	
GGAAT1B07	√		√	DYS576		√	
YCAIIa	√	√	√	DYS570		√	
YCAIIb	√	√	√	CDYa		√	
Y-GATA-A10	√		√	CDYb		√	

There are several other companies that specialize in DNA testing for genealogy, most notably, Oxford Ancestry (OA) was founded by Dr. Bryan Sykes in 2001 in response to the success of his book The Seven Daughters of Eve. The company originally offered only mtDNA testing, but in 2003, OA expanded its product line to include haplogroup typing services based on Y-chromosome STR analysis. For a complete list of DNA testing companies, see[52] http://www.duerinck.com/dnalabs.html.

Family Tree DNA (www.familytreedna.com or www.ftdna.com)

Family Tree DNA was founded in 1999 by Bennett Greenspan and Max Blankfeld in conjunction with Dr. Mike Hammer, Director of the Genomic Analysis and Technology Core testing facility at the University of Arizona, Tucson, AZ. Dr. Hammer's laboratory offers multi-user state-of-the-art facilities for the development of new biotechnologies, and meets the stringent peer-review requirements of the biotechnology research community. Dr. Hammer, along with Dr. Alan Redd, was responsible for the discovery of many of the markers that are commonly used by testing companies for both forensic and genealogical STR analysis[53].

Relative Genetics (www.relativegenetics.com)

Relative Genetics, located in Salt Lake City, serves as the business unit of Sorenson Genomics, the DNA processing laboratory founded by the Sorenson Molecular Genealogy Foundation (www.smgf.org)[54]. SMGF is a nonprofit organization that offers a free on-line database of Y-chromosome haplotypes linked to surnames, dates, and places of births[55].

The Sorenson testing facilities are International Standards Organization (IOS) 17025-accredited by the National Forensic Science Technology Center (NFSTC), meaning that the facilities comply with international testing standards developed for genetic testing by the National Institute of Standards and Technology (NIST). The Sorenson facilities are also accredited for paternity testing by the American Association of Blood Banks (AABB). Through Relative Genetics and Gene Tree, Sorenson Genomics offers DNA testing for genetic genealogy and for verifying extended family relationships. GeneTree also offers paternity testing.

DNA Heritage (http://www.dnaheritage.com)

DNA Heritage (DNAH) was founded in 2002 to service the growing genetic genealogy market in Europe. In August 2004 DNAH opened a North American office in Rochester, New York. DNAH has made an agreement with Relative Genetics to use their ISO17025 certified testing laboratories. DNAH specializes in Y-chromosome testing only. DNAH offers the flexibility of a per-marker price for testing and allows the customer a choice of which will be tested, with a minimum of 23 alleles. DNAH does not sell lower resolution Y-chromosome tests. DNAH tests all markers at one time; when an upgrade is ordered, the results are delivered immediately.

Testing Options

All three major companies offer STR testing to determine a man's haplotype. A testee's results are compared with others in his surname study. A perfect match between two people indicates a close genetic relationship. One or two mismatches indicate a more distant relationship. More than two mismatches are not usually considered as showing a relationship within the recent past, although there are exceptions if the two people belong to separate branches of an extensive family tree.

RG and FTDNA also perform testing on SNP markers existing on both the Y-chromosome and mtDNA. Because of the slow mutation rates of SNP markers, SNP testing is not useful for determining family relationships. It can however be used to determine which haplogroup someone belongs to. Y-chromosome SNP testing can only be done on males, and indicates haplogroup membership along the exclusively male line of a family. mtDNA SNP testing can be done on both males and females and indicates haplogroup (clade) membership along the exclusively female line of a family. Note that Y-chromosome and mtDNA SNP testing is not valid for tracing mixed-gender family lines, for example, through the maternal grandfather or paternal grandmother. It is useful for tracing the heritage of only the exclusively male or exclusively female lines of a family.

Because of the high cost of SNP testing, FTDNA provides with its Y-STR results an estimate of which haplogroup an individual belongs to, based on a comparison of the results with its database of people who have been tested on both STR and SNP markers. An SNP test to verify its estimate of the most probable haplogroup is available at low additional cost. If the SNP test gives negative results - that is, the person does not belong to the predicted haplogroup - FTDNA will continue, at no further cost to the customer, to test closely related SNPs until a match is made or until it has tested all the SNPs within its capabilities. The average number of additional SNP tests required is about three, but in rare cases, it can be as many as 15[56].

Due to the high interest in Native American and African American ancestry, RG offers testing options specifically for these ancestries on both Y-chromosome and mtDNA SNPs. RG collaborates with AfricanAncestry.com to provide African-American male and female SNP testing. Results are compared to a large database of patrilineages and matrilineages from over 135 African populations, compiled from published research results and from SNP tests of living Africans. The database concentrates on African regions that were prominent in the European slave trade. Note that there is as high as a 30% chance that testing for African ancestry will give negative results because the person belongs to a European haplogroup along the line being tested.

RG also offers six levels of extended-family testing including: Full- or Half-Siblingship, Duo-Grandparentage, Single Grandparentage, Avuncular (Aunt or Uncle), First Cousin and Twin

Zygosity (testing for fraternal or identical twins). Paternity testing is available through RG's sister company GeneTree. Results are reported in terms of a Relationship Index, the probability of relationship of testees compared to the probability of relationship of two people tested at random from the total human population.

ONLINE DATABASES

There are several on-line databases that are useful for comparing Y-STR results to widen a search for genetic connections beyond a surname study. Along with the name and contact information for any matches that are found, they often give you additional information on haplotype and marker value frequencies and the geographical distribution of participants. Some will also predict haplogroup membership based on haplotype.

http://www.smgf.org – The Sorenson Molecular Genealogy Foundation database correlates genetic and genealogical information. As of January 2005, it contains nearly 10,000 haplotypes, associated with 6,594 surnames and 8507 distinct paternal lineages including over 320,217 individuals. The www.smgf.org site provides a drop-down menu where you can enter your haplotype for easy comparison with the database. Closely matching haplotypes are returned with a table indicating the status of the match for each marker, but without giving the actual value of any of the markers. The table is linked to the pedigrees of each matching haplotype and to an estimate of the MRCA for each match. Names of living individuals are not provided with the pedigrees for privacy reasons.

To add your haplotype to the SMGF database, you must request a GentiRinse test kit and return the samples to the Sorenson laboratory. No personal results are provided back to the testee. All results are added to the publicly accessible database on the site, but personal information on haplotype composition and vital statistics (name, birth date, etc.) are never provided with match information. Sorenson actively recruits individuals with extensive genealogies, family surname groups, and members of specific populations. A list of surnames and geographical locations that are in the database is given, along with the statistics, the physical properties of, and references to scientific research papers for each marker.

www.ysearch.org is provided by Family Tree DNA. It accepts Y-STR results from all the other testing laboratories for comparison with its database. It also accepts family trees in GEDCOM format. As of January 2005, the YSearch database contained 9,971 surnames, 8,022 unique haplotypes and 10,381 records. To access the database, a user must create an account by submitting his Y-STR results and providing information on his most distant known ancestor along the direct male line. The number of markers and mismatches to search on are user-selectable. A search can be limited on the basis of surname, surname variants, geographical location, and haplogroup. A user can also search on a specific surname or user ID. There are Y-search Compare and Genetic Distance™ Report facilities for comparing specific user IDs in the database. The site offers a MRCA calculator supported by technical references for those interested in the derivation of MRCA estimates. Statistics on the haplogroup composition of the database are also provided by the site.

www.y-base.org is sponsored by DNA Heritage. It provides a user-friendly way of comparing haplotypes to a growing database and for submitting your haplotype through a drop-down menu of marker values for inclusion. There is a search engine based on both haplotype and surname that provides the contact information of contributors. The site also provides a 'haplomatic' for predicting your haplogroup from your STR profile, along with statistics on the allele value and haplogroup composition of the database.

www.yhrd.org – The Y Chromosome Haplotype Reference Database was created by the Forensic Y-User Group. This database is a successor to the www.ystr.org database. The website provides haplotype frequency estimates for both forensic and genealogical use, and also for wider studies of population composition. As of January 2005 the database contains 28,650 haplotypes drawn from 249 populations worldwide.

The www.yhrd.org website provides useful information on haplotype frequencies, the statistical distributions of the various markers' allele values, the mutation rate of the Y Users Group-defined core and extended group of Y-STR markers, and the position of each of these markers on the Y-chromosome. It is possible to search the database for anonymous matches to a haplotype and obtain information on the geographical location of its donor. The site only accepts submissions from laboratories that pass a quality control exercise involving the evaluation of blind samples supplied by the Institut für Rechtsmedizin, Humboldt-Universität, Berlin, Germany. There is a list of contributing laboratories on the site with contact information.

http://www.cstl.nist.gov/biotech/strbase/index.htm was created by John M. Butler and Dennis L. Reeder of the National Institute of Standards and Technology (NIST) as a repository of information relating to the use of STRs in human identity testing. The site covers many more markers than the core or extended STR set. It presents an excellent library of information on STRs more suited to the experienced forensic researcher, including information on the properties of the markers, information on the FBI use of STRs, quality assurance testing standards and population data.

www.mitosearch.org is provided by Family Tree DNA for matching mtDNA results. Use of the database requires the creation of an account through the submission of mtDNA results. Searches can be performed on the basis of mtDNA SNP results or on haplogroup. Statistics for this site are still unavailable since it is relatively new.

THE DETAILS OF DNA MARKERS AND THEIR GENEALOGICAL USES

Short Tandem Repeats (STRs)

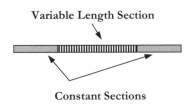

Figure 5a. Each locus has a variable section bracketed by two constant sections.

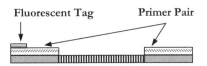

Figure 5b. A primer pair attaches itself to either side of the variable section. A fluorescent tag allows the measurement of the length.

Each STR marker is composed of three regions, two constant regions that bracket a variable region (Figure 5a). The chemical protocol used to analyze each marker involves a primer pair that latches on to each of the constant regions. One component of the pair is tagged with a fluorescent molecule that produces an optical signal when exposed to laser light in a genetic analyzer. DNA segments having shorter lengths travel faster through the analyzer than those that are longer, so that the time when the fluorescent signal appears depends on the length of a marker. Several markers can be tested at one time by using tags that fluoresce at different wavelengths. The results are calibrated against known standards to deduce the length of the variable region, which is reported as the allele value for that marker (Figure 5b.)

A few loci appear in multiple locations on the Y-chromosome. These include **DYS385**, **DYS459**, **DYS464**, and **YCAII**. (See Figure 6a.) In these cases, alleles are reported separately for each of the positions. Note that **DYS389** is not considered a multiple marker. During analysis one of the components of the **DYS389** primer pair latches onto a region on one end of an STR segment, while the other component latches onto two different regions at the other end (Figure 6b). In this case, two overlapping regions of DNA are tagged so that the length measured for **DYS389I** is included in that reported for **DYS389II** and the number of repeats is determined by both alleles. If the values of **DYS389I** and **DYS389II** both show a change of 1, this is counted as one mutation. If **DYS389II** shows a change of 1, but **DYS389I** has not changed, this is also counted as a single mutation. If **DYS389I** has changed by 1, but **DYS389II** has not changed, this is counted as two mutations to account for the reverse mutation **DYS389II** had to experience to keep its total length unchanged. For example, if **DYS389I** = 12, **DYS389II** = 28 for one person, and **DYS389I** = 11, **DYS389II** = 27 for a second person, the second person only exhibits one mismatch with the first, caused by a mutation of **DYS389I**.

A typical haplotype is shown in Table 6, along with the name of each locus and its value for a particular person's haplotype. By comparing haplotypes within a study group, mismatches in allele values caused by mutations can indicate how closely individuals are related. It is common to find that a study group contains subgroups of participants who are more closely related to each other than to anyone else in the study. More closely related participants have fewer mismatches.

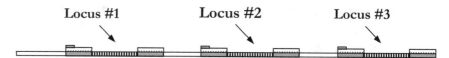

Figure 6a. Some markers are found at more than one location, and are associated with more than one allele.

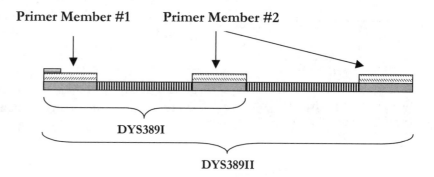

Figure 6b. DYS389I is included in DYS389II. The number of mutations must take into account both alleles.

Table 7 shows the results for five related groups of our Fitzpatrick study. Three groups consist of only one person, but might include others in the future as our test group is expanded. Because of the similarity of the haplotypes of all five groups, it is probable that they all had a common ancestor some time in the recent past. The shaded alleles clearly show the unique characteristics defining each group. An expanded version of this table showing other Fitzpatricks who differ from these by two or more mismatches appears later in Table 20 in the section Cladograms and Pairwise Mismatches.

Single Nucleotide Polymorphisms (SNPs)

<u>Y-Chromosome SNPs and Haplogroups</u>

An SNP on the Y-chromosome involves the substitution of one base pair for another (for example, a change from ACGGCTAA to ATGGCTAA). There are 153 haplogroups and subgroups that have been identified[57] based on Y-chromosome SNP mutations. They are named according to the hierarchical nomenclature system or Phylocode[58] developed by the International Society for Phylogenetic Nomenclature and by the Y-Chromosome Consortium[59]. The 19 major haplogroups

Table 6. A typical haplotype.

	Marker Names & Values																								
	385a	385b	388	389	389b	390	391	392	393	394	426	437	438	439	447	454	455	460	461	462	B07	A11a	A11b	A10	C4	H4
69D	11	14	12	13	29	21	11	13	13	14	12	15	12	12	25	11	11	10	12	11	10	22	23	13	23	12

Table 7. Several subgroups of the Fitzpatrick DNA study. Subgroups can be identified by their variations with the most common values in the group.

	Marker Names & Values																								
	385a	385b	388	389	389b	390	391	392	393	394	426	437	438	439	447	454	455	460	461	462	B07	A11a	A11b	A10	C4	H4
Group 1																										
15853	11	14	12	13	29	21	11	13	13	14	12	15	12	12	25	11	11	10	12	11	10	22	23	13	23	12
69D	11	14	12	13	29	21	11	13	13	14	12	15	12	12	25	11	11	10	12	11	10	22	23	13	23	12
21477	11	14	12	13	29	21	11	13	13	14	12	15	12	12	25	11	11	10	12	11	10	22	23	13	23	12
Group 2																										
69G	11	14	12	13	29	21	11	13	13	14	12	15	12	12	25	11	11	10	12	11	**11**	22	23	13	23	12
Group 3																										
11682	11	**15**	12	13	29	21	11	13	13	14	12	15	12	12	25	11	11	10	12	11	10	22	23	13	23	12
Group 4																										
22104	11	14	12	13	29	21	11	13	13	14	12	**14**	12	12	25	11	11	10	12	11	10	22	23	13	23	12
Group 5																										
10108	11	14	12	13	29	21	11	13	13	14	12	15	12	12	25	11	11	**11**	12	11	10	22	23	13	23	12
3011	11	14	12	13	29	21	11	13	13	14	12	15	12	12	25	11	11	**11**	12	11	10	22	23	13	23	12
11299	11	14	12	13	29	21	11	13	13	14	12	15	12	12	25	11	11	**11**	12	11	10	22	23	13	23	12
11294	11	14	12	13	29	21	11	13	13	14	12	15	12	12	25	11	11	**11**	12	11	10	22	23	13	23	12

are designated by upper case letters of the alphabet, including the letter Y which is used to signify the haplogroup including haplogroups **A** through **R**. The names of nested haplogroups alternate alphanumeric characters[60]. For example, **R1b**, also known as the Atlantic Modal Haplotype (**AMH**), is the most common haplogroup in European populations. It is believed to have spread into Europe about 10,000 to 12,000 years ago after the end of the last Ice Age.

Super-haplogroups include one or more haplogroups. Some super-haplogroups are labeled with single uppercase letters. Others unlabeled super-haplogroups are named by concatenations of their constituent haplogroups to designate the most recent common ancestor of these haplogroups plus all of his descendents. For example, in Figure 7, the **CR** superhaplogroup designates those branches of the phylogenetic tree derived from mutations **M168** and **P9**. This includes all groups except for **A** and **B**. Super-super-haplogroups such as the pre-**CR** group are denoted by adding pre- to the super-haplogroup name.

A haplogroup may be composed of subhaplogroups that by definition share the same SNPs defining that haplogroup, but that differ from each other on one or more other SNPs. There may also be individuals that belong to the haplogroup who do not belong to any one of its subgroups. These individuals form a para-haplogroup, labeled with an asterisk. For example, referring to Figure 7[61], members of the para-haplogroup **B*** have the **M60** and **M181** mutations required for membership in group **B**, but lack mutation **M146** defining sub-haplogroup **B1** and mutation **M182** defining sub-haplogroup **B2**. At a later date, mutations might be found that will identify some or all members of the **B*** paragroup as a **B3** sub-haplogroup. There is ongoing research to further define the sub-haplogroups of the Y-chromosome SNP phylogenetic tree.

Mitochondrial (mtDNA) SNPs and Clades

The double helix of the human genome contains 3 billion base pairs. The mitochondrial genome is a circular structure that is only 16,569 base pairs long. The mtDNA regions typically tested are Hypervariable Region 1 (**HVR1**, including base pairs 16001 through 16540) and Hypervariable Region 2 (**HVR2**, including base pairs 61 through 570). These regions are part of the control region, also called the D-loop, where mtDNA starts the unzipping process during replication. New mutations, which can take the form of substitutions, deletions or additions of a base pair, occur in the **HVR1** region at the rate of 7.96×10^{-6} per locus per generation or 0.33 per locus per million years[62]. This is equivalent to a new mutation appearing among the 540 **HVR1** markers once every 5,800 years. Because of its very slow mutation rate, mtDNA is useful for exploring deep genetic roots along the exclusively female line of a family.

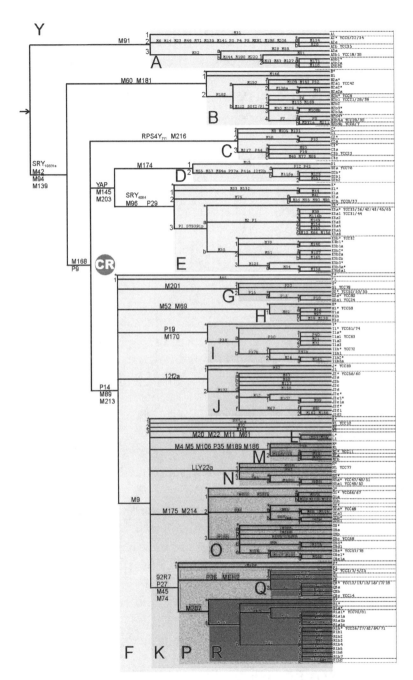

Figure 7. Phylogenetic tree of Y-chromosome SNP haplogroups[59]. The **CR** super haplogroup is differentiated by mutations **M168** and **P9**.

Mitochondrial DNA was first sequenced in 1981, creating the Cambridge Reference Sequence (CRS)[63]. It is the mtDNA profile of an arbitrary member of clade **H** (the clan Helena), the most common female clade found among people with Western Eurasian ancestry[64]. In a slightly modified form the revised CRS[65] is used as a master template against which to compare all other mtDNA profiles. The CRS for the **HVR1** and **HVR2** regions is shown in Table 8.

Mitochondrial DNA clades are labeled similarly to Y-chromosome haplogroups. Major mtDNA clades are designated by uppercase letters of the alphabet, with the names of nested subclades alternating numbers and lower case letters. Superclades that contain two or more clades are named with a concatenation of their two uppercase letters to designate the most recent common ancestor of these superclades plus all of her descendents, for example, the **HV** clade. Super-superclades that include these superclades are denoted by adding pre- in front of the superclade name, as pre-**HV**.

A clade may be composed of subclades that share the same SNPs defining that clade, but that differ from each other on one or more other SNPs. There may also be individuals that belong to the clade but who do not belong to any one of the subclades. These individuals form a paraclade and are labeled with an asterisk. Clade **H** (Helena) is by far the largest mtDNA clade in Europe. (See Table 3). It has not yet been fully resolved into subclades. Although until recently there were 11 subclades identified for haplogroup **H**, that is, **H1**, **H2**, ……**H11**, 17% of the people who tested positive for **H** tested negative for its known subclades. These individuals are labeled **H***, implying that they belong to an as-yet unidentified **H** subclade[66]. Recently new research by *Achilli et al*[67] has identified four more **H** subclades, **H12** through **H15**, but does not rule out the possibility of the existence of additional **H** subclades.

Results of individual mtDNA analyses are usually given in terms of deviations from the CRS. The sample results for the **HVR1** region shown in Table 9[68] indicate seven substitutions relative to the CRS. The number indicates the position in the mtDNA genome where the substitution occurs, with the letter indicating which base has been substituted into the mtDNA. For example, the notation **16129A** stands for the substitution of Adenine (A) for Thymine (T) in position No. **16129** in the CRS. Table 10 shows an explicit comparison between these **HVR1** results and the CRS.

Sample results for the **HVR2** region shown in Table 11 indicate substitutions, additions, and deletions of bases relative to the CRS. Additions are indicated by the number of the position in the genome after which the addition takes place, followed by a decimal point, a digit, and the initial of the added base. If the numeral is a 1, the notation indicates the addition of a base directly after the position. If the digit is a 2, the base is the second addition after that position. For example, the notation **309.1C** means that Cytosine (C) was added after position 309, and **309.2A** means that a adenine was added after the cytosine. A deletion is indicated by the number of the position followed by a minus sign, so that **523-** means that the base at position **523** has been deleted. An explicit comparison between these **HVR2** results and the CRS appears in Table 12.

Table 8. The Cambridge Reference Sequence (CRS) for Hypervariable Regions 1 (**HVR1**) and Hypervariable Region 2 (**HVR2**).

HVR1 Reference Sequence

16010►	16020►	16030►	16040►	16050►	16060►	16070►	16080►
ATTCTAATTT	AAACTATTCT	CTGTTCTTTC	ATGGGGAAGC	AGATTTGGGT	ACCACCCAAG	TATTGACTCA	CCCATCAACA
16090►	16100►	16110►	16120►	16130►	16140►	16150►	16160►
ACCGTATGT	ATTTCGTACA	TTACTGCCAG	CCACCATGAA	TATTGTACGG	TACCATAAAT	ACTTGACCAC	CTGTAGTACA
16170►	16180►	16190►	16200►	16210►	16220►	16230►	16240►
TAAAAACCCA	ATCCACATCA	AAACCCCCTC	CCCATGCTTA	CAAGCAAGTA	CAGCAATCAA	CCCTCAACTA	TCACACATCA
16250►	16260►	16270►	16280►	16290►	16300►	16310►	16320►
ACTGCAACTC	CAAAGCCACC	CCTCACCCAC	TAGGATACCA	ACAAACCTAC	CCACCCTTAA	CAGTACATAG	TACATAAAGC
16330►	16340►	16350►	16360►	16370►	16380►	16390►	16400►
CATTTACCGT	ACATAGCACA	TTACAGTCAA	ATCCCTTCTC	GTCCCCATGG	ATGACCCCCC	TCAGATAGGG	GTCCCTTGAC
16410►	16420►	16430►	16440►	16450►	16460►	16470►	16480►
CACCATCCTC	CGTGAAATCA	ATATCCCGCA	CAAGAGTGCT	ACTCTCCTCG	CTCCGGGCCC	ATAACACTTG	GGGGTAGCTA
16490►	16500►	16510►	16520►	16530►	16540►		
AAGTGAACTG	TATCCGACAT	CTGGTTCCTA	CTTCAGGGTC	ATAAAGCCTA	AATAGCCCAC		

HVR2 Reference Sequence

70►	80►	90►	100►	110►	120►	130►	140►
CGTCTGGGGG	GTATGCACGC	GATAGCATTG	CGAGACGCTG	GAGCCGGAGC	ACCCTATGTC	GCAGTATCTG	TCTTTGATTC
150►	160►	170►	180►	190►	200►	210►	220►
CTGCCTCATC	CTATTATTTA	TCGCACCTAC	GTTCAATATT	ACAGGCGAAC	ATACTTACTA	AAGTGTGTTA	ATTAATTAAT
230►	240►	250►	260►	270►	280►	290►	300►
GCTTGTAGGA	CATAATAATA	ACAATTGAAT	GTCTGCACAG	CCACTTTCCA	CACAGACATC	ATAACAAAAA	ATTTCCACCA
310►	320►	330►	340►	350►	360►	370►	380►
AACCCCCCCT	CCCCCGCTTC	TGGCCACAGC	ACTTAAACAC	ATCTCTGCCA	AACCCCAAAA	ACAAAGAACC	CTAACACCAG
390►	400►	410►	420►	430►	440►	450►	460►
CCTAACCAGA	TTTCAAATTT	TATCTTTTGG	GGGTATGCAC	TTTTAACAGT	CACCCCCAA	CTAACACATT	ATTTTCCCCT
470►	480►	490►	500►	510►	520►	530►	540►
CCCACTCCCA	TACTACTAAT	CTCATCAATA	CAACCCCCGC	CCATCCTACC	CAGCACACAC	ACACCGCTGC	TAACCCCATA
550►	560►	570►					
CCCCGAACCA	ACCAAACCCC	AAAGACACCC					

Table 9. Sample mtDNA **HVR1** results.

| 16129A | 16223T | 16391A | 16085G | 16172C | 16311C | 16519C |

Table 10. **HVR2** mtDNA results from in Table 8 compared to the Cambridge Reference Sequence (top line of each row). Mutations are indicated in bold and underlined. To calculate the position of a mutation: 1) locate the cell where the mutation is shown, 2) add the number at the top of the previous column to the number at the beginning of the row, 3) count starting at 1 from the first entry in the cell to the position of the mutation. For example, the substitution of A in the second row is located at 16020 + 100 + 9 = 16129.

Add	16010	16020	16030	16040	16050	16060	16070	16080	16090	16100	Add
Add	ATTCT AATTT	AAACT ATTCT	CTGTT CTTTC	ATGGG GAAGC	AGATT TGGGT	ACCAC CCAAG	TATTG ACTCA	CCCAT CAACA	ACCGC TATGT	ATTTC GTACA	Add
									ACC**G**G TATGT		
100	TTACT GCCAG	CCACC ATGAA	TATTG TACGG	TACCA TAAAT	ACTTG ACCAC	CTGTA GTACA	TAAAA ACCCA	ATCCA CATCA	AAACC CCCTC	CCCAT GCTTA	100
			TATTG TAC**AG**					A**C**CCA CATCA			
200	CAAGC AAGTA	CAGCA ATCAA	CCCTC AACTA	TCACA CATCA	ACTGC AACTC	CAAAG CCACC	CCTCA CCCAC	TAGGA TACCA	ACAAA CCTAC	CCACC CTTAA	200
			CC**T**TC AACTA								
300	CAGTA CATAG	TACAT AAAGC	CATTT ACCGT	ACATA GCACA	TTACA GTCAA	ATCCC TTCTC	GTCCC CATGG	ATGAC CCCCC	TCAGA TAGGG	GTCCC TTGAC	300
		CACAT AAAGC							**A**TCCC TTGAC		
400	CACCA TCCTC	CGTGA AATCA	ATATC CCGCA	CAAGA GTGCT	ACTCT CCTCG	CTCCG GGCCC	ATAAC ACTTG	GGGGT AGCTA	AAGTG AACTG	TATCC GACAT	400
500	CTGGT TCCTA	CTTCA GGGTC	ATAAA GCCTA	AATAG CCCAC							500
		CTTCA GGGCC									

Table 11. Sample **HVR2** results.

73G	199C
203A	204C
250C	263G
309.1C	(insertion of a C after location 309)
309.2A	(insertion of an A after the previous insertion)
315.1C	(insertion of a C after location 315)
455.1T	(insertion of a T after location 455)
523-	(base pair at location 523 is missing)
524-	(base pair at location 524 is missing)

The clade an individual belongs to is determined by comparing his mtDNA mutations to those characteristic of the various mtDNA haplogroups. In the example given in Tables 9 through 12, the **HVR1** mutations at **16129, 16223, 16391** and the **HVR2** mutations at **199, 204,** and **250** are indications of Clade **I**. The additional mutations in **HVR1** (**16311C, 16172C**) and in **HVR2** (**203A**) are indications of subclade **I1**. The remaining mutations could be random mutations that either define an as yet unidentified subsubclade of Clade **I** or are random mutations that are not shared by a large enough population to define a subsubclade. The relationship between these mutations and Clade **I** can be seen in the upper left hand area of Figure 8[69].

THE MOST RECENT COMMON ANCESTOR (MRCA)

The Most Recent Common Ancestor (MRCA) is just what the name implies, the most recent ancestor shared by a group of two or more people. The most probable haplotype of the MRCA can be constructed from the most frequent allele at each site. This assumes that since the original haplotype from which the group descends has existed longer than any mutated version, it will be the most frequent. Table 13 shows the same five groups of Fitzpatricks that were shown earlier in Table 7. The presumed haplotype of the MRCA of this group has been added in the top line of the table. It was composed from the most frequent allele values at each site. Note that Group 1 is not the largest of the groups, but that the Group 1 haplotype has the fewest deviations with respect to that of the MRCA.

The number of mutations or mismatches between the haplotypes of two individuals can be used to estimate a time period for their MRCA.

The MRCA calculation is an estimate of how recently two people might have had the same ancestor. Since mutation rates are statistical, a MRCA calculation can only provide the probability that a common ancestor lived within a given number of generations, based on how many loci are tested, how many mismatches are observed between the two people, and the estimated mutation rate. The probability of finding the MRCA in any generation can be calculated, but MRCA results are usually presented either in terms of the generation associated with a 50% probability of finding the MRCA more recently, or the generations between which there is a 95% probability of finding the ancestor.

Table 12. **HVR2** mtDNA results from Table 10 compared to the Cambridge Reference Sequence (top line of each row). Substitutions, additions, and deletions are indicated in bold and underlined. To calculate the position of a mutation: 1) locate the cell where the mutation is shown, 2) add the number at the beginning of the row to the number at the top of the previous column, and 3) count starting at 1 from the first entry in the row to the position of the mutation. For example, the substitution of C at the end of the second row is located at 100 + 90 + 9 = 199. Note that this numbering scheme is different from the one used in Table 8.

	10	20	30	40	50	60	70	80	90	100	
Add							CGTCTG GGGG	GTATGC ACGC	GATAG CATTG	CGAGA CGCTG	**Add**
								GT**G**TG CACGC			
100	GAGCC GGAGC	ACCCTA TGTC	GCAGT ATCTG	TCTTTG ATTC	CTGCCT CATC	CTATTA TTTA	TCGCAC CTAC	GTTCAA TATT	ACAGG CGAAC	ATACTT ACTA	**100**
										ATACTT AC**C**A	
200	AAGTG TGTTA	ATTAAT TAAT	GCTTGT AGGA	CATAAT AATA	ACAATT GAAT	GTCTGC ACAG	CCACTT TCCA	CACAGA CATC	ATAACA AAAA	ATTTCC ACCA	**200**
	AA**ACGT**GTTA				ACAATT GAA**C**		CC**G**CTT TCCA				
300	AACCCC CCCT	CCCCCG CTTC	TGGCC ACAGC	ACTTAA ACAC	ATCTCT GCCA	AACCCC AAAA	ACAAA GAACC	CTAACA CCAG	CCTAAC CAGA	TTTCAA ATTT	**300**
	AACCCC CCC**CA**T	CCCCC**C** GCTTC									
400	TATCTT TTGG	CGGTAT GCAC	TTTTAA CAGT	CACCCC CCAA	CTAACA CATT	ATTTTC CCCT	CCCACT CCCA	TACTAC TAAT	CTCATC AATA	CAACCC CCGC	**400**
						ATTTT**T** CCCCT					
500	CCATCC TACC	CAGCAC ACAC	ACACCG CTGC	TAACCC CATA	CCCCGA ACCA	ACCAAA CCCC	AAAGA CACCC				**500**

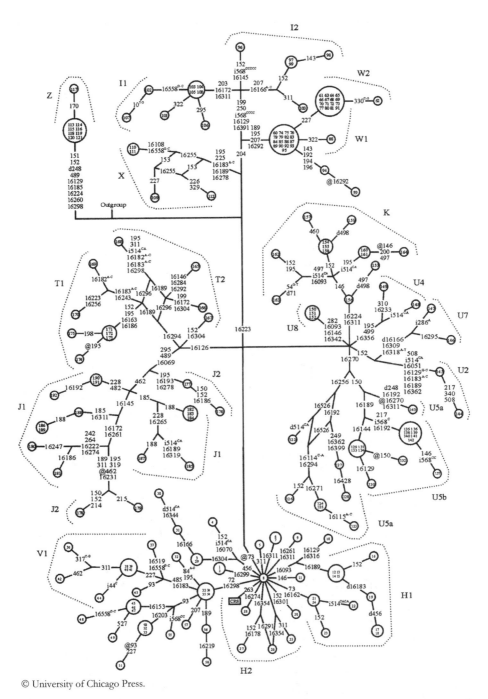

Figure 8. Diagram of mutational differences among European mtDNA subclades[69].

Table 13. MRCA haplotype.

	385a	385b	388	389	389b	390	391	392	393	394	425	437	438	439	447	454	455	460	461	462	1307	A1a	A1b	A10	C4	H4
MRCA	11	14	12	13	29	21	11	13	13	14	12	15	12	12	25	11	11	10	12	11	10	22	23	13	23	12
Group 1																										
15853	11	14	12	13	29	21	11	13	13	14	12	15	12	12	25	11	11	10	12	11	10	22	23	13	23	12
21477	11	14	12	13	29	21	11	13	13	14	12	15	12	12	25	11	11	10	12	11	10	22	23	13	23	12
69D	11	14	12	13	29	21	11	13	13	14	12	15	12	12	25	11	11	10	12	11	10	22	23	13	23	12
Group 2																										
69G	11	14	12	13	29	21	11	13	13	14	12	15	12	12	25	11	11	10	12	11	10	22	23	13	23	12
Group 3																										
11682	11	15	12	13	29	21	11	13	13	14	12	15	12	12	25	11	11	10	12	11	10	22	23	13	23	12
Group 4																										
22104	11	14	12	13	29	21	11	13	13	14	12	14	12	12	25	11	11	10	12	11	10	22	23	13	23	12
Group 5																										
10108	11	14	12	13	29	21	11	13	13	14	12	15	12	12	25	11	11	11	12	11	10	22	23	13	23	12
3011	11	14	12	13	29	21	11	13	13	14	12	15	12	12	25	11	11	11	12	11	10	22	23	13	23	12
11299	11	14	12	13	29	21	11	13	13	14	12	15	12	12	25	11	11	11	12	11	10	22	23	13	23	12
11294	11	14	12	13	29	21	11	13	13	14	12	15	12	12	25	11	11	11	12	11	10	22	23	13	23	12

There are several analogies that can help to explain how the number of mismatches between haplotypes relates to how long ago the MRCA lived. One of the cleverest involves two Mexican jumping beans sitting at about the same place on a table. As they jump, they get father apart. If you observe the beans and they are positioned close to each other, you would guess that they started out close by and that not much time has passed since they started jumping. If they are farther apart, more time has passed if they started out together. Knowing the average distance of a jump and having a rough idea about how often they jump will give you an estimate of how much time has gone by since the beans might have been at the same position on the table. If the beans are extremely far apart, you can conclude that a very long time has elapsed.

Likewise, by observing how far apart the haplotypes of two individuals are (how many mismatches they exhibit) it is possible to estimate the amount of time that has passed since their MRCA existed based on how often mutations occur. If two haplotypes are very far apart (with many mismatches), you can conclude that they are probably unrelated or that they have a MRCA in the very distant past.

About MRCA Calculations

In general, if the haplotypes of two individuals do not mismatch on any of the markers tested, they probably had a common ancestor who lived within the recent past. Is it possible that their MRCA lived many generations ago? Sure, but probably not, otherwise there would probably have been enough time for a mutation to occur. Is it possible that one or both of the participants had a marker that changed and then changed back to its original value, pushing the date of the MRCA further into the past? Sure, but very unlikely. On the other hand, if the two haplotypes show several mismatches, the MRCA probably lived in the remote past, allowing enough time for the markers to mutate. Is it possible that their MRCA lived only two or three generations ago? Sure, but highly unlikely. It is important to emphasize that a MRCA calculation is only to be used as a guideline for determining relationships. It can only give an estimate of when a common ancestor existed.

A MRCA calculation depends on three things: 1) how many markers are tested, 2) how many mismatches are observed, and 3) the mutation rate estimate used. The greater the number of markers that are tested, the more refined the estimate of the MRCA will be. Testing on at least 20 markers will give a reasonable estimate of which individuals are related in the last few hundred years. Testing on more than about 20 markers can confirm this relationship[70]. Because genealogical documentation usually exists only back as far as five hundred to a thousand years, it is not often useful to calculate the MRCA for individuals who show more than two or three mismatches, although there are exceptions for groups if there is an extensive family tree with a large number of participants.

A MRCA calculation is not difficult. The full mathematical expressions are complex, but for the cases that are usually of interest to genealogists, that is, relationships within the last few hundred years for families derived from large populations, the math reduces to common algebra and the results can be summarized in a couple of simple tables. If you are interested in creating your own Excel® spreadsheets to do the calculations yourself, instructions are included in the section How to Construct an Excel® Spreadsheet for MRCA Calculations. There are also premade spreadsheets included on the Forensic Genealogy CD and on the website www.forensicgenealogy.info that you can adapt for your own calculations without having to enter the formulas yourself. If you are interested in doing the math to derive the your own results, you will find helpful information in the section A Short Discussion on the Mathematical Models Used for MRCA Calculations.

MRCA Lookup Tables

Since the leading DNA testing companies offer testing options based on only particular numbers of markers, and because more than a small number of mismatches is not meaningful, it is possible to use a lookup table to obtain a MRCA estimate. If you'd rather experiment with the effect of different numbers of markers and mismatches or with different mutation rates, the equations and instructions necessary to do so are included in the next section.

Tables 14 and 15 are lookup tables that can be used to find the number of generations associated with a 50% chance and a 95% chance of finding the MRCA of two individuals using specific numbers of markers and assuming 0, 1, 2, and 3 mutations. Usually more than three mutations results in too many generations to be of interest. The calculations are based on the commonly accepted average mutation rate of two tenths of one percent (= 0.002 = 2/10% = 0.2%) per marker per generation. A higher mutation rate would mean that mutations happened more often, decreasing the number of generations to the MRCA.

Table 14. MRCA calculation results for the 50% confidence level.*

50%		Number of Markers				
		12	25	26	37	42
Number of Mismatches	0	14.5	6.9	6.7	4.7	4.1
	1	35.0	16.6	15.9	11.1	10.1
	2	55.8	26.8	25.7	18.1	15.9
	3	76.5	36.8	35.3	24.9	26.9

*Based on a mutation rate of 0.002.

To use Table 14 choose the column representing the number of markers tested. Go down the column to the row representing the number of mismatches of interest. The number in the cell at this intersection tells you that there is a 50% chance of finding the MRCA as recently as this many generations ago. Repeating the same procedure with Table 15 gives you the number of generations between which there is a 95% chance of finding him.

For example, if there is one mismatch on a test of 25 markers, the 50% confidence level is 16.6 generations, and the 95% level is found between 2.4 and 55.5 generations.

Table 15. MRCA calculation results for 95% the confidence level.*

95%		Number of Markers				
		12	25	26	37	42
Number of Mismatches	0	0.5 to 77	0.26 to 37.0	0.25 to 35.5	0.17 to 24.8	0.15 to 22.0
	1	5.1 to 116	2.4 to 55.5	2.4 to 53.5	1.7 to 37.5	1.5 to 33.0
	2	13 to 150.5	6.2 to 72.5	6 to 69.3	4.2 to 48.8	3.7 to 43.1
	3	23 to 182.5	11 to 87.5	10.7 to 84.5	7.5 to 59.3	6.6 to 52.0

*Based on a mutation rate of .002.

How to Construct an Excel® Spreadsheet for MRCA Calculations

An Excel® spreadsheet is a great way to gain insight into the meaning of MRCA calculations. Having your own spreadsheet to play with allows you the flexibility to experiment with different numbers of markers, different numbers of mismatches, and different mutation rates, without needing to understand detailed mathematics. If you want to experiment with the various parameters but you are not interested in constructing your own spreadsheet to do so, you can use the premade spreadsheets on the accompanying Forensic Genealogy CD, or obtain them from the website: www.forensicgenealogy.info.

MRCA calculations are performed based on the number of possible transmission events where a mutation can take place. A transmission event refers to the transfer of a single DNA marker to an offspring, independent of which marker is transmitted and in which generation the transmission occurs. If an offspring can inherit a mutation on any one of **n** markers from his father, then **G** generations up the family tree to the MRCA there are **n*G** possible occasions where a mutation can occur. Likewise back down the family tree to a different offspring in the same generation there are **n** times **G** (or **n*G**) possible chances for a mutation to occur, so that the total number of transmission events is **t = 2*n*G**. For a single marker, if the MRCA is 10 generations in the past, there are 20 transmission events to consider, ten from the first individual up to the MRCA, and ten back down to the second individual sharing the ancestor.

It is important to keep track of the difference between what we commonly refer to as a 'generation' meaning a collection of people with the same parents, same grandparents, or same great-grandparents, etc., and a 'transmission event' meaning the passing of a DNA marker to an offspring. Two brothers who are in the same generation in common terminology are separated in DNA-speak by two transmission events for each marker transferred, one from the first brother up to their father, and the other from their father back down to the second brother. For simplicity MRCA calculations assume that the number of generations up to the common ancestor is the same as the number of generations back down from the common ancestor to the present. This accounts for the factor of two in the expression for the number of transmission events **t**. In reality this might not be the case, with one or more ancestors having children either very early or very late in life, increasing or reducing the number of generations in a family line, respectively. But for a given number of transmission events and markers, the total number of generations is constant, so that an increase in the number of generations in one direction along the family tree must be accompanied by a corresponding decrease in the number of generations in the other direction.

To get a general idea of what is involved in a MRCA calculation, consider two participants, A and B, in a study who are one mismatch apart, and that from other DNA profiles of the group, we can assume that the mutation occurred in A's family line. If we could research the DNA profile of A's line, generation by generation, starting at the present and moving backwards along his family tree, we would find that over the centuries, A's family's DNA mutated many times. The last mutation to take place accounts for the one difference observed between A and B. Since A has this mutation but B does not, the mutation must have happened in some generation **G(1)** after their MRCA. If we search only up to and including **G(1)**, we have not searched far enough back to find the MRCA. For example, the mutation could have occurred in the grandchild of their MRCA.

If we continue to search further back we will find a generation **G(2)** where A's family DNA shows a second mutation. Since this mutation does not show up as a difference between A and B, it must have occurred in an ancestor they share, and their family lines must have branched off after **G(2)**. Their MRCA must have been born after **G(2)** but before **G(1)**.

The probability that A and B's MRCA lived up through a generation **G** is the probability that more than one mutation happened since this generation. This is the mathematical equivalent of

$$1 - [\text{the probability of 0 plus the probability of 1 mutation occurring by generation G}]$$
$$= 1 - [P(0) + P(1)] \qquad \text{Eq. 1}$$

In general, the probability of finding the MRCA based on **k** mismatches on **n** markers is

$$1 - [P(0) + P(1) + P(2) + \ldots + P(k)] \qquad \text{Eq. 2}$$

Binomial Expansion & Poisson Distribution Spreadsheets

The binomial expansion and the Poisson distribution are equivalent ways of calculating a MRCA. Both give the same results in the limit of very low mutation rates and the large number of markers common to single-name studies. By copying the formulas shown in Tables 16 and 18 into an Excel® spreadsheet, you can perform your own MRCA calculations using these two methods with only minimal understanding of the mathematics behind the calculations. There are also premade Excel® spreadsheets included on the accompanying Forensic Genealogy CD and on the

Table 16. Excel® spreadsheet showing binomial formulas needed for MRCA calculations.

	A	B	C	D	E	F	G	H
1	n	G	R	2nG	(1-R)^2nG	(1-R)^(2nG-1)	(1-R)^(2nG-2)	(1-R)^(2nG-3)
2	25	6.9	0.002	0	=(1 – C2)^D2	=(1 – C2)^(D2-1)	=(1 – C2)^(D2-2)	=(1 – C2)^(D2-3)
3						2nGR	½(2nGR)^2	(1/6)*(2nGR)^3
4						=2*A2*B2*C2	=0.5*(2*A2*B2*C2)^2	=(1/6)* (2*A2*B2*C2)^3
5								
6								
7	Terms	(1-R)^(2nG)	(1-R)^(2nG-1)	(1-R)^(2nG-2)	(1-R)^(2nG-3)			
8	1	=E2						
9	2nGR		=F2*F4					
10	½(2nRG)^2			=G2*G4				
11	(1/6)*(2nGR)^3				=H2*H4			
12								
13	SUM0							
14	SUM1							
15	SUM2							
16	SUM3							
				Prob the MRCA will Occur within G Generations Assuming k Mismatches on n Markers				
				k	0	1	2	3
				Probability	=1-B13	=1-B14	=1-B15	=1-B16

Table 17. Excel® spreadsheet showing model results for binomial calculations.

	A	B	C	D	E	F	G	H
1	n	G	R	2nG	(1-R)2nG	(1-R)(2nG-1)	(1-R)(2nG-2)	(1-R)(2nG-3)
2	25	6.9	0.002	345	0.5	0.5	0.5	0.5
3								
4								
5								
6						2nGR	½(2nGR)^2	(1/6)*(2nGR)^3
7	Terms	(1-R)2nG	(1-R)(2nG-1)	(1-R)(2nG-2)	(1-R)(2nG-3)	0.69	0.24	0.05
8	1	0.5						
9	2nGR		0.35					
10	½(2nRG)^2			0.12				
11	(1/6)*(2nGR)^3				0.03			
12				Probability	k			
13	SUM0	0.5						
14	SUM1	0.85		Prob the MRCA will Occur within G Generations Assuming k Mismatches on n Markers				
15	SUM2	0.97		0.499	0	0.152	0.032	0.005
16	SUM3	1.00				1	2	3

188

Table 18. Excel® spreadsheet showing Poisson formulas needed for MRCA calculations.

	A	B	C	D	E	F	G	H
1	n	G	R	2nGR	½(2nGR)^2	(1/6)*(2nGR)^3	Exp(-2nGR)	
2	25	6.9	0.002	=2*A2*B2*C2	=(0.5)*D2^2	=(1/6)*D2^3	=exp(-D2)	
3								
4								
5	Terms	Exp(-2MRG)						
6	1	=G2						
7	2nGR	=G2*D2						
8	½(2nRG)^2	=G2*E2						
9	(1/6)*(2nGR)^3	=G2*F2						
10								
11								
12					Prob the MRCA will Occur within G Generations Assuming k Mismatches on n Markers			
13	SUM0	=B6		K	0	1	2	3
14	SUM1	=B6+B7		Probability	=1-B13	=1-B14	=1-B15	=1-B16
15	SUM2	=B6+B7+B8						
16	SUM3	=B6+B7+B8+B9						

189

Table 19. Excel® spreadsheet showing intermediate results for Poisson calculations.

	A	B	C	D	E	F	G	H
1	n	G	R	2nG	½(2nGR)^2	(1/6)*(2nGR)^3	Exp(-2nGR)	
2	25	6.9	0.002	0.69	0.24	0.5	0.5	
3								
4								
5	Terms							
6	1	0.5						
7	2nGR	0.35						
8	½(2nGR)^2	0.12						
9	(1/6)*(2nGR)^3	0.03						
10								
11								
12					Probability	k		
13	SUM0	0.5						
14	SUM1	0.85			Prob the MRCA will Occur within G Generations Assuming k Mismatches on n Markers	0		
15	SUM2	0.97				0.5		
16	SUM3	0.99				0.15	1	
						0.03	2	
						0.005	3	

190

website www.forensicgenealogy.info for those who want to experiment with the calculations without having to construct their own spreadsheets.

The three parameters that can be varied are the number of markers n (entered in cell **A2**), the number of generations of interest **G** (**B2**), and the mutation rate **R** (**C2**). If you have set your spreadsheet up correctly, you should get the intermediate results shown in Tables 17 and 19 for n = 25, **G** = 6.9 and **R** = 0.002. The probabilities associated with **k** = 0, 1, 2, and 3 mismatches will appear in the lower right hand corner, in cells **E16**, **F16**, **G16**, and **H16**, in Tables 17 and 19. Using your spreadsheet you should be able to duplicate the results in Table 14 for the 50% confidence level for **k** = 0, 1, 2, and 3 mismatches. You should also be able to duplicate the results in Table 15 for the 95% confidence level. The lower value of **G** in Table 15 gives the 2.5% probability of finding the MRCA for a given number of mismatches, and the upper value of **G** in the table gives the 97.5% confidence level. Between these two values of **G** there will be a 95% chance of finding the MRCA.

To find the generation associated with any other probability level using Tables 17 and 19, use the iterative approach. For example, to find which generation gives a 30% probability with **n** = 25 markers, **k** = 0 mismatches, and **R** = 0.002, adjust the number of generations G in cell B2 until the probability in cell **E16** is 0.3. The answer is 3.5 generations.

What is a Generation?

One last comment. To make a MRCA calculation fit in with other genealogical materials it is necessary to convert generations to years. Although it is common practice to equate a generation with 25 years, recent research indicates that a generation for people living over the last few hundred years is closer to 30 years for males[71]. In the sample calculation in Table 14, for an exact match on 25 markers there is a 50/50 chance of finding the MRCA within 6.9 generations, or about 6.9*30 = 207 years.

A Short Discussion of the Mathematical Models Used for MRCA Calculations

If you are not interested in an explanation of the mathematical basis of a MRCA calculation, you can skip this section. Although I only give a few mathematical details along with some references for further investigation, it's OK to proceed to the next section if you are not a math enthusiast.

MRCA calculations are based on Bayes' theorem that relates to the probability that an event happened in the past based on something that is observed in the present, in other words, the probability that event **X** happened, if event **Y** is observed, **P(X|Y)**. This is a sensible approach to use for genealogy because DNA analysis tells us how many mismatches **k** occur on **n** markers between two individuals tested in the present (event **Y**) and, from this, we want to deduce the likelihood that they had a common ancestor who lived a certain number of generations **G** in the past (event **X**), or **P(G|k)**.

Another way of saying this is that the Bayesian approach to MRCA calculations depends on the probability of finding individuals within a population who have two characteristics in common. Not only do they show **k** mismatches on **n** markers, they also have a MRCA ancestor exactly **G** generations ago. There will be many people who have only one of these characteristics that will not qualify for the group. Many people will have **k** mismatches, but they will not have a MRCA exactly **G** generations ago, and many people will have a MRCA exactly **G** generations ago, but will not exhibit **k** mismatches. If we find the fraction of people in the general population who have both characteristics, we can calculate the MRCA estimate.

In searching for this group, it does not matter which of the two attributes we investigate first. We could start with the fraction of people whose DNA profiles mismatch **k** times out of **n** markers, **P(k)**, and then select from them only those with a MRCA exactly **G** generations ago **P(G|k)**. The total probability of finding those with both characteristics is the product of these two quantities, or **P(G|k)*P(k)**. (Call this the forward direction). Or we could do it the other way around. We could find the fraction of the people in the general population who share a MRCA exactly **G** generations ago **P(G)** and then select from them, narrow the group down to only those who show **k** mismatches on **n** markers **P(k|G)**. The total probability of finding those with both characteristics is the product of these two quantities, or **P(k|G)*P(G)**. (Call this the backward direction). Either way, we will arrive at the same group of people who both have a MRCA exactly **G** generations ago and exhibit **k** mismatches out of **n** markers.

In other words, the forward probability is equal to the backward probability, or

$$P(G|k)*P(k) = P(k|G)*P(G) \qquad \text{Eq. 3}$$

This is Bayes' theorem.

The term we are after in Eq. 3 is the first one on the left, **P(G|k)**, which can be obtained from an evaluation of the other three terms in the equation as follows.

P(k) = the probability that two randomly selected individuals will show **k** mismatches out of **n** markers. This is a constant **α** that can be obtained empirically from DNA testing on a large number of randomly selected people. Alternatively, this constant can be determined by a mathematical process called normalization that involves summing the probabilities on the right hand side of the equation for all values of **k** and adjusting the sum so that it equals unity.

P(G) = the probability that two randomly selected individuals have a common ancestor exactly **G** generations ago. Since the amount of effort required to experimentally determine this factor would be prohibitive for now, it must be modeled through coalescence population theory. This theory indicates that, for a sample drawn from a population greater than about 250 individuals within which marriage occurs, **P(G)** can be set to unity without a significant effect on the calculations. Genealogical studies usually meet this criterion unless they involve very limited populations such as Stone Age tribes on isolated islands in the Indian ocean. The reader is referred to Hudson[72] for more information on coalescence theory.

So for populations of more than 250 individuals, Eq. 3 reduces to:

$$P(G|k) * \alpha = P(k|G) * 1 \qquad \text{Eq. 4}$$

or

$$P(G|k) = P(k|G)/\alpha \qquad \text{Eq. 5}$$

The remaining term to evaluate is **P(k|G)**, the probability that two individuals mismatch on **k** out of **n** markers given that they have a MRCA **G** generations ago. **P(k|G)** can be calculated using either the infinite-allele or stepwise model of mutations. The infinite allele model assumes that the possible outcomes of a mutation are infinite, that is, they do not occur through discrete changes in length. This implies that there is a negligible chance that two different loci will mutate in the same way, so that each mutation is unique. Using this model the only way two individuals can match on a marker is for that marker not to have changed. This model does not take into account the possibility of multiple mutations, including those where a mutation might have canceled itself out in a two-step process, changing in one direction the first time and then in the reverse direction the second time. The model also does not distinguish a multiple-step from a single-step mutation. The infinite-allele model for **k** mutations on **n** markers is nothing more than the binomial distribution representing the number of ways **k** items can be chosen from a pool of **n** total items. In the limit of very low mutation rates the binomial expansion reduces to the Poisson probability distribution:

$$P(G|k) = \frac{(2nG)!}{k!(2nG-k)!} R^k (1-R)^{2nG-k} = \frac{e^{-2nGR}(2nGR)}{k!} \qquad \text{Eq. 6}$$

where **R** is the mutation rate, 2nG! = 2nG * (2nG-1) * (2nG-2) *......* 1 and t = 2nG is the total number of chances for a mutation to occur (transmission events).

The stepwise model of mutations assumes that the length of a marker changes in discrete steps, adding or subtracting one unit of length during each mutation. The stepwise model considers that a (+1) mutation, where the allele increases by one, has the same probability of a (–1) mutation, where the allele decreases by one. The stepwise model allows for multiple discrete mutations at a single marker, including pairs of mutations that cancel out. The stepwise model also includes the possibility that two separate family lines have experienced the same mutations on the same markers, maintaining a perfect match on these markers. Since the stepwise model includes the possibility of mutations that have reversed themselves, it gives a higher estimate for the number of generations back to a MRCA than the infinite allele model as long as enough time has gone by such that there is a non-negligible chance that more than one mutation has occurred.

In practice, MRCA calculations depend on many empirical parameters that have not yet been accurately determined, such as mutation rates of individual markers. Stepwise calculations are much more difficult than infinite-allele calculations. Although the stepwise approach is closer to the physical phenomena being modeled than the infinite allele method, both models give the same results within the margin of error in cases where the probability of more than one mutation is low, or where the number of generations $G < 0.25/R$. For the mutation rate of $R = 0.002$, $G = 125$ generations[73]. Considering a generation as 25 to 30 years, this means between 3125 and 3750 years, well outside the range of conventional genealogy.

In spite of the detailed discussion about Bayes' probability distributions and the various mutation models, most MRCA calculations are trivial. The formulas used for these calculations based on the infinite-allele model and assuming a large sample population are nothing more than the well known binomial expansion and the Poisson probability distribution, as given by Eq. 6. For genealogical purposes MRCA calculations involve common algebra and can be performed with a calculator. They can also be programmed into an Excel® spreadsheet. See the accompanying Forensic Genealogy CD or visit the website www.forensicgenealogy.info for model spreadsheets you can adapt for your own calculations.

CLADOGRAMS AND PAIRWISE MISMATCHES

As a single-name study becomes large it is useful to create a diagram to show the genetic structure of the group. A clade is a biological term meaning a group of animals or people who descend from a common ancestor. A cladogram is a diagram of the genetic relationships joining the members of a clade. In genetic genealogy the term cladogram is applied more broadly to mean a diagram of the genetic relationships among all members of a DNA study.

The Basics of Cladograms

Figure 9 shows a simple cladogram representing the haplotypes in Table 7. Each open circle represents one or more participants with an identical haplotype, the number represented by the size of the circle. Links that form the web of the network are labeled with the names of the mutations that mismatch for nearest neighbors. This can be verified by comparing the

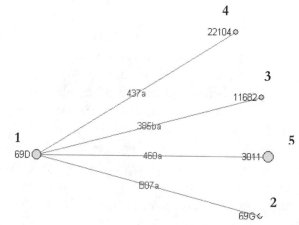

Figure 9. Simple cladogram of the haplotypes shown in Table 7, identified by id number and group.

mutations indicated in the diagram with the haplotypes in the table. Group 1 (which has the haplotype matching that assumed for the MRCA) is separated by one mutation from each of the other groups.

Table 20 shows the haplotypes for six additional people who might have the same MRCA as those in Table 7. These six differ by more than one mutation from the haplotype of this MRCA. When these new haplotypes are added to the original cladogram, the result is a more complicated structure.

There are several possible networks that can be created to describe the relationships within this enlarged population. Figure 10 shows one of them. The small solid circles (known as median vectors) represent hypothetical haplotypes that are created by software to join the known haplotypes into the most efficient network. The median vectors do not represent anyone presently in the study, but could belong to a future study participant or to a common ancestor whose haplotype has died out. The difference between any two haplotypes (both current study participants and median vectors) can be found by tracing a path through the network from one node to the other and noting which mutations appear along the way. For example, node #**3011** is connected to #**21472** in the upper left of the diagram by two mutations, one at **DYS385bd** and the other at **DYS390a**.

The cladogram of this expanded population includes the structure of the original diagram showing the same core at #**69D** connected to four nodes (**#3011**, **#22104**, **#69G**, and **#11682**) each through a single mutation. The new haplotypes connect to the core structure either along new lines or as extensions of existing lines.

A cladogram of the entire Fitzpatrick DNA study group as of August 2004 is shown in Figure 11, with the exception of three people who are separated from the others by so many mutations (15 or more) that they cannot conveniently fit on the page. The diagram is only one of several similar diagrams that could represent the relationships among the haplotypes of the 52 participants. The two sets of closely

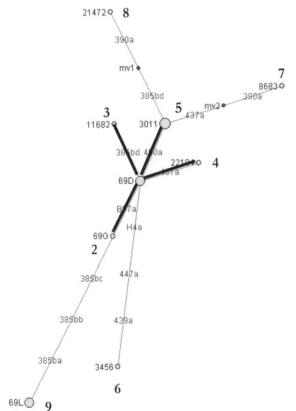

Figure 10. Cladogram of expanded set of haplotypes shown in Table 20. Bold lines show the original cladogram in Figure 9.

Table 20. More haplotypes within a few mutations of the MRCA in Table 13.

	385a	385b	388	389	389b	390	391	392	393	394	426	437	438	439	447	454	455	460	461	462	B07	A11a	A11b	A10	C4	H4
MRCA	11	14	12	13	29	21	11	13	13	14	12	15	12	12	25	11	11	10	12	11	10	22	23	13	23	12
Group 6																										
3456	11	14	12	13	29	21	11	13	13	14	12	15	12	12	25	11	11	10	12	11	10	22	23	13	23	11
Group 7																										
8683	11	14	12	13	29	20	11	13	13	14	12	15	11	24		11	11	10	12	11	10	22	23	13	23	
Group 8																										
21472	11	15	12	13	29	20	11	13	13	14	12	15	12	12	25	11	11	11	12	11	10	22	23	13	23	
Group 9																										
69L	11	11	12	13	29	21	11	13	13	14	12	15	12	12	25	11	11	10	12	11	11	22	23	13	23	12
7349	11	11	12	13	29	21	11	13	13	14	12	15	12	12	25	11	11	10	12	11	11	22	23	13	23	12
9252	11	11	12	13	29	21	11	13	13	14	12	15	12	12	25	11	11	10	12	11	11	22	23	13	23	12

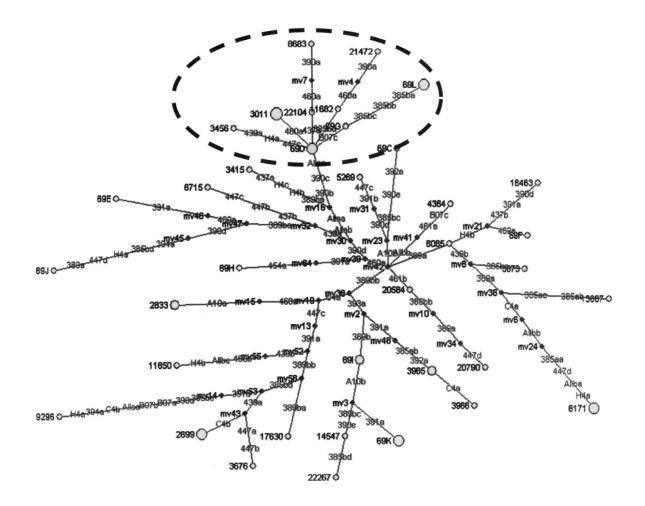

Figure 11. Cladogram of the Fitzpatrick DNA study as of August 2004. The dotted oval shows the location of the group of Fitzpatricks listed in Table 20 who appear in the cladograms in Figures 9 and 10.

related Fitzpatricks shown in Figures 9 and 10 appear at the top of the diagram separated from the rest of the network. There is a third set at the bottom (at about 6 o'clock), consisting of nodes labeled **69I, 69K, 14547,** and **22267** that has a structure similar to that found within the first two sets, and that likewise forms its own branch within the network. This third set of Fitzpatricks is known to have originated in County Down. To obtain a copy of the dataset from which the cladogram in Figure 11 was derived, please visit the Fitzpatrick study web site at http://www.genealogy.com/genealogy/users/f/i/t/Colleen-Fitzpatrick-CA/index.html[74]. You can also find it on the accompanying Forensic Genealogy CD or on the website www.forensicgenealogy.info.

What Can Cladograms Tells You About Your Family History?

A cladogram is useful for visualizing the genetic distance between various clusters that can occur in a study. When results are viewed in tabular form it is not always obvious which haplotypes belong to which cluster, but with a cladogram this can be easily determined. The structure of a cladogram can indicate much about the groups who adopted the surname.

Cladograms are useful in large surname studies that include many different haplotypes. Many Irish surnames fall into this category. Cladograms are not very useful for a group involving only a few participants who have a very rare surname, or for a group who descends from only a very few known common ancestors. The Barton Study (http://www.bartondna.info[75]) is a good example. Most of the participants descend from three Bartons who arrived in America in the mid to late 1600s. The haplotypes of most of the 125+ participants in the Barton study are very closely matched, so that the cladogram they would create would consist of only a very few large nodes connected through only one or two mutations. As an aside, there is at least one surname that died out because it was possessed by only one person who had no male children. In 1932 the Turkish nation became the last in Europe to adopt family names. They were usually chosen through personal preference based on a family characteristic or as a matter of personal pride. Kemel Ataturk was the leader of Turkey who initiated this change in his drive to bring the country into the modern era. The surname he chose for himself, 'Ataturk', means 'Father of the Turkish Nation'. Since he had no male children and was such a hard act to follow, it is appropriate that the world will only know one Ataturk. The Ataturk surname cladogram looks like ○ .

★ I have found cladograms to have a tremendous value in discovering the historical context for my family. Yet their value in uncovering deep family pedigrees has yet to be exploited by the majority of genealogists. As part of this discussion of the various uses for cladograms, I include several examples from my own research that I hope will suggest interesting approaches for others in their search for their family roots. Each of these examples is marked with a star.

The Wedge Effect

When participants in a DNA study exhibit more than two or three mismatches, it is often assumed that their MRCA lived too long in the past to be genealogically significant. This is not always a correct assumption. It is possible that as more results come in, relationships can be discovered through the development of a network of haplotypes linking people who are otherwise assumed to be unrelated.

⭐ An example of what I call The Wedge Effect is shown in Figure 12. It is an enlargement of the far right area of the general Fitzpatrick cladogram shown in Figure 11. Early in our study, participants **#69F** and **#5873** mismatched on four single step mutations on the markers **DYS385b, DYS462, DYS439, Y-GATA-H4**. (This can be confirmed by noting the mutations appearing along the path linking these two participants.) For this reason, we initially believed they were only remotely related through a common ancestor very far in the past.

Subsequently, the haplotype of participant **#6085** 'wedged' itself between those of the first two, creating the three-way relationship shown in the figure. **#6085** mismatched **#69F** on the first two markers **Y-GATA-H4** and **DYS462**, and mismatched **#5873** on the second two markers **DYS439** and **DYS385b**. This indicates that **#69F** and **#5873** are related through **#6085** much more recently than we initially expected, and that the three share a common ancestor. Sometime in the not so distant past the two branches of the family represented by **#69F** and **#5873** separated from the branch of the Fitzpatrick family represented by **#6085**. **#69F**'s line accumulated two mutations, and **#5873**'s line accumulated two different mutations, while **#6085**'s family haplotype did not change. Note that these results do not imply that **#69F**'s and **#5873**'s branches separated in the same generation from the main line, only that the probability of their doing so is the same over the same time period.

There are many great hints on family history that you can get by looking beyond the lines and numbers to understand what the cladogram is saying in the context of known genealogies. The three Fitzpatricks used to illustrate the wedge effect apparently descend from a non-paternity event. This could have been an adoption, a name change, or illegitimacy. Two of them (**#5873** and **#6085**) live in the United States and descend from Joseph, the third son of William Fitzpatrick and his wife Sarah Breckinridge, who emigrated from Ulster to America in about 1720. The third one, **#69F**, has an unknown pedigree and still lives in Ireland. None of them shows the DNA profile of the descendents of William and Sarah's older sons William and Thomas.

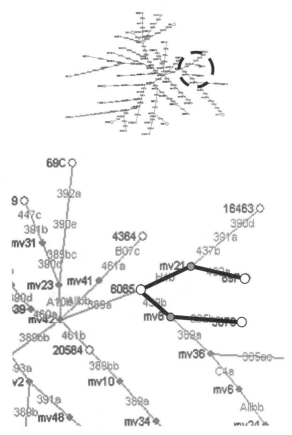

Figure 12. Illustration of the wedge effect. This diagram is an enlargement of branches of the cladogram appearing at about 3 o'clock in Figure 11, as indicated on the inset.

The most convenient way to explain **#69F**'s presence in Ireland is to assume that either Sarah Breckinridge had a child by another Fitzpatrick before the couple left for America (after which this other Fitzpatrick had at least one additional son) or that William and Sarah adopted the son of another Fitzpatrick and brought him to America with them, leaving his brother behind in Ireland. This Fitzpatrick back in Ireland could have resulted from a non-paternity event himself, so that the DNA of his descendents would not match William's.

There are still other ways to explain why these three related Fitzpatricks live on both sides of the Atlantic Ocean. For example, two orphaned brothers from another family could have been adopted, one by William who eventually took him to America, and the second one by a Fitzpatrick who remained in Ireland. No matter what explanation is given, DNA results indicate that there were two related Fitzpatricks who were not genetic children of William and Sarah, one taken with them to America, and the other who remained in Ireland. William and Sarah's geographically divided history – half in Ireland and half in America, gives an indication that the date of the MRCA for Fitzpatricks **#5873**, **#6085**, and **#69D** is no later than 1720.

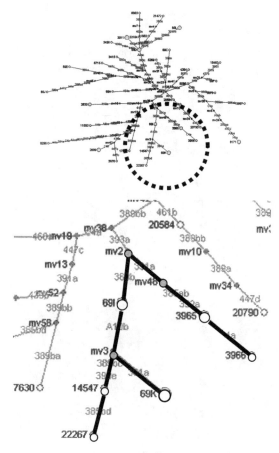

Figure 13. Cladograms can indicate historical significance. This diagram is an enlargement of branches of the cladogram appearing at about 6 o'clock in Figure 11, as indicated on the inset.

Teasing Family History from a Cladogram

Cladograms can be used to connect the histories of clusters in a surname study. This is the same as the wedge effect, but for two groups instead of two individuals. If one group appears in a cladogram separated from another by only a couple of mismatches, the two can compare written genealogies to check for common names and dates. Finding they have ancestors by the same name who lived during the same time period lends credibility to both sets of research and suggests the identity and date of their MRCA. If one of the groups has gaps in its pedigree it can get hints on its origins from the history of the other.

★ The great Irish historian Edward MacLysaught noted in his *Surnames of Ireland*[76] that a Fitzpatrick changed his name to Shera in honor of his uncle Jeffry (the English equivalent of the name). Three men with the surname Shera joined the Fitzpatrick study hoping to confirm this legend. The results showed that all three Sheras are closely related, and on comparing written genealogies, they discovered that two out of three of them had traced their ancestry to a Caleb Shera, born about 1740, probably in County Roscommon, Ireland. The two Calebs could be the same ancestor.

The Sheras do not match any Fitzpatricks, but they fall close to a Fitzpatrick cluster originating in County Down. Figure 13 shows the bottom area of the Fitzpatrick cladogram in Figure 11 including the three Sheras (two at #**3965** and one at #**3966**) and six Fitzpatricks from County Down (one each at #**14547** and #**22267**, two at #**69I**, and three at #**69K**). Shera #**3965** is located only four mutations away from Fitzpatrick #**69I**. It is possible that a future participant will join the study who will wedge himself along the path joining the two families, indicating a more recent connection between the two clans than is now evident. This would not only help to confirm MacLysaght's statements about the name change from Fitzpatrick to Shera, it would also give hints at a geographical location with an estimated time period for the change.

Using a Cladogram to Reach Beyond Written History

Valuable information on the ancient origins of a surname can be derived from cladograms. This type of analysis is commonly used by genetic anthropologists to research the origins of specific populations, but it can be just as relevant to genealogists studying surname groups who have occupied the same geographical location for a long time.

Many surnames are associated with ancient tribal locations. For example, the Fitzpatricks, Butlers, O'Rourkes, and O'Reillys are only a few of the Clans that have occupied specific areas of Ireland from as early as the first millennium. Although such a surname group may ascribe to a common written genealogy, perhaps starting with a famous ancestor who lived long in the past, its structure is likely to show up in a cladogram as a cluster of several small groups of very similar haplotypes, separated from each other by only one or at most two mismatches. People with identical haplotypes probably have the same MRCA, and people belonging to a cluster of nearly identical haplotypes are probably related through a MRCA of their MRCAs. The greater the number of different yet closely related haplotypes, the more likely it is that present descendents come from several parallel family lines originating well before written history. It is likely that many members of the group are descended not from the family ancestor, but from his brothers, cousins, and other known male relatives, and that over the years, family lore has blended the descendents into a single family line.

In a cladogram of a surname, a core group surrounded by diverse sets of haplotypes is an indication of an older dominant branch of a family. Since wealthy families adopted surnames centuries before common folk due to the need to establish inheritance, the progenitors of this older core group were probably powerful and influential in their geographical area. When most common Europeans adopted surnames during the Industrial Revolution, there was a natural tendency to take the name of the important family in their area.

The cladogram of the Fitzpatricks in Figure 11 shows this structure. Genealogies of the members of the core group, used in conjunction with DNA results, indicate that they descend from the noble line of the family from County Laois that includes Bryan MacGiollaPhadraig, who received the title of First Lord and Baron of Upper Ossory from King Henry VIII in the early 1500s. But, because of the number of satellite clusters around the two main groups represented by **#3011** and **#69D**, the MRCA of the whole core group probably lived well before the 16th century, and not all of the present Fitzpatricks in the core descend from Bryan himself.

In fact, the MacGiollaPhadraig (who later anglicized their name to Fitzpatrick) did not arrive in Upper Ossory just at the moment Bryan appeared on the scene. There is a tradition that their ancestors might have been there before 200 BCE. Written history begins around 996 CE when Gilla Pátraic assumed the kingship of the Clan[77]. About the year 1003 there is evidence that a split occurred in the Clan when the Clan chief was slain by his cousin Donnchadh (later anglicized to Donoghoe). This split continued for generations. After the death of the king Giolla Pháttraicc Ruadh in 1103, the main branch maintained its hold on the large middle portion of the kingdom (possibly the northern two-thirds of modern County Kilkenney), while a more junior branch laid claim to the southern portions of the kingdom. Plausibly, the two largest groups inside the main cluster of our cladogram are derived from the two groups that resulted from this family schism (represented by **#69D** and **#3011**). It would be interesting to compare the haplotypes of these core groups of Fitzpatricks with those of the Donoghoe (Donohoe) clan.

Creating a Cladogram

A freeware program called NETW41XX (where XX represents the current version number) for generating your own cladogram from STR data can be found at http://www.fluxus-engineering.com/sharenet.htm[78]. It is self extracting, meaning it will install itself. It comes with several different kinds of sample files you can experiment with, including a file of STR marker values. The technical language used by the HELP menu might seem complicated, but the program is straightforward, so you should not be deterred. Using NETW41XX you can generate a basic cladogram in only a few easy steps, even if your single-name study group's relationships are complex.

The following instructions are meant as a basic guide for creating a cladogram from Y-STR data. They are not meant as an exhaustive tutorial on the principles of cladogram generation. The following explanation is as technically accurate as possible, keeping in mind this chapter is meant for the intelligent reader, and not exclusively for someone with an advanced degree in genetics. The NETW41XX program can be used for analysis of other types of data such as amino acid sequences that will not be discussed here. For more advanced users the HELP menu of the NETW41XX program provides references for further research. The following instructions are based on NETW4108 as this is the current version as of the creation of this chapter.

There are three steps to using the NETW4108 program:
1. Creating the program's input file from your group of haplotypes,
2. Calculating the cladogram,
3. Drawing the cladogram.

Step #1 - Creating a Database

You can create a database to use with NETW4108 in either of two ways. You can create the file manually with the built-in editor included in the program under the File menu or you can create your file using Microsoft Notepad® or Wordpad®. It is not advisable to use Word for Windows® to create the input data file because it inserts extra characters that can cause the program to generate wrong results.

To use the built-in NET4108 editor, first click on **File**, then **New**. The program will ask you what type of file you want to create. In this case, the answer is **Y-STR data** (Figure 14). When you click on **Continue**, the next screen asks you to enter the **Number of Taxa** (participants or haplotypes), the **Number of Loci** (STR markers) you want to enter and the **Default Weight** you want to give each locus (default is 10). (See Figure 15.) The weight can be changed to reflect the variation of a marker within a group. If you assign a lower weight to a marker with a higher variability, the cladogram will exhibit a shorter distance between nodes that are separated by a mutation of this marker. This will influence the calculation of the most efficient (most

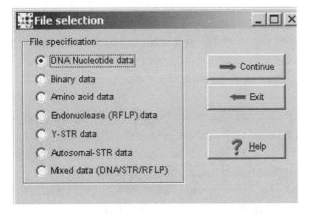

Figure 14. Data type selection menu.

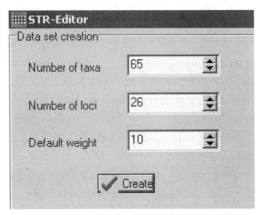

Figure 15. Data set creation.

parsimonious) network in the calculation step. Enter the number of participants and loci, for now leaving weight = 10 for all loci. The cladogram of the Y-STR data in Table 7 uses taxa = 9 and loci = 26. Click on **Continue**.

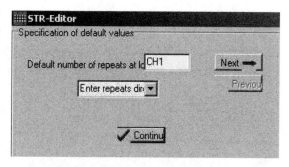

The final menu asks you to enter the **Default Number of Repeats** at each of the loci (Figure 16). If some of the marker values appear frequently among your group members, those values can be set here as defaults, eliminating the need to enter the same numbers many times. You can change specific marker values in the next step to take into account any variations on the default profile you have set up.

Figure 16. Specification of default values.

The data editor is self-explanatory (Figure 17). Enter the names of the markers along the top row labeled **Locus**. Enter the names or identification numbers of the participants in the first column labeled **Taxon**. In each case names of taxa are limited to 6 characters and names of loci are limited to five

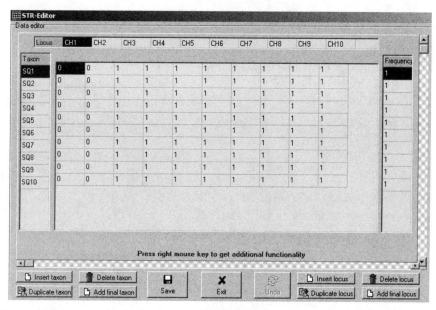

Figure 17. Data editor.

characters, so the longer locus names must be abbreviated; for example, you can use **C4** for **Y-GATA-C4**. There are buttons on this screen for inserting, duplicating, deleting, and adding additional participants (taxa) or loci. There are also **Save**, **Exit**, and **Undo** features. The file will be saved with a .ych (Y-chromosome) extension.

To create a data file with Notepad® use the format shown in Figure 18. You can also use the sample data file included on the Forensic Genealogy CD and on the www.forensicgenealogy.info site as a template to create your own input file. The sample data in the figure represent the haplotypes in Table 7. Enter the names of the markers on the first line separated only by commas. If the data requires more than a single line, allow the line to wrap without using a carriage return. Follow this with at least one blank line. The next three lines form a set that is repeated for each

```
385a,385b,388,389,389b,390,391,392,393,394,426,437,438,439,447,454,455,
460,461,462,B07,Alla,Allb,A10,C4,H4
15853
11,14,12,13,29,21,11,13,13,14,12,15,12,12,25,11,11,10,11,11,10,22,23,13,23,12
1
69D
11,14,12,13,29,21,11,13,13,14,12,15,12,12,25,11,11,10,11,11,10,22,23,13,23,12
1
21477
11,14,12,13,29,21,11,13,13,14,12,15,12,12,25,11,11,10,11,11,10,22,23,13,23,12
1
69G
11,14,12,13,29,21,11,13,13,14,12,15,12,12,25,11,11,10,11,11,11,22,23,13,23,12
1
11682
11,15,12,13,29,21,11,13,13,14,12,15,12,12,25,11,11,10,11,11,10,22,23,13,23,12
1
22104
11,14,12,13,29,21,11,13,13,14,12,14,12,12,25,11,11,10,11,11,10,22,23,13,23,12
1
10108
11,14,12,13,29,21,11,13,13,14,12,15,12,12,25,11,11,11,11,11,10,22,23,13,23,12
1
```

Figure 18. Data format required for the NETW4108 program.

individual and consist of the participant's name or identification number on a line by itself, his marker values in the same order that the marker names are entered on the first line of the file and separated only by commas (no spaces) with a carriage return at the end of the list and, finally, the number 1 on the last line of each set to denote the end of that participant's data. (If more than one person has the same haplotype, you can invent a name for the group and enter the number of participants belonging to the group in place of the number 1.) Repeat these last three instructions for each participant in the study. Do not leave any blank lines between participants.

Notepad will save the file with a **.txt** extension, but you must change it to **.ych** by renaming the file using Windows Explorer®. Windows® will warn you that doing so might make the file unstable, but change the extension anyway.

Step #2 - Calculating the Network

Now that you have created a data file, you are ready to calculate the network for your cladogram. This could be a challenge without a computer, considering the large number of possible connections between members of the group and the goal of finding the tree that connects all the haplotypes through the smallest number of steps. Such a network is called the Maximum Parsimony or MP tree and is assumed to be the route taken by nature for the evolution of related haplotypes. It is also referred to as a Steiner tree if the loci weights are not all the same. Because the relationships among haplotypes are often highly complex, the calculations can result in several plausible MP trees, each with an equal probability of representing 'the' path through which the haplotypes developed. The collection of all of these MP trees is known as the MP network.

There are two main algorithms you can use to calculate your cladogram, the Median Joining (MJ) algorithm and the Reduced Median (RM) algorithm. These algorithms use different criteria for identifying and joining closely related haplotypes into a network, therefore they can produce somewhat different cladograms. They can also result in multiple paths connecting the same pairs of haplotypes (called reticulations) that represent ambiguities in the calculations. To eliminate such redundancy from the cladogram, the output of the MJ or RM algorithms can be post-processed by the Maximum Parsimony (MP) algorithm.

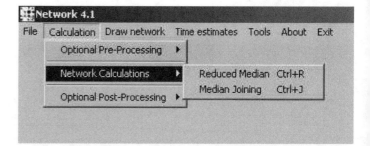

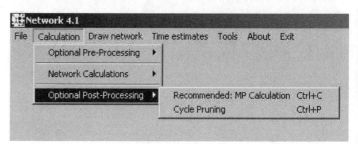

Figure 19. Network calculation and optional post processing menus.

The Median Joining (MJ) algorithm found in the Calculation menu (Figure 19) first calculates the distance between each pair of haplotypes. It starts building the network by joining nearest neighbors and then adding other haplotypes in order of proximity until all have been included. The MJ algorithm then examines sets of three haplotypes in the network, starting with the triplets that are most closely related. If there is an economy in connecting a triplet through a common intermediate point instead of pairwise (as in Figure 20), the algorithm connects it via a median vector created from the most common values (the consensus values) of the three haplotypes. Of course, if the median vector is the same as a haplotype that is already part of the triplet, it does not duplicate the haplotype. Median vectors can represent future participants in the study or

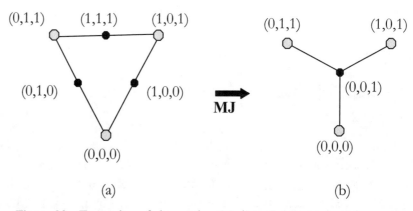

Figure 20. Example of how the Median Joining algorithm uses median vectors to economize on network connections. (a) Pairs connected through median vectors, (b) Triplets connected through a single median vector.

206

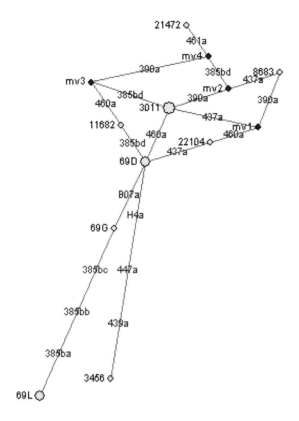

Figure 21. Median Joining cladogram of the Fitzpatricks included in Table 20.

ancestors whose haplotypes have become extinct.

The algorithm then adds the new median vector haplotype to the dataset and repeats the process of creating the network from the expanded set. It repeats the process until no new median vectors are created. A final MJ cladogram often results in multiple paths connecting pairs of haplotypes.

A simple example of how the MJ algorithm connects related haplotypes is illustrated in Figure 20[79]. The example assumes that a marker has one of two values, represented by a 0 or a 1.

Each pair of haplotypes in the triplet (0,0,0), (0,1,1) and (1,0,1) is a distance d = 2 apart, since changing one haplotype into another requires changing two of the markers by a single step each. The haplotypes could be joined into the network pictured in Figure 20a, but the MJ algorithm economizes on the lengths of network connections by joining the haplotypes through a median vector as in Figure 20b. Note that all pairs are still separated by a distance d = 2.

In constructing the MJ cladogram of the Fitzpatricks in Figure 21 (from Table 20), for example, the algorithm first builds the basic skeleton of the network through joining nearest neighbor haplotypes. It then examines haplotype triplets to find three median vectors:
- **mv1** connecting the triplet [**3011**, **22104** and **8683**] at a cost of three steps,
- **mv2** connecting [**3011**, **8683**, and **21472**] at a cost of four steps, and
- **mv3** connecting [**3011**, **69D** and **21472**] at a cost of four steps.

In the second iteration, the MJ algorithm includes the least expensive median vector **mv1** in its network calculation. No new median vectors are discovered at the same or lower cost. A third iteration of the algorithm adds **mv2** and **mv3** at the slightly higher cost of four steps each to the set of original haplotypes plus **mv1**. This third iteration discovers a fourth median vector **mv4** that was previously not possible that connects [**mv2**, **mv3** and **21472**] at a cost of three steps. **mv4** also reduces the cost of including **mv2** and **mv3** to three steps each, as they now both connect to **mv4** instead of **21472**. Subsequent iterations do not produce any new median vectors.

The MJ network shown in Figure 21 contains four cycles and four median vectors, **mv1** through **mv4**. This network is not optimized yet as it has cycles where pairs of haplotypes (such as **3011** and **21472**) are joined by more than one path. They can be resolved in post-processing by the Maximum Parsimony algorithm.

The Reduced Median (RM) algorithm examines each allele individually and splits the haplotypes into groups that share the same values. As each successive allele is analyzed, groups formed during previous stages are subdivided into smaller groups until all alleles have been exhausted. For example[80], analysis of the first allele of the haplotypes (0,0), (0,1), (1,0) and (1,1), causes them to be separated into the two groups [(0,0) + (0,1)] (at the left of Figure 22a), and [(1,0) + (1,1)] (at the right of Figure 22a), since the first pair of haplotypes has 0 as its first value and the second pair has a 1 in this position. Analysis of the second allele splits the first group into the two subgroups (0,0) and (0,1) (on the left side of the square in Figure 22b) and the second group into the two subgroups (1,0) and (1,1) (on the right side of the square in Figure 22b).

Joining these four subgroups leads to several equivalent paths through which the haplotypes can be connected. The RM algorithm may resolve them based on the relative weight (frequency of occurrence) of a mutation and on the population having certain haplotypes.

Because unmutated markers have existed longer, we assume that the less frequent marker values represent mutations. In this example 0 represents an unmutated marker and 1 represents a mutated marker. Splitting on the first allele produces three people who have 1 on this allele (their first marker has mutated). Splitting on the

Haplotype	Population
(0,0)	4
(0,1)	3
(1,0)	2
(1,1)	1

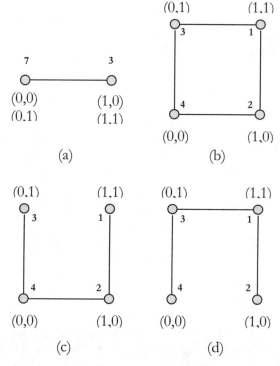

Figure 22. Sample results of the Reduced Median algorithm. (a) Splitting on the first allele; (b) forming subgroups by splitting on the second allele; (c) and (d) alternate paths that result by assuming a mutation on the second allele is more frequent than on the first. If more people have (0,0) and (1,0) haplotypes than (0,1) and (1,1), the path shown in (c) is output by the RM algorithm.

second allele produces four people with the second allele equal to 1 (their second marker has mutated). Since mutations on the first marker occur less frequently than on the second, the algorithm retains either horizontal line in the figure but not both. The most likely paths are shown in Figures 22c and 22d. In this case, since more people have the (0,0) and (1,0) profiles at the bottom corners of the square than have (0,1) and (1,1) profiles at the top corners, based on the surplus of people at the bottom, the path in Figure 22c is the diagram the algorithm outputs.

Once the RM algorithm has set up the framework of the network, it examines triplets of haplotypes separated by more than one mutation to determine the position of the median vectors required for the most economical connections. There may still be loops in the network if there are ambiguous paths that include values with the same weight or that involve haplotypes with equal frequencies. The cladogram created by the RM algorithm for the groups of Fitzpatricks from Table 20, shown in Figure 23, has two such cycles [**3011** + **69D** + **11682** + **mv1**] and [**3011** + **69D** + **22104** + **mv2**] that cannot be resolved. Each of them includes values that have been given the same weight for the calculation, [**385b** and **460a**] in the

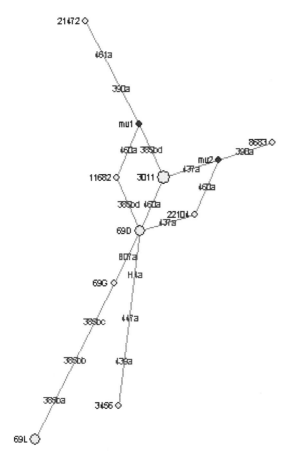

Figure 23. Reduced Median cladogram of the Fitzpatricks included in Table 20.

cycle on the left and [**437** and **460**] in the cycle on the right so that neither cycle can be broken into favored paths. Since the RM algorithm does not resolve cycles only on the basis of relative haplotype frequencies, both cycles remain part of the final cladogram.

The Maximum Parsimony (MP) algorithm is a post-processing step to resolve cycles that remain in networks produced by the MJ and RM algorithms. The MP algorithm searches for the shortest paths through the network. In cases where the input network contains cycles, there may be more than one path with the same length. In this case, the NETW4108 software provides the option of showing each MP tree individually or all of them together in a single MP network. Figure 24 shows the MJ network after MP post-processing. Figures 25a, b, and c show three equivalent MP trees obtained by post-processing the RM network. Figure 25d combines these three MP trees into a MP network. Note that all MP trees have a similar structure, with haplotypes **#3011**, **#69D**, **#69G**, and

#69L lying on a central axis connected with the other haplotypes through an open network of branches.

There is a preprocessing option that will be mentioned here only briefly. If your study group contains more than a couple of hundred people, you will probably want to preprocess your data using the Star Contraction algorithm on the Optional Preprocessing Menu. The network for very large and complex datasets can be time consuming to calculate and the resulting cladograms are often too complicated to read. In such cases, the star contraction algorithm can be used to identify star-like clusters in the network and condense them into a single node. The star-contracted dataset can then be put into the MJ or RM algorithm to generate the basic skeleton of network. Post-processing with the MP algorithm can be done as before.

Step #3 - Displaying the Results

After you have finished calculating your network, you can draw its cladogram by clicking on **Draw Network** on the main menu. Click on **File**, then **Open**, and select the name of the file you wish to draw. MJ and RM networks have the extension **.out**. MP networks have the extension **.sto**. In the case of an MP network, the program gives you the option of either drawing the MP trees as freestanding networks or highlighting them as part of the original (not optimized) MJ or RM network (Figure 26.) Once the cladogram is drawn, there are formatting options for changing the font and the node size and for turning on and off the display of mutations, node names, and median vectors (Figure 27). You can move nodes and connections to make the diagram more readable. The program also has the capability of displaying the statistics of your group, so that you can recalculate the network using different relative weights for the various alleles to explore their effects on the cladogram.

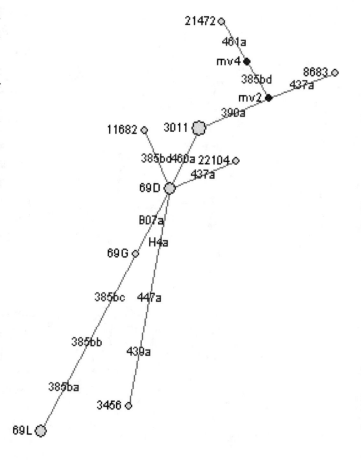

Figure 24. Maximum Parsimony cladogram created from the Median Joining network of Figure 21.

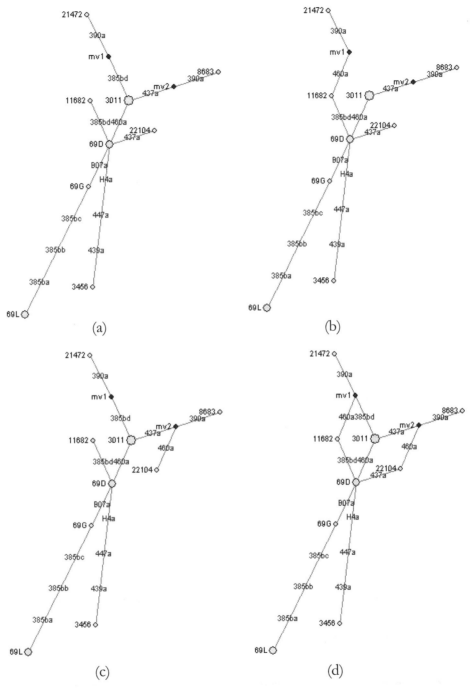

Figure 25. (a) – (c) Maximum Parsimony trees generated from the Reduced Median network shown in Figure 23; (d) Maximum Parsimony network that is a combination of these trees.

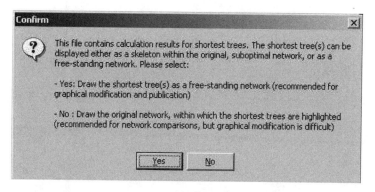

Figure 26. Options for drawing a Maximum Parsimony or Steiner network.

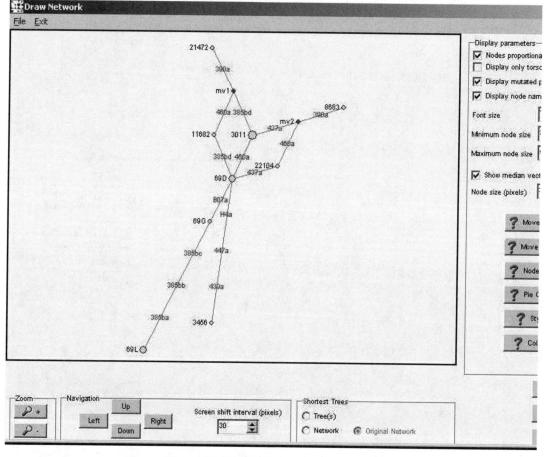

Figure 27. The Draw Network screen.

Pairwise Mismatches

One aspect of STR testing that is often overlooked is the analysis of pairwise mismatches. Most studies are interested in examining the relationship between individual pairs of participants, both in the recent past and more remotely. But there is value in examining the collective relationships among all members of a study. The number of mismatches between two people gives you an indication of how recently they are related; the average number of mismatches for the group can tell you about how far in the past the group itself might have been formed. This analysis is most valuable for large, genetically diverse studies.

The NETWORK4108 program has the option on the **Tools** menu of graphing the distribution of pairwise differences in a study group. (See Figure 28.) A plot of the frequency associated with specific numbers of pairwise mismatches for a group can indicate whether more than one haplogroup is present. Having pairs of participants that mismatch on a very large number of markers is an indication that your cladogram will have long branches and could be very complicated.

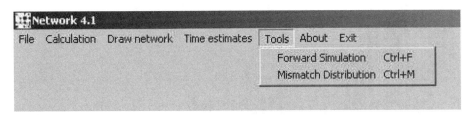

Figure 28. The NETW4108 software package has the option of plotting pairwise mismatches.

The pairwise mismatches for our Fitzpatrick study shown in Figure 29 fall into four groups:
- Those near the origin who are closely related and who show only 0, 1 or 2 mismatches.
- A second large group centered at about 10 mismatches.
- Two small groups involving outliers located to the far right at about 30 and 38 mismatches.

Note that the peak close to the origin includes exact or close matches between pairs of outliers. Note also that the right edge of this peak is partially covered by the left edge of the large middle peak.

The third and fourth groups of outliers far to the right represent people with unusual haplotypes who probably do not belong to the same haplogroup as the majority. Of the three participants responsible for these two small peaks, two probably belong to the I1c haplogroup that appears along the west cost of Ireland and the third probably belongs to the J2 haplogroup that originated in the northern part of the Middle East and then later spread throughout central Asia, the Mediterranean, and south into India[81]. The J2 haplogroup is found in Jewish populations.

213

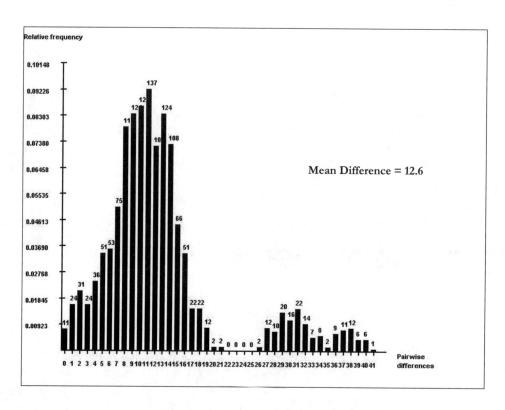

Figure 29. Pairwise mismatches found in the Fitzpatrick study including outliers.

When the outliers are eliminated from the pairwise mismatch calculation, the graph shown in Figure 30 is the result. The first and second peaks represent people who belong to the same haplogroup. Considering the Irish origins of the name Fitzpatrick, it is most likely the R1b haplogroup. While the participants in our study have not been tested on SNP markers to verify membership in the R1b haplogroup, the haplogroup predictor found at[82] http://www.newscientist.com/news/news.jsp?id=ns99992716 gives the highest probability of R1b to all of these participants.

Pairwise Mismatches Can Give Hints on Family History

For a diverse family group the average number of pairwise mismatches (excluding outliers) can provide hints of the time period when the family group was formed. In the Pairwise Mismatch graph of closely related Fitzpatricks in Figure 30, the average number of mismatches for the group is 9.7 out of 25 markers. A MRCA calculation can be performed with $n = 26$, $k = 9.7$, and $R = 0.002$ to generate a plot of the probability of a match as a function of the number of generations G. See

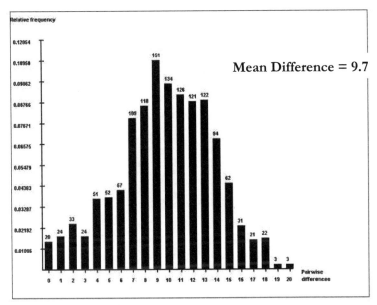

Figure 30. Pairwise mismatches found in the Fitzpatrick study not including outliers.

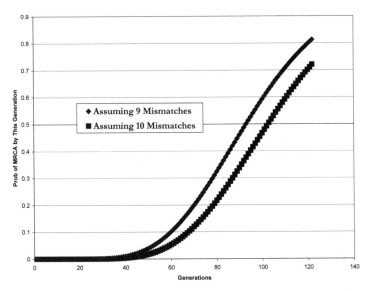

Figure 31. Cumulative probability of MRCA versus generation for an average number of pairwise mismatches.

Figure 31 for the calculations based on 9 and 10 mismatches. The results for 10 mismatches are used in the plot instead of those for 9.7 because they are easier to calculate. Based on 10 mismatches, there is a 50% probability that the MRCA for the group lived as long as 102 generations or 2550 - 3060 years[83] ago, or around 550 - 1060 BCE.

 It is interesting to compare this estimate with ancient Irish history. (Non-Irish historians call it mythology.) Celts of Ireland are descended from the three sons of King Milesius of Spain[84] who ruled Ireland under one hundred eighty-three monarchs from about 1700 BCE until they submitted to King Henry II of England in 1186 CE. In particular, the royal house of Ossory, from which the Fitzpatricks descend, is descended from Heremon the seventh son of Milesius, and the third of the three sons who had male descendents. Irish nobility accordingly originated about 3700 years ago.

This estimate date can be checked against that obtained from DNA results by taking into account that the sons of Milesius originally settled in the north of the island. Considering that the rate of population expansion into Europe from Africa has been estimated at 300 meters per year, it would have taken several centuries for their settlements to become established in County Laois located in the center of the island, approximately 280 km from the north coast. Assuming that the Fitzpatrick Clan formed from this early County Laois population, an additional $280/0.3 = 933$ years can be subtracted from the timeline. This dates the origins of the Clan to about $1700-933 = 766$ BCE. This is in good agreement with the 50/50 estimate of $550 - 1060$ BCE provided by the analysis of the group's pairwise mismatches.

THERE WILL ALWAYS BE MYSTERIES LEFT

Genealogists realize that for every mystery that is solved, ten more take its place. Participating in a DNA study does not change this. No matter how many relationships are discovered through DNA, there will always be many more that remain hidden. Even those that are found might never be explained.

Perhaps the most interesting aspect of any DNA study is not the large networks of cousins that are uncovered but the residue of participants who remain genetically unconnected to anyone else in the study, with the exception of known family members. Even if family folklore tells of a connection with a famous (or infamous) person in history, DNA testing might be unable to confirm it. All you can say is that a connection has not been established 'yet'.

A family might have a recent connection to a study group but, because the family has no males to take an STR test, DNA cannot be used to prove it. Once in a desperate search for a DNA sample to use for testing a family with no remaining males, I investigated using hair follicles from a deceased father's hairbrush or skin shards from his razorblades. But these items are not appropriate for use in a test set up for extracting DNA from the epithelial cells from the inside of the cheek. Because this deceased father had been the last known male in his family, the family's hope of finding a genetic link through STR testing had vanished pending the future discovery of a more distant male relative.

In the long run there will be a fraction of participants who never connect with anyone else simply because they never connect with anyone else. We know who we are, we are sure of our patronage, at least in the recent past, yet we remain STR orphans. It could be that somewhere along the generations, all descendents were female, causing related male lines to become extinct. It also could be that we just haven't found a match yet. In my own case, I am enrolled in DNA studies covering both my father's and my mother's sides through my brother and my mother's male cousin, respectively. Yet I have not found a match on either side. There is only one conclusion I can draw from this. I have always thought my family was from another planet, and now it seems I have found proof.

[1] http://www.accessExcel®lence.org/AB/BC/1900-1953.html

[2] http://sumagazine.syr.edu/summer01/features/brightideas/ and M. Menotti-Raymond et al., "Pet cat hair implicates murder suspect," *Nature*, **386**(774), 1997.

[3] http://www.ornl.gov/sci/techresources/Human_Genome/elsi/forensics.shtml

[4] http://www.innocenceproject.org

[5] http://www.amazon.com/exec/obidos/tg/detail/-/0345406400/qid=1099499480/sr=8-5/ref=pd_csp_5/103-4253549-7236611?v=glance&s=books&n=507846

[6] http://www.ornl.gov/sci/techresources/Human_Genome/elsi/forensics.shtml#4

[7] Ryder et al., ECOLOGY:DNA Banks for Endangered Animal Species, *Science 2000* **288**: 275-277

[8] Steve Bunk, "Forensics Fights Crimes Against Wildlife," *The Scientist* **14**(7):24, Apr. 3, 2000

[9] http://www.ornl.gov/sci/techresources/Human_Genome/elsi/forensics.shtml

[10] Julianna Kettlewell, ""Junk" Throws Up Precious Secret," BBC Online, http://news.bbc.co.uk/1/hi/sci/tech/3703935.stm

[11] Anne E. Peaston, Alexei V. Evsikov, Joel H. Graber, Wilhelmine N. de Vries, Andrea E. Holbrook, Davor Solter, and Barbara B. Knowles: "Retrotransposons Regulate Host Genes in Mouse Oocytes and Preimplantation Embryos,"*Developmental Cell*, **7**(4), pages 597–606, October 2004.

[12] http://science.howstuffworks.com/dna-evidence2.htm

[13] J. W. Schumm, Promega Corporation, "New Approaches to DNA Fingerprint Analysis," *Notes Magazine*, **58** 1996, p. 12.

[14] Alan J. Redd et al, "Forensic value of 14 novel STRs on the human Y-chromosome," *Forensic Science International*, **3460** (2002), pp 1 – 15.

[15] A good reference on forensic science use of DNA is John Butler's book, *Forensic DNA Typing*, available through Amazon.com at http://www.amazon.com/exec/obidos/ASIN/012147951X/anilaggrawasi-20/103-4253549-7236611.

[16] If the STR markers used for genealogical analysis were used to identify someone who committed a crime, about 580 markers would have to match to have a 90% probability that the person who left the DNA sample at the scene of a crime shared a MRCA with the suspect within 1 generation. This is about ten times the number of markers that are presently known. If the probability were lowered to 50%, roughly 380 markers would be required.

[17] A recent discovery has shown that it is possible, although very rarely, to inherit at least of fraction of one's mtDNA from the mother. See http://www.newscientist.com/news/news.jsp?id=ns99992716, or *New England Journal of Medicine* **347**, p576.

[18] http://www.amazon.com/exec/obidos/tg/detail/-/0393323145/103-8588707-5017455?v=glance

[19] http://en.wikipedia.org/wiki/DNA

[20] E. Heyer, J. Puymirat, P. Dieltjes, E. Bakker, P. de Knijff, "Estimating Y chromosome specific microsatellite mutation frequencies using deep rooting pedigrees," *Hum Mol Genet* **6** (1997) 799-803, also M. Kayser, L. Roewer, M. Hedman, L. Henke, J. Henke, S. Brauer, C. Krüger, M. Krawczak, M. Nagy, T. Dobosz, R. Szibor, P. de Knijff, M. Stoneking, A. Sajantila, "Characteristics and frequency of germline mutations at microsatellites from the human Y chromosome revealed by direct observation in father / son pairs," *American Journal of Human Genetics* **66** (2000) 1580-1588, also G. Cooper, N.J. Burroughs, D.A. Rand, D.C. Rubinsztein, W. Amos, "Markov Chain Monte Carlo analysis of human Y-chromosome microsatellites provides evidence of biased mutation," *Proceedings of the National Academy of Sciences USA*, **96**, 11916-11921, (1999).

[21] B. Myhre Dupuy, M. Stenersen, A. G. Flones, B. Olaisen, "Mutations at Y-STR Loci: a study of 1767 Father-Son Pairs of Norwegian Origin," *Proc. of the Third International Y-Users Workshop, Y-chromosome haplotype database(s): state of the art and future developments*, November 7 – 9, 2002, Porto, Portugal.

[22] http://www.dnaheritage.com/glossary.asp

[23] See the Y-STR Database description at http://www.ystr.org/index_usa_gr.html

[24] Y_STR Profiles in DNA, March 2003, www.promega.com

[25] http://www.ornl.gov/sci/techresources/Human_Genome/faq/snps.shtml

[26] The Y Chromosome Consortium , "A Nomenclature System for the Tree of Human Y-Chromosomal Binary Haplogroups," **12**(2)**,** 339-348, February 2002.

[27] http://www.kerchner.com/haplogroups-ydna.htm with permission from Family Tree DNA.

[28]

[29] Cann, R.L., Stoneking, M., and Wilson, A. C., "Mitochondrial DNA and human evolution," Nature, 1987 Jan 1-7;**325**(6099):31-6; and Stoneking, M., Mitochondrial DNA and human evolution," *J Bioenerg Biomembr.*, Jun; **26**(3):251-9, 1994.

[30] http://www.genomenewsnetwork.org/articles/04_02/mito_dna.shtml

[31] See http://www.newscientist.com/news/news.jsp?id=ns99992716 or *New England Journal of Medicine*, **347**, p576 for a rare exception.

[32] Bryan Sykes, *The Seven Daughters of Eve*. Also see http://www.oxfordancestors.com/your-maternal.html and http://www.roperld.com/mtDNAdaughters.htm#haplogroups

[33] Used with the permission of Bennett Greenspan, Family Tree DNA.

[34] J. F. O'Connell, "Genetics, archeology, and Holocene hunter-gathers," Proc *Natl Acad Sci U S A*, September 14; **96** (19): 10562–10563, 1999.

[35] J. F. O'Connell, "Genetics, archeology, and Holocene hunter-gathers," *Proc Natl Acad Sci U S A*, September 14; **96** (19): 10562–10563, 1999.

[36] Annette Gordon-Reed, *Thomas Jefferson and Sally Hemmings: An American Controversy*, University of Virginia Press, Charlottesville, 1998) as discussed in Thomas H. Roderick, "The Y-Chromosome in Genealogical Research: 'From Their Ys a Father Knows His Own Son', *National Genealogical Society Quarterly* 88 (June 2000), p. 122-143.

[37] E. A. Foster et al, :Jefferson Fathered Slave's Last Child," *Nature* **396** (5 November) 1998:27-28.

[38] Thomas H. Roderick, "The Y-Chromosome in Genealogical Research: 'From Their Ys a Father Knows His Own Son', National Genealogical Society Quarterly 88 (June 2000), p. 122-143.

[39] http://www.wouldfamilies.net

[40] http://www.familytreedna.com/surname_join.asp?code=F86325&special=True.

[41] http://www.bartonsite.org/ie_index.html

[42] http://www.duerinck.com/privacy.html

[43] *Descendants of Bryan Fitzpatrick, Lord and First Baron of Upper Ossory*, S. Zalewski and R. Fitzpatrick, 2002.

[44] http://indigo.ie/~wildgees/lally.htm

[45] http://www.breckinridge.com/Man_of_Fr.htm

[46] http://genealogy.about.com/gi/dynamic/offsite.htm?site=http%3A%2F%2Fwww.rootsweb.com%2F%7Ecanqc%2Fangloabc.htm

[47] Marion L. Smith, "American Names/Declaring Independence," http://genealogy.about.com/gi/dynamic/offsite.htm?site=http%3A%2F%2Fwww.immigration.gov%2Fgraphics%2Faboutus%2Fhistory%2Farticles%2Fnames.htm

[48] Marian L. Smith, op cit.

[49] Mark Haacke, private communication.

[50] http://web.staffs.ac.uk/schools/humanities_and_soc_sciences/census/illegit.htm

[51] http://www.encyclopedia.com/html/A/Armada-S1.asp, as taken from G. Mattingly, The Armada (1959); A. McKee, From Merciless Invaders (1964); W. Graham, The Spanish Armadas (1972).

[52] http://www.duerinck.com/dnalabs.html

[53] See for example, Alan J. Redd et al, "Forensic value of 14 novel STRs on the human Y-chromosome," *Forensic Science International*, **3460** (2002), pp 1 – 15.

[54] http://www.relativegenetics.com. Click on "About Relative Genetics".

[55] http://www.smgf.org

[56] Bennett Greenspan, Family Tree DNA, private communication.

[57] http://ycc.biosci.arizona.edu/nomenclature_system/fig1.html

[58] http://www.ohiou.edu/phylocode/art9.html and http://www.miketaylor.org.uk/dino/faq/s-class/phyletic/

[59] http://ycc.biosci.arizona.edu/nomenclature_system/results.html

[60] The Y Chromosome Consortium , "A Nomenclature System for the Tree of Human Y-Chromosomal Binary Haplogroups," **12**(2), 339-348, February 2002.

[61] http://www.familytreedna.com/haplotree.html or http://ycc.biosci.arizona.edu/nomenclature_system/fig1.html

[62] S. Siguraordottir, Agnar Helgason, Jeffrey R. Gulcher, Kari Stefansson, Peter Donnelly, "The Mutation Rate in the Human mtDNA Control Region," *Am. J. Hum. Genet.,* **66**:1599-1609, 2000.

[63] Anderson S., A. T. Bankier, B. G. Barrell, et al. (14 co-authors), "Sequence and organisation of the human mitochondrial genome," *Nature*, **290**:457-465, 1981.

[64] http://www.oxfordancestors.com/glossary.html

[65] Andrews R. M., I. Kubacka, P. F. Chinnery, R. N. Lightowlers, D. M. Turnbull, N. Howell, "Reanalysis and revision of the Cambridge reference sequence for human mitochondrial DNA," *Nat. Genet.*, **23**:147, 1999.

[66] Bennett Greenspan, Family Tree DNA, private communication.

[67] A. Achilli et at, "The Molecular Dissection of mtDNA Haplogroup H Confirms that the Franco-Cantabrian Refuge Was a Major Source for the European Gene Pool," *Am. J. Hum. Genet.*, **75**, 910-918, 2004.

[68] Information in Tables 8, 9, 10, and 11 and information included in the accompanying discussion are used with the permission of L. David Roper, http://www.roperld.com/mtDNA.htm

[69] http://www.journals.uchicago.edu/AJHG/journal/issues/v68n6/002593/fg2.h.gif. Figure 2 from Finnila, S., Lehtonen, M.S., Majamaa, K., Phylogenetic Network for European mtDNA," *Amer. J. of Human Genetics*, **68**: 1475-1484 (2001).

[70] B. Walsh, "Estimating the Time to the Most Recent Common Ancestor for the Y chromosome or Mitochondrial DNA for a Pair of Individuals" , *Genetics*, **158**: 897 – 912 (June 2001).

[71] M. Tremblay and Helene Vesina, "New Estimates of Intergenerational Time Intervals for the Calculation of Age and Origins of Mutations," *Am. J. Hum. Genet.*, **66**:651-658, 2000.

[72] Hudson, R. R., "Gene genealogies and the coalescence process," *Oxford Surveys in Evolutionary Biology*, D. J. Futuyama and J. Antonovics, eds., Oxford University Press, Oxford, pp. 1 – 44.

[73] B. Walsh, "Estimating the Time to the Most Recent Common Ancestor for the Y chromosome or Mitochondrial DNA for a Pair of Individuals," *Genetics*, **158**: 897 – 912 (June 2001).

[74] If this link does not work, an alternate route to the site is to go to www.genealogy.com, click on My Community on the banner, click on F, click on FI, click on FIT, then search for "DNA" or "Colleen" on the page.

[75] http://www.bartondna.info

[76] http://www.amazon.com/exec/obidos/tg/detail/-/0716523663/qid=1099517562/sr=8-1/ref=sr_8_xs_ap_i1_xgl14/103-4253549-7236611?v=glance&s=books&n=507846

[77] http://www.rootsweb.com/~irlkik/history/ossory.htm

[78] http://www.fluxus-engineering.com/sharenet.htm

[79] H.-J. Baldelt, P. Forster, A. Röhl, "Median Joining Networks for Inferring Intraspecific Phylogenies," *Mol. Biol. Evol*,. **16**(1): 37-48 (1999).

[80] H.-J. Baldelt, P. Forster, B. C. Sykes, and M. B. Richards, "Mitochondrial Portraits of Human Populations Using Median Networks," *Genetics*, **141**: 743-753 (October 1995).

[81] http://www.kerchner.com/haplogroups-ydna.htm

[82] http://www.newscientist.com/news/news.jsp?id=ns99992716

[83] While it is true that Trembly et al, "New Estimates of Intergenerational Time Intervals for the Calculation of Age and Origins of Mutation," *Am. J. Hum. Genet.*, **66**:651-658 (2000) found that a generation over the last few centuries is about 30 years, the average lifespan of males for the last few thousand years was probably much shorter.

[84] Irish Pedigrees or the Origin and Stem of the Irish Nation, by John O'Hart. http://www.accessExcel®lence.org/AB/BC/1900-1953.html